Rhododendrons
in the Landscape

Rhododendrons in the Landscape

Sonja Nelson

Illustrations by Nicholas Brown

Sonja Nelson

TIMBER PRESS
Portland, Oregon

Published in 2000 by
Timber Press, Inc.
The Haseltine Building
133 S.W. Second Avenue, Suite 450
Portland, Oregon 97204, U.S.A.

Printed in Hong Kong

Library of Congress Cataloging-in-Publication Data

Nelson, Sonja.
     Rhododendrons in the landscape / Sonja Nelson; illustrations by
   Nicholas Brown.
          p.   cm.
     Includes bibliographical references (p.   ) and index.
     ISBN 0-88192-440-7
     1. Rhododendrons. 2. Landscape gardening. I. Title.
   SB413.R47N45   2000
   635.9'3366—dc21   99-31316
                                                                CIP

Contents

Preface   7
Acknowledgments   9
List of Tables   11

CHAPTER 1. The History of Landscaping with
        Rhododendrons   13
        Plant Hunters—Introduction of New Species—
        Landscaping Origins in Britain—Landscaping Origins in
        North America—The Rhododendron Boom—Suggested
        Reading

CHAPTER 2. Designing by Principle   29
        Strive for Site Unity—Strive for Plant Harmony—Create
        Movement—Garden Tours—Suggested Reading

CHAPTER 3. Planning the Landscape   51
        Taking Inventory of the Site—Narrowing the Choices—
        Drawing the Plan on Paper—Planting—Garden Tours—
        Suggested Reading

CHAPTER 4. The Woodland Garden   71
        Taking Inventory of the Site—Narrowing the Choices—
        Improving the Site—Planting—Companions—Garden
        Tours—Suggested Reading

CONTENTS

CHAPTER 5. The Rock Garden   93
   Taking Inventory of the Site—Narrowing the Choices—
   Improving the Site—Planting—Companions—Garden
   Tours—Suggested Reading

CHAPTER 6. The Mixed Border   111
   Taking Inventory of the Site—Narrowing the Choices—
   Improving the Site—Planting—Companions—Garden
   Tours—Suggested Reading

CHAPTER 7. The Collector's Garden   129
   Species Collections—Hybrid Collections—Geographic
   Collections—Aesthetic Collections—Garden Tours—
   Suggested Reading

CHAPTER 8. The Native Plant Garden   143
   Taking Inventory of the Site—Narrowing the Choices—
   Improving the Site—Planting—Companions—Garden
   Tours—Suggested Reading

CHAPTER 9. The Small Garden   159
   Taking Inventory of the Site—Narrowing the Choices—
   Improving the Site—Planting—Garden Tours—Suggested
   Reading

CHAPTER 10. Special Features   175
   Hedges—Islands—Foundation Plantings—Single-
   Specimen Accents—Bonsai, Espalier, and Topiary—
   Containers—Raised Beds—Water Features—Plantings for
   Fall Color—Plantings for Fragrance—Garden Tours—
   Suggested Reading

Bibliography   193
Index of Plants   203

Color plates follow page 128

Preface

THIS BOOK is an effort to advance the use of the genus *Rhododendron* and to usher these magnificent plants into their rightful place of distinction and influence in today's gardens.

The rhododendron story is an epic one, ranging from wild habitat to grand estates in Britain, and from elite specimen to common shrub in North America. The rhododendron's regal bearing and stunning flowers have fired the horticultural interests of Western gardeners for more than a century. It is no wonder that many gardeners have been blinded into planting more and more rhododendrons, crowding out other garden-worthy plants only to end up with dull rhododendron monocultures. However, the genus *Rhododendron*, with its nearly 1000 species and thousands of hybrids, offers a remarkable range of plant form, foliage texture, and flower color. In addition, the marvelous versatility of rhododendrons makes them useful as companions to many other genera. Today's gardeners wanting to fit a rich palette of plants into a small space will find unlimited possibilities within the genus *Rhododendron*.

The versatility of rhododendrons is no secret to many contemporary garden builders. Many began with rhododendron gardens and gradually enhanced the plantings with companions from other genera. Others began with a favorite garden feature, such as a woodland or planting of natives, and found that rhododendrons would enhance it. Still others began with a difficult garden site and found rhododendrons that would thrive. The experiences of these gardeners have been invaluable to me in writing this book. I have passed on their successes in the "Garden Tours" section of each chapter—hopefully these will be inspiring to you who are looking for new ideas and new plants to make your gardens ever more beautiful and satisfying.

I have used botanical nomenclature of *Rhododendron* following the Sleumer/Edinburgh revision of the genus, as published in the 1998 Royal Horticultural Society *Rhododendron Handbook*. The fancy cultivar names I have used are included in the International Rhododendron Register.

Acknowledgments

I GIVE my profound thanks to Neal Maillet, executive editor at Timber Press, for his encouragement and guidance throughout the process of writing this book, and to Ellen Kussow of Timber Press for her editing of the text. For their review of the manuscript, I am grateful to landscape architect Clive Justice of Vancouver, British Columbia; landscape architect Mai Arbegast of Berkeley, California; nurseryman Larry Allbaugh of Everson, Washington; colorist Woody Ching of Bellingham, Washington; and fellow gardener Rosemary Read. My thanks also go to North American Registrar of Plant Names Jay Murray for her review of *Rhododendron* cultivar names.

Numerous gardeners, many members of the American Rhododendron Society, have generously shared with me their experiences or invited me to their gardens: Larry and Alma Allbaugh, Susan Baker, Dalen and Lori Bayes, Warren Berg, Stephen Brainard, Julia and Chris Cutler, Dee and Dick Daneri, Arthur Dome, Laura Eisener, Wing Fong, Frank Fujioka, Jean Furman, George Gray, J. Powell Huie, Howard Kline, Steve Krebs, Connie LeClair, Barbara and Richard Levin, Bill Moynier, Chip Muller, Niki Muller, Walter Ostrom, Don Paden, Eleanor and Bruce Philp, John Platt, Jim and Suzanne Ramsey, George Ring, June Sinclair, Jeanine and Rex Smith, Parker Smith, Herb and Betty Spady, Pat and Judy Stephens, Bill and Mary Stipe,

Pete Sullivan, Harriet Waldman, and Gordon and Linda Wylie. Public gardens have also made generous contributions of information: Winterthur (in Winterthur, Delaware), Descano (in La Cañada, California), the Arnold Arboretum (in Jamaica Plain, Massachusetts), the Holden Arboretum (in Madison, Ohio), the Washington Park Arboretum (in Seattle, Washington), and the Rhododendron Species Foundation's Rhododendron Species Botanical Garden (in Federal Way, Washington).

I also thank Antique Collectors Club for permission to reprint excerpts from Gertrude Jekyll's *Wall, Water and Woodland Gardens* and *Colour Schemes for the Flower Garden*.

I am indebted to Nicholas Brown for his line drawings that illustrate rhododendrons in diverse landscapes. And thank you to the following people for photographs used in the book: Kay Anderson, Arthur Dome, Wing Fong, Herb Spady, J. Powell Huie, Linda Eirhart, Jean Furman, Earl Sommerville, William Moynier, Gordon Wylie, Tom Ahern, Susan Baker, Nicholas Brown, and George Ring.

Finally, I wish to thank the American Rhododendron Society, whose journal I edit and through which I have been introduced to inspiring gardens and, more importantly, to generous and enthusiastic gardeners.

List of Tables

T HE PLANTS listed in the tables are intended as suggestions only. Size refers to plant size at ten years as listed in *Greer's Guidebook to Available Rhododendrons* (Greer 1996). The following terms of plant size indicate the corresponding heights:

ground cover (gc)	(to 1½ feet, 0.5 meters)
dwarf shrub	(1½ to 3 feet, 0.5 to 1 meter)
small shrub	(3 to 4½ feet, 1 to 1.5 meters)
medium shrub	(4½ to 6½ feet, 1.5 to 2 meters)
large shrub	(6½ to 9 feet, 2 to 3 meters)

Table 1. Evergreen rhododendrons with traditionally shaped leaves (elliptic) page 36

Table 2. Evergreen rhododendrons with narrow leaves (lanceolate) page 38

Table 3. Evergreen rhododendrons with egg-shaped or oval leaves (obovate or orbicular) page 39

Table 4. Deciduous rhododendrons page 40

Table 5. Sun-tolerant rhododendrons page 54

Table 6. Rhododendrons making single- or multi-stemmed trees when mature page 74

Table 7. Companion plants: trees page 75

Table 8. Evergreen azaleas page 81

Table 9. Rhododendrons with creeping habit   page 101
Table 10. Companion plants: shrubs   page 121
Table 11. Companion plants: herbaceous perennials   page 122
Table 12. Companion plants: ferns and mosses   page 125
Table 13. Vireya rhododendron hybrids   page 137
Table 14. Native North American companions:
    small trees   page 151
Table 15. Native North American companions:
    shrubs   page 152
Table 16. Native North American companions:
    herbaceous perennials   page 153
Table 17. Native North American ericaceous
    companions   page 154
Table 18. Rhododendrons suitable as single
    specimens   page 180
Table 19. Fragrant rhododendrons   page 190

The History of Landscaping with Rhododendrons

THE RHODODENDRON landscapes in our modern gardens were first inspired by the sight of rhododendrons growing in the wild. When the early Western plant hunters, especially those adventurers who explored western China and the Himalayas, first beheld the beauty of wild rhododendron landscapes they were awed by the majesty of the land and the plants that inhabited it. So powerful were their impressions that they wrote home to tell about them, building a literature that describes landscapes previously never seen by Western gardeners. Those wild rhododendron landscapes were the seeds of our modern rhododendron gardens. They were the power source behind the development of man-made designs in the British Isles and later in North America.

Plant Hunters

For more than a century explorers re-created through words and photographs the sights of wild rhododendron landscapes for plant lovers at home. As early as 1854 the Englishman Sir Joseph Dalton Hooker wrote in *Himalayan Journals* of seas of mist floating in the deep valleys beneath him, reminding him of the lochs of Scotland, while above him in the alpine meadows the bells of rhododendrons glowed brightly in their various colors.

Rhododendrons often grow precariously on cliffs and ledges in wild mountain landscapes of China and the Himalayas. Such natural formations have long inspired landscape designers.

In a 1917 issue of *Gardener's Chronicle* the Scotsman George Forrest tried to relay to his countrymen the vastness and immensity of the landscapes of dwarf rhododendrons he had found in the Yunnan Province of China. He resorted to comparing them to mile after mile of heather. Reginald Farrer, on the other hand, was not at a loss for words when he described in his 1921 book *The Rainbow Ridge* an alpine meadow at the Mekong-Salween Divide: "one simultaneous riot of colour, laid on, not in dottings and pepperings, but in the broadest and most massive sweeps such as might satisfy the most opulent day-dreams of a herbaceous borderer."

In 1913, Ernest H. Wilson wrote home of cliffs, glens, steep mountainsides, and razor-sharp ridges where rhododendrons grew. He described forests of 30-foot high (9-meter) tree rhododendrons, the archetypal *Rhododendron sutchuenense.* He found groves where rhododendrons grew as the understory, "their flowers making one blaze of color." He wrote of the *Primula, Hydrangea,* and *Acer* companions of the blue-flowered, willow-leafed shrub *R. augustinii*. He described narrow wooded valleys and acres of *R. calophytum*, gigantic in flower and leaf. And he wrote of the subalpine regions where the small-leafed species grew amid the *Saxifraga, Sedum, Primula*, and *Rheum*. Such epic natural landscapes had to be greatly scaled down for gardens, but they provided new inspiration for garden design (Plate 1).

Modern day plant hunters continue the tradition of motivating gardeners with reports of wild landscapes. Peter Cox of Perth, Scotland, is an avid plant hunter. He seeks out remote valleys and mountain passes in western China to collect seed and experience the habitats of *Rhododendron* species. In the *Journal American Rhododendron Society* (spring 1991), he tells of standing at a lookout point over a glacier and deep valley, while behind him on the cliffs cling plants of the shaggy-barked *R. longesquamatum*, its dark, shiny green leaves familiar to many gardeners. He recounts finding the finest group of the elegant *R. edgeworthii* he had ever seen, growing in open areas of virgin forest of 150-foot conifers (46 meters).

Warren Berg of Port Ludlow, Washington, has made numerous treks to China. His photographs capture the dramatic, pristine rhododendron landscapes of western China—the golden-brown leaves with indumentum, or hairy covering, of *Rhododendron phaeochrysum* against a mountain backdrop in the glow of early morning sun, or the dark green leaves of the prostrate *R. forrestii* spreading over rock and moss.

Although North American rhododendrons were discovered some 200 years before, in 1951 Henry T. Skinner, a director of the U.S. National Arboretum, set out to search for native azaleas in the southeastern United States. Gardeners still read his accounts of the red *Rhododendron calendulaceum* blooming on precarious rocky cliff faces and on Gregory Bald in vast expanses of yellow, salmon, pink, and red. They read of *R. prunifolium* blooming on the sides of steep gullies in Georgia and Alabama. Such sights fire the imagination of many a gardener who wishes to grow native azaleas in an appropriate landscape.

Modern plant hunters have been moved to poetry by the breathtaking range of colors and intoxicating fragrance of the swarms of deciduous azaleas on Gregory Bald on the North Carolina-Tennessee border. George McLellan and Sandra McDonald recounted in 1996, "Suddenly we burst into the open of a grassy bald covered with hundreds upon hundreds of brightly colored azaleas in full bloom. All the while our sense of smell was overwhelmed by a wonderful fragrance." Roan Mountain, also on the border between North Carolina and Tennessee, is home to a sea of blooming *Rhododendron catawbiense* that has captivated many photographers. And even those plant hunters who grow *R. occidentale*, the native U.S. West Coast azalea, in their home gardens seek out each spring the fog-drenched streamside and hillside habitats of the species to view firsthand in the wild its shiny green leaves and exquisite pink and white flowers (Plate 2).

Introduction of New Species

The late David Leach traces the history of rhododendron cultivation in the British Isles in his book *Rhododendrons of the World.* He begins in 1656 with the introduction to Britain of the alpenrose, *Rhododendron hirsutum* of the European Alps. Almost 100 years elapsed before the North American native species were exported to England: the eastern deciduous azaleas *R. canescens* and *R. viscosum* and the elepidote, or non-scaly, evergreen *R. maximum.* In 1752 *R. ferrugineum*, also from the European Alps, was brought to England, and soon after, *R. ponticum* found its way to Britain from Gibraltar. Among the last eighteenth-century introductions was *R. dauricum* from Siberia, which has become a parent for many worthy and hardy hybrids including the *Rhododendron* PJM Group.

Early in the nineteenth century more species gradually appeared in cultivation, including the hardy *Rhododendron catawbiense* from North America, which has become a supremely useful parent. But in 1811, the magnificent tree *R. arboreum* arrived from India, the first of the great influx of Asian species that would so transform gardens of the West.

Then, in 1850, Sir Joseph Dalton Hooker changed forever the role rhododendrons would play in garden design. He introduced forty-five new species from Sikkim in the eastern Himalayas, some of which have developed into the greatest of all rhododendrons: the dark red-flowering *Rhododendron thomsonii*, the smooth-barked *R. hodgsonii*, the large-leafed *R. grande*, and the tall, columnar *R. falconeri*. Soon following Hooker's example, Robert Fortune brought from China *R. fortunei*, which would impart sublime fragrance and large, lush flowers to its progeny. Several French missionaries also introduced species from China in the late 1800s. And at about the same time, Augustine Henry introduced the wonderful landscape species *R. augustinii* with its blue-violet flowers and multi-stemmed form. By the end of the nineteenth century nearly 300 species of rhododendrons had been made available to Western gardeners.

The introduction of new species continued into the twentieth century. Among Ernest H. Wilson's many finds was *Rhododendron williamsianum* from China, with its bell-shaped flowers, heart-shaped leaves, and mounding form. In 1917, Wilson also contributed *R. schlippenbachii*, the elegant native azalea of Korea, although rhododendron taxonomist H. H. Davidian mentions that it had previously been introduced by Veitch nursery in England from a Japanese garden. Among the discoveries of George Forrest was the lovely, red-flowering, prostrate, alpine *R. forrestii* from Yunnan Province in China. The great finds made by Frank Kingdon-Ward in China and Tibet included *R. wardii*, which has imparted its bright yellow flower color to many yellow hybrids. The popular garden shrub *R. yakushimanum*, loved for its compact, mounding form and silver indumentum on the upper leaf surface, reached Britain in 1934 when Lionel de Rothschild received two plants from a nursery in Japan. (Taxonomists have recently reclassified *R. yakushimanum* as a subspecies of *R. degronianum*, but for this book the older nomenclature has been retained because of its familiarity among gardeners.) Reginald Farrer and Joseph Rock made further collections in Asia.

The excitement created by the new wealth of *Rhododendron* species was tremendous among both botanists and gardeners. Here was new plant material in dazzling variety with which gardeners could create new landscapes. Excitement centered in Britain, with its long tradition of gardening that had prepared it

17

to take advantage of these new prizes. But news—and seeds— were distributed around the world like foreign spices to people bored with a bland diet of the same handful of garden plants.

Landscaping Origins in Britain

The tremendous wealth of new Asian species forced gardeners to unearth new ways to display the plants' advantages. At the turn of the twentieth century, many growers attempted to make the plantings as visually attractive as possible. Our gardens today are living testament to the many successful arrangements developed to solve the challenge of rhododendron display.

Since those who supported the plant hunters financially tended to be estate owners, nurseries, and botanic gardens, they were the primary recipients of the new *Rhododendron* seed. They devised grand landscapes where the exotic new plants could reside almost naturally while their attributes were shown to best advantage. Nowhere was the endeavor for the grandest rhododendron display more assiduously pursued than in Scotland.

Arduaine, an estate overlooking the sea from Argyll on the west coast of Scotland, was a leading promoter of the new rhododendrons. James Arthur Campbell bought the property in 1897 and built Arduaine. He imported Himalayan rhododendrons in tea crates, and by the 1920s had a collection of some 220 different plants, mostly species. The 20-acre site (8 hectares) needed shelter planting to create a protected environment for the rhododendrons. Two landscaping features are particularly noteworthy: the Woodland Garden and the Gully Path. The Woodland Garden is protected from wind by a shelter of towering trees, and it is planted with an array of rhododendrons, from the dainty, fine-textured *Rhododendron luteiflorum* to the heavy *R. praestans*. Dappled shade gives exactly the right amount of light, with shafts of sun spotlighting first one plant and then another in a most dramatic way. The Gully Path, which follows a deep ravine, is even more sheltered. The plants along its sides are protected from frost with a steep gradient that allows cold air to flow down the slope. And a canopy of Japanese larch (*Larix kaempferi*)

18

adds an insulating layer of vegetation and air over the plants beneath them. The somewhat tender tree *R. arboreum* and the even more tender, fragrant shrubs *R. formosum* and *R. maddenii* thrive here. Woodland and ravine gardens are two landscape features seen again and again where rhododendrons are grown.

Arduaine, still flourishing, exemplifies many landscape features that work for rhododendrons. The pond is adorned with mixed plantings at its edges, a mixed border combines trees, shrubs, and herbaceous perennials, and a rockery has been developed on a natural rock outcrop. The Arduaine gardens use a wide variety of genera that grow happily and beautifully alongside rhododendrons. Perhaps the most significant lesson that can be taken from Arduaine is the overall design of the garden: the distinct features induce visitors to pass from one to the next with a feeling of anticipation, always expecting something new and different ahead.

Stonefield is another historic garden that is home to some of the first rhododendrons. This site, also in Argyll, at the edge of Loch Fyne, raised the seeds collected in 1850 from Sikkim by Sir Joseph Dalton Hooker. Here mature specimens of many Himalayan species now thrive with astounding vigor: *Rhododendron arboreum, R. campanulatum, R. thomsonii, R. cinnabarinum, R. falconeri, R. grande,* and *R. campylocarpum* (Plate 3, Plate 4). So much at home are these Asian rhododendrons that they seed naturally and give rise to so-called Stonefield seedlings. Those who have visited the Himalayas and have seen these species in their native land claim that Stonefield is reminiscent of the country near Darjeeling where many grow. In the mild climate of Scotland's west coast, protected by magnificent stands of conifers and broadleafed trees on the slopes leading down to Loch Fyne, these historic rhododendrons and their companions, in combination with the mansion house itself, illustrate the grand English landscape style that can still be used to grow and display these equally grand rhododendrons.

The English landscape style, in which estate plantings evoke the natural lay of the land with curves, slopes, and ponds, developed in the eighteenth century when it gradually replaced the seventeenth-century formality that had come from French and

Italian influences. This more naturalistic style was brought to its height by Lancelot "Capability" Brown, a landscape designer who lived from 1715 to 1783. He directed installations at Kew and Blenheim, earning a reputation for using simple materials and techniques to achieve natural harmony. His style and that of the time made extensive use of trees and grand expanses of green lawn. An adjunct to the style was the "American garden," in which were planted newly imported American species, later including rhododendrons. Also, the "shrubbery" developed as an alternative to the formal clipped hedge. The naturalistic English landscape style prepared designers and gardeners with an approach that proved receptive to the flood of rhododendrons to come in the nineteenth century.

Even before the great influx of rhododendrons, new plant material was arriving in Britain from around the world. Collecting exotic plants and developing the horticultural skills to grow them came more into favor. During the sixty-four-year reign of Queen Victoria, from 1837 to 1901, the glasshouse was home to many exotic plants, including the newly discovered Malaysian rhododendrons of section *Vireya*. At first, not only these truly tender rhododendrons were housed under glass, but new, hardier ones were protected until their tolerance to the climate was tested. The Victorian innovation of bedding schemes, where plants are laid out in geometric designs, was fashionable at the time but proved ineffective at highlighting rhododendrons.

The designer William Robinson led the way late in the nineteenth century toward answering the question of how to use the new rhododendrons in the landscape. He took the eighteenth-century concept of creating the natural landscape and applied it to groups of garden plants that require the same growing conditions. He encouraged the plants to grow naturally as they might in the wild. In his gardens, the design was subordinate to the plants' natural growth and beauty, an approach well suited to the growing of rhododendrons.

Once the new Asian species were established in Britain, a new wave of activity began: hybridizing. *Rhododendron griffithianum* proved to be a wonderful parent, producing *Rhododendron* 'Cynthia', 'Pink Pearl', and the Loderi Group, including 'Loderi

King George' and 'Loderi Venus', which all are still on the market (Plate 5). It also combined with *R. campanulatum* to produce the still popular 'Beauty of Littleworth'. And 'Shilsonii' owes its parentage to *R. thomsonii* and *R. barbatum.*

Finally, the question of color had to be addressed if rhododendron species and hybrids were to be used to their fullest in garden design. It was Gertrude Jekyll, a colleague of William Robinson, who approached the matter of color head-on. In her 1908 book *Colour Schemes for the Flower Garden* she divided rhododendrons into six classes of color combinations, warning against the use of crimsons and purples together and the planting of rhododendrons and azaleas side by side. Traditional designs such as the woodland garden continue to find favor among many British gardeners and offer splendid solutions for rhododendron lovers.

Landscaping Origins in North America

Before the mid-nineteenth-century introduction of Asian rhododendrons, gardens in North America undoubtedly contained native species, such as *Rhododendron catawbiense, R. maximum, R. minus,* and the East Coast azaleas. In the 1700s, John Bartram, the first American botanist, kept his collection of some 2000 native plants in a garden on the Schuylkill River outside Philadelphia. He discovered *R. arborescens* and introduced British gardeners to *R. maximum.* Thomas Jefferson was another early gardener with a strong interest in native plants. He grew *R. periclymenoides* (wild honeysuckle) and *R. maximum* (rosebay rhododendron) at Monticello. Jefferson's landscapes were influenced by the naturalistic eighteenth-century British styles, reflected in Monticello's walks and beds that curved between groves of trees.

In 1841, at a time when interest in gardening and plants was growing rapidly in America, an influential publication appeared by horticulturist Andrew Jackson Downing. His *Landscape Gardening: A Treatise on the Theory and Practice of Landscape Gardening Adjusted to America, with a View to the Improvement of Country Residences* advocates the English landscape style modified by the

North American environment. Reminding gardeners to adhere to the common principles of design, Downing directs that the natural beauty of the site be the beginning of the design, along with the house itself.

In 1870, Frank J. Scott in *Victorian Gardens: The Art of Beautifying Suburban Homes, A Victorian Handbook* instructed American homeowners to create a refuge from the bustle and grime of the city. Scott envisioned garden designs that invited the neighbors rather than fencing them out, as was most common in the city. He suggested planting large, long expanses of lawn that would preserve the line of sight from house to street and vice versa. Instead of the enclosed garden favored by the British, Scott encouraged Americans to create views from the street toward the house, and to decorate the foundations with plantings. The expanses of lawn could be divided and particular views defined by planting shrubs and trees in belts or groups radiating from the house to the street. Rhododendrons could be massed under and between the trees, along with spireas (*Spiraea* spp.), lilacs (*Syringa* spp.), and weigelas (*Weigela* spp.), with dwarf rhododendrons and other small plants in front. Rhododendrons of medium size could be planted under bay windows.

The Art of Landscape Gardening, published in 1907 by the American Society of Landscape Architects, looks at the influence of horticulturist Andrew Jackson Downing on the leading American landscape architect at the end of the nineteenth century—Frederick Law Olmsted. Along with his two sons, Olmsted dominated American landscape design for the greater part of the nineteenth century. His style is characterized by the creation of a highly complex texture in a mixed planting, alternated with broad expanses of lawn. He was always looking for the broad landscape effect. In fact, he considered gardens visually separate from the spaces he designed for landscape effect and often walled them in.

The Olmsted influence extended from small gardens to country estates and to public parks. His pastoral design of New York's Central Park—a place for workers to find relief from urban stress—was precipitated by both Downing's theories and the English landscape tradition. Olmsted's home and office from 1883 to 1895, Fairsted in Brookline, Massachusetts, is an example of his early landscape style. The design makes ample use of American natives allowed to grow in a wild manner. Specific features at Fairsted include the incorporation of plants already growing on the site, a rolling lawn, a dell called the Hollow where *Rhododendron maximum* is planted, a rock outcrop for a rock garden, and a bank of trees and shrubs—which all flow in an unbroken design. The U.S. National Park Service is now restoring Fairsted based on the site as it existed in the 1920s, which is changed from the original design by having a smaller and less diverse number of shrubs. The plant list for the restored Hollow includes *R. maximum* and *R. schlippenbachii.*

In 1888 Olmsted designed Biltmore near Asheville, North Carolina, for George W. Vanderbilt. His instructions for planting the approach to the estate give an idea of his grand landscape style. First would be 10,000 plants of the native American *Rhododendron maximum* as background, to be fronted by a variety of evergreen plants, including "five thousand of the most splendid hybrid rhododendrons such as they exhibit under tents at the horticultural gardens of London" (Beveridge and Rocheleau 1995). These would be supplemented by Himalayan and alpine rhododendrons, and among these would be scattered laurel (*Laurus* spp.), native and Japanese andromedas (*Andromeda* spp.), Japanese euonymus (*Euonymus* spp.), aucubas (*Aucuba* spp.), and mahonias (*Mahonia* spp.), under-planted with low-growing evergreen plants. Olmsted was ever on the lookout for plant material to create the effect of "complexity of light and shadow near the eye" that was essential to his "picturesque" style (Beveridge and Rocheleau 1995). The Edward B. Dunn Garden in Seattle, a more modest project done in 1915 by the Olmsted firm, shows the same principles at work.

As in Britain, botanic gardens and the owners of private estates were the main collectors of rhododendrons in America. At the turn of the century the Asian rhododendrons were expensive garden plants only the wealthy could afford. The owners and designers of these turn-of-the-century American country estates used the growing number of cultivated rhododendrons in the trade to help build their grand family seats. And, as the British had, the Americans gradually relied less and less on formal Italianate design and more and more on the English landscape style and the design ideas of the Olmsteds. The North American native *Rhododendron maximum* was often used, as at the Biltmore estate, but the Asian natives and new hybrids slowly filtered in.

Garden designer Beatrix Jones Farrand lived from 1872 to 1959 and studied in Jamaica Plain, Massachusetts, at the Arnold Arboretum, which had been designed by Olmsted, and where the new rhododendrons had been planted by Charles Sprague Sargent, the arboretum's director from 1873 to 1927. Farrand wrote after an arboretum visit, "The rhododendrons, if possible, are finer than ever! All agree there is no shrub to compare with them for grand effect" (Brown 1995).

At the London, Connecticut, estate of Edward S. Harkness, Farrand combined the hybrids *Rhododendron* 'Mrs. Milner' (red), 'Giganteum' (rosy crimson), and 'Album Elegans' (white) at the periphery of a formal planting (Brown 1995). All three cultivars, similar in leaf shape, are crosses made by Anthony Waterer of England. They all carry *R. catawbiense* in their parentage for hardiness. In the rock garden at Oakpoint, Bayville, on Long Island, Farrand planted rhododendrons to give shade, and at Reef Point, her home in Maine, she planted both rhododendrons and azaleas and discovered that azaleas loved the sea mists. Farrand went on to design the Dumbarton Oaks estate in Washington, D.C., with its dazzling azalea plantings.

Many other estates across the country used rhododendrons in their plantings. They adorned a walled shrub garden at Edgewood in Millbrook, New York. At Planting Fields on Long Island, another Olmsted garden, the woods were under-planted with rhododendrons. At Box Hill, also on Long Island, a long line of rhododendrons edged the drive. Rare dwarf rhododendrons were used in the rock garden at Moggy Hollow in New Jersey. In Akron, Ohio, Frank Sieberling's Stan Hywet displayed an allé of rhododendrons and azaleas with the London plane tree (Platanus ×acerifolia).

Estate owners in the Pacific Northwest were discovering that many Asian species and hybrids were well suited to the moderate maritime climate. At Elk Rock, a 13-acre estate (5 hectares) near

Portland, Oregon, designed by the Olmsted firm, Peter Kerr established his rhododendron collection amid native flora, including coast redwoods (*Sequoia sempervirens*), magnolias (*Magnolia* spp.), and witch-hazels (*Hamamelis* spp.). In the mild Coast Range south of San Francisco, the Filoli estate, though formal and Italianate in design, placed rhododendrons at the perimeter in an informal, relaxed manner.

The Rhododendron Boom

Through the increasing use of rhododendrons in botanical gardens and the estates of America's upper classes, the rhododendrons became known as the elite among evergreens, news which spread rapidly to the rest of the continent. And as more and more gardeners discovered the species and hybrids, availability of the plants through nurseries grew with demand.

The surge in rhododendron popularity included the excitement of hybridizing that drew both professional and amateur American growers. They created fantastic varieties suitable for American climates. A cross by Charles Dexter of Sandwich, Massachusetts, made between 1925 and 1942 resulted in *Rhododendron* 'Scintillation', which still flourishes in many of today's gardens. Two East Coast hybridizers, Joseph Gable and Guy Nearing, were busily hybridizing during the 1930s and 1940s, trying for hardy hybrids suitable for the East Coast. Two of their numerous lasting creations are Gable's *Rhododendron* 'Caroline' with its pale orchid-pink flowers and glossy leaves, and Nearing's 'Wyanokie' with its abundance of small white flowers on a small bush. In 1939 Benjamin Yeo Morrison of Washington, D.C., introduced the first of his Glenn Dale hybrids, a group of evergreen azaleas bred for cold hardiness and large flowers. James Barto of Eugene, Oregon, selected superior forms from the vast collection of species planted in his Pacific Northwest woodland.

Nursery catalogs extolling the beauty of the new hybrids entranced gardeners. Few could resist when the 1962 catalog from Bovees nursery in Portland, Oregon, presented new hybrids entering the market such as *Rhododendron* 'Goldbug': "a most attractive dwarf plant . . . most unusual flowers at first scarlet then changing to orange, then to cream yellow heavily spotted dark red." The species *R. yakushimanum* was also making its entry into the market, and Bovees listed it in the 1962 catalog: "For the first time we have a few small plants three years old from selfed seed from our award plant. Probably the most famous and one of the most beautiful dwarf rhododendrons and exceedingly rare."

The democratization of the genus *Rhododendron* gained even more momentum with the founding of the American Rhododendron Society in 1945. Though based in Portland, Oregon, and American in name, the society held strong ties to Britain. John Henny, first president of the new society, traveled to England to meet rhododendron growers, among them Edmund de Rothschild, founder of Exbury Gardens. Along with the excitement of discovering new species and hybrids suitable for North America came British ideas on how to use the new-found wonders in the landscape. Through articles and tours, members were introduced to North American and British gardens that enabled them to see for themselves landscape designs that might work on their own garden sites. By its fiftieth anniversary in 1995, the American Rhododendron Society had amassed a generous body of literature on landscape design available to all its members.

An early successful landscaping venture of the society was, in 1950, to establish a rhododendron garden at Crystal Springs Lake in Portland under the shade of a native tree canopy. Many species were grown from seed collected in the Himalayas and China, and others were given by early Portland-area nurserymen and hybridizers. Two forty-year-old plants of *Rhododendron* 'Cynthia' were brought to the garden for its dedication in 1951. Forty-five years later a grove of old 'Loderi King George' and 'Loderi Venus' create their own canopy of green and, in spring, a roof of rapturously fragrant blossoms. Though grand in its scale, the Crystal Springs Rhododendron Garden is instructive in ways to use rhododendrons within a natural site to complement the land's existing features, in this case woodland, lakeside, stream gully, and grassy areas. The garden also exemplifies ways to incorporate suitable companion plants.

Besides introducing the world of rhododendrons to the American gardener of modest means, the American Rhododendron Society made it possible for its growing legion of members to participate in a uniquely British and upper class activity— the support of plant exploration in Asia in exchange for seed collected in the wild. Americans could now follow a tradition started more than a century before with Sir Joseph Dalton Hooker's first journey into the high Himalayas in search of new species. In 1948, the American Rhododendron Society supported Joseph F. Rock, a research fellow at Harvard University and respected plant hunter, in an expedition to the Yunnan-Tibet border. Thus began a series of letters published in the society's *Quarterly Bulletin of the American Rhododendron Society* from Rock to the society's members telling of the seed enclosed with his correspondence. One 1948 letter explains, "I have had a man collect seeds on the snow range here, only a few miles from here, and as I write the snow peak is aglow from the setting sun. I thought that you would like to have fresh seed of some of the rhododendrons growing in the snow range, and so I enclose seeds of the following. . . ."

As the fever of rhododendron collecting increased, so did questions of how to place the plants attractively and healthily in the landscape. From the beginning, gardeners were overjoyed with the versatility of their new plants. They could be used as foundation planting around the house, as screen plantings, as crevice plants in a rock garden, as part of a formal setting, and, especially, as an understory in the woodland garden. In 1946, an article by O. E. Holmdahl appeared in the American Rhododendron Society *Rhododendron Yearbook* detailing the myriad of landscape uses for the "monarch of all ornamental shrubs." As early as this, the rhododendron's versatility for the garden was recognized, along with potential problems, such as overgrown foundation plantings and the heavy monotony that can result from overplanting. Through the society's quarterly journal, gardeners were being instructed in the many aspects of landscape design: color in rhododendron plantings, ground covers for rhododendrons, foliage interest, trees to associate with rhododendrons, naturalistic planting of native azaleas, companion plants, design principles, evergreen azaleas in the landscape, the rock garden, shade gardens, and container gardening.

Yet today new challenges present themselves as gardens become smaller, new plants enter the market to compete with rhododendrons, ecology becomes a design factor, and gardeners' tastes change. But with a century-old tradition of landscaping with rhododendrons behind them and an enduring love of the genus within them, gardeners are meeting these challenges with innovation and creativity.

Suggested Reading

Elliott, Brent. 1996. Rhododendrons in British gardens: a short history. In *Rhododendron Story*, Ed. Cynthia Postan. London: Royal Horticultural Society.

Hobhouse, Penelope. 1992. *Gardening Through the Ages*. New York: Simon and Schuster.

Leach, David G. 1961. *Rhododendrons of the World*. New York: Charles Scribner's Sons.

Lyte, Charles. 1983. *Plant Hunters*. London: Orbis.

CHAPTER 2

Designing by Principle

B ASIC DESIGN principles can be tools as useful as spades or trowels for the job of garden building. Many gardeners know these fundamentals instinctively but disregard them in the heat of enthusiasm over this plant or that. When shaping a landscape, gardeners cannot ignore the basics of design if they hope to satisfy the eye and spirit. Be aware of the site unity, plant harmonies, and movement in the garden. Be aware of the effect each plant and the placement of each plant have on these principles. To garden by principle requires a certain amount of self discipline but will, in the long run, save time, effort, and money.

The distinction between "landscaping" and "garden building" is significant for a better understanding of design. Landscaping refers to the enhancement of property with plantings, which may include a garden. Garden building or making, in the classic sense, is the creation of an enclosed space safe and separate from the surrounding world. For instance, the foundation of a house can be decorated with landscaping, but the planting itself is not a garden.

Strive for Site Unity

The principle of unity, in which all elements contribute to a main theme, is as basic to garden building as to any artistic endeavor.

A central idea must bind the parts together to create a satisfying piece of work. In landscaping and, specifically, garden building, the goal is to create a place, an ideal sort of place, where mind and spirit will be happily engaged without distraction. A united landscape, in which every component makes its contribution to the main theme, lifts a place out of the ordinary, giving it impact and making it a place in which you yearn to be. Plants and structures are extraneous if they do not make their contribution. Without unity a garden is merely a smattering of plants.

Nature undisturbed by the human hand reveals much about unity. For good reason the wild rhododendron landscapes described by plant hunters have fired the imaginations of gardeners for more than a century. These natural creations have a unity that appeals to our deepest sense of beauty. In the best natural landscapes, plants clearly belong together; they are bound by an essential unity that arises from the site through repetition, balanced scale, and simplicity.

Site unity in a landscape can be created through the repetition of plants. Consider the meadow described by George Forrest in the alpine reaches of the Yunnan Province of China. One plant, a dwarf rhododendron, repeated itself over the landscape, mile after mile. Forrest was in awe. Would the picture have been improved, for example, by adding a single tree of the columnar *Rhododendron arboreum*? The uninterrupted, vast rhododendron sea created a sense of unity. Few garden sites offer "mile after mile" to work with, but the lesson is the same. A stunning landscape can result from repeating a plant or planting throughout the garden. The Royal Botanic Garden Edinburgh and the Rhododendron Species Botanical Garden in Federal Way, Washington, both exhibit excellent examples of the technique at work.

Another aspect of natural landscapes that affects their site unity is scale. Unity of scale contributed to the powerful effect of the rhododendron sea; the planting was in perfect proportion to the open expanse of sky above it. Modern plant hunters at the Doshong La in Tibet in June 1995 witnessed an alpine meadow in which red-flowering dwarf rhododendrons, *Rhododendron forrestii* and *R. chamaethomsonii*, violet individuals of *Primula* and *Bergenia*, and yellow plants of *Diapensia* happily shared the same bed (Muller and White 1996). Despite the variety in flower color and foliage textures, the plants were drawn together by their similarity in scale. The low, ground-hugging stature of all the plants connected one to the other in a unified whole. The wildflower meadows of the Great Plains, the heaths of England, and the tundra of the North are nature-made examples of plantings in which a variety of characteristics succeed through unity of scale.

Simplicity also can contribute to site unity. Ernest H. Wilson was impressed with a stand of virgin forest he encountered in western China. Here the landscape was layered, with a tree canopy of silver firs (*Abies alba*) and birches (*Betula* spp.), under which grew a dense undergrowth of four species of rhododendrons, *Rhododendron oreodoxa* var. *fargesii*, *R. maculiferum*, *R. sutchuenense*, and *R. adenopodum*, "most of them bushes ten to twenty feet tall, their flowers making one blaze of colour" (Wilson 1913). These species produce flowers from pink to deep rose to pale lilac, all capable of having purple blotches, although Wilson never mentioned this characteristic. Here site unity results from the simplicity of a tree canopy of only two genera and an understory of exclusively rhododendrons of the same height with flower colors adjacent on the spectrum—and they might all have had purple blotches. In spite of the layered composition of the forest, simplicity unifies the many components of the site.

Plants growing in wild locations have similarities in aspect simply for their survival. Alpine rhododendrons need their tiny leaves to withstand the bright sunlight of the mountain air, but the forest-dwelling species have large leaves and need shade overhead. Although landscaped sites are designed and planted by humans and otherwise influenced by human activity, they are tied to nature through the site's climate, soil, terrain, and native vegetation. When you carry out a site's natural demands, a unified landscape emerges in which all parts relate to the site. Though you may at times curse the land or the climate for its unrelenting hostility to certain plants, the site is, in fact, a design blessing, because complying with its standards will help bring about unity.

But when designing a landscape, you must also cater to the structures existing on a site, such as the house, outbuildings, and large trees, for they will either contribute to or detract from the overall unity. The house itself is the most significant influence. Its style—country, colonial, modern, formal, and so on—and scale will indicate the style and scale you must give to the garden to bring unity between the house and the landscape. Garden structures also need to be of a style and scale in keeping with the house and site in order to sustain unity. For formal gardens, clipped hedges and walls belong with their strong geometry, but fences and shrubberies lend themselves to informal styles.

According to garden designer Joe Eck, "The house that sits in the center of a garden is one of the two principal factors that determine its scale. The other is what lies beyond [the garden], be it adjacent buildings or nature itself" (Eck 1996). The neighboring environment will present limitations on the design, but in return, the environment will help bind the house to a unique location. A landscape that connects to the nearby environment —be it farmland, ocean beach, wilderness, or city block—will look and feel natural and comfortable because of the unity with its larger setting. Using native plants is one satisfying way to connect the site to its neighboring environment.

Strive for Plant Harmony

Site unity is the foundation for making satisfying landscapes and gardens, but how do we use the rich array of plants at our disposal without sacrificing unity? Even within the genus *Rhododendron* the variation is so great that trying to create unity in a planting is often baffling. The primary principle upholding site unity in the garden is plant harmony, which is the agreeable combination of plant parts. Achieving harmony begins with an in-depth knowledge of the form, texture, and color of plants (Plates 6, 7, and 8).

PLANT FORM

Awareness of plant form is a good place to begin building plant knowledge. The genus *Rhododendron* includes such forms as single-trunked and multi-stemmed, upright-growing and wide-spreading, open-growing and compact, and mounding and pros-

32

trate (Plate 9). The great diversity in size varies through ground cover, dwarf shrub, medium shrub, large shrub, and tree. Garden builders must remember that form and size change over time and, as a result, change the landscape and garden. Landscape architect Clive Justice (personal communication) of Vancouver, British Columbia, explains the multitude of considerations professional garden designers must make when evaluating the many rhododendron plant-form choices for a garden:

> A landscape architect wants to know whether a rhododendron will be a tree, a shrub, or a ground cover. . . . A designer wants to know what shape and habit the plant will assume. If a tree, whether it will be small or medium, whether single-stemmed or multi-stemmed, narrow or upright, spreading or round-headed. If a shrub—and we can assume that most rhododendrons will fall into this classification of landscape plant material—whether it will be small, medium, or large, compact or open, upright or spreading. Looking for a rhododendron ground cover, a landscape architect wants to know if the selection will be creeping, mounding, or arching in habit or whether it will grow flat, low, or high.

The variation within the genus allows rhododendrons to play many roles in a landscape. Some grow as wide-spreading trees, such as *Rhododendron calophytum* or the hybrid *Rhododendron* 'Loderi King George'. Others are upright-growing, multi-stemmed shrubs, such as *R. augustinii*, which is useful as a screen. The open-growing form of *R. nuttallii* reveals a rich, dark red bark. The distinctly mounding form of *R. yakushimanum* in new growth creates a perfect silver dome. Spreading its shiny leaves and bright red flowers along the ground is the prostrate *R. forrestii*. Form can be repeated in plants of different genera, as well, to create a harmonious chord, as in a planting of the mounding *R. williamsianum* with the mounding *Acer palmatum* 'Ever Red'.

FOLIAGE TEXTURE

The visual texture that a plant gives to a design derives mainly from its foliage. Among rhododendrons, textures range from fine to coarse, from airily delicate to ponderously heavy. A great many evergreen rhododendrons are of medium texture, lending stability and strength with their reassuringly substantial leaves that survive all seasons.

Leaf size greatly affects texture. The minuscule ½-inch leaf (1.3 centimeters) of *Rhododendron calostrotum* subsp. *keleticum* Radicans Group creates a fine-textured carpet under the single, violet flowers. The canoe-paddle-sized leaf of *R. sinogrande*, which can reach 30 inches in length (75 centimeters), creates a coarse texture that can be dramatic. Grouping leaf sizes together or grading leaf sizes from large to medium to small in a planting of rhododendrons are suggestions for creating textural harmony (Grant and Grant 1954).

Leaf shape also affects texture and can vary from the narrow, lanceolate leaves of *Rhododendron roxieanum*, which grow in upright, staccato-like whorls, to the round, orbicular leaves of *R. orbiculare*, appropriately named. How the leaves attach to the branches also contributes to texture: pointing upright in the case of *R. roxieanum* or folding downward and forming a collar for the bright truss of flowers in the case of *R. sutchuenense*.

The tactile texture of a plant's leaves also affects the visual texture of a planting. In keeping with the characteristic variety within the genus, the surface texture of rhododendron leaves ranges from the shiny leaves of the hardy Siberian native *Rhododendron dauricum* to the matte surface of the splendid dark green leaves of *Rhododendron* 'Taurus'. New foliage often adds a whole new and striking dimension, coming on like a second season of bloom after the flowers. The upright new foliage of *R. macabeanum* is covered with a white indumentum in contrast to the shiny green of old leaves, and it is further decorated with red leaf bracts along the leaf stems. The magnificent new foliage of *R. yakushimanum* is also decorated with white indumentum on its gracefully curving, convex leaves, with their added surprise of fawn-colored indumentum on the undersides.

Similar foliage textures can be used to link rhododendrons and their companions in harmonious combinations. For instance, the taxonomically related *Rhododendron augustinii*, *R. lutescens*, and *R. yunnanense* all have fine-textured, lanceolate

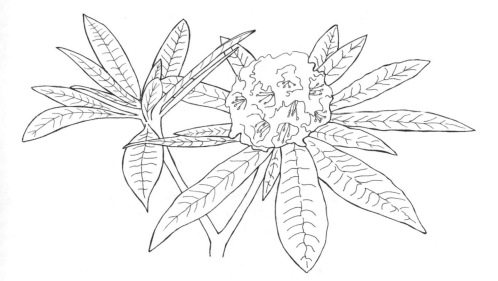

The coarse foliage texture of *Rhododendron sinogrande* is a result of its large leaf size. The gloss on leaf surfaces and silver indumentum on leaf undersides draw attention to the magnificent foliage.

leaves of approximately the same size. Leaf color, however, varies from the dark green leaves of *R. augustinii* to the bright green leaves of *R. yunnanense* to the bronze-red leaves of *R. lutescens*. The narrow, lance-like leaf shape of these three rhododendrons could be repeated in a planting of bamboo, with even more lance-like foliage and an even more upright growing habit (of course, take precautions against choosing an invasive bamboo).

A member of the American Rhododendron Society with a keen interest in the texture of rhododendrons is Wing Fong of Cherry Hill, New Jersey. He points out that each part of a rhododendron—foliage, bud, and flower—has its own shape, pattern, line, and color. These can be played against each other to create harmonies, for instance, oval leaves against narrow leaves, shiny leaves against matte leaves, oval buds against lance-shaped buds, white flower color against bright flower color. Fong explains, "We usually don't associate lines with rhododendrons, but there are many: in *Rhododendron calendulaceum*, the long, thin line of stamens and pistils contrasts with petals; in *R. racemosum*,

Table 1. Evergreen rhododendrons with traditionally shaped leaves (elliptic)

	USDA hardiness zone	Plant size in ten years	Plant form	Foliage texture	Flower color
argyrophyllum subsp. *nankingense*	7	medium shrub	rounded	medium, white ind	p
barbatum	7	medium shrub	upright	medium, bristly	r
brachycarpum	4	small shrub	compact, rounded	medium, brown ind	w, p
bureavii	6	small shrub	rounded	medium, rust ind	w, p
campanulatum subsp. *aeruginosum*	6	small shrub	rounded	medium, bluish ind	w, v
fortunei	5	medium shrub	open, upright	medium	w, p
maximum	4	medium shrub	compact	medium, glossy	w, p
phaeochrysum	7	medium shrub	compact, upright	medium, brown ind	w, p
smirnowii	5	small shrub	open, upright	medium, brown ind	v
ungernii	8	small shrub	open, upright	medium, gray ind	w, p
wardii	7	small shrub	open	medium	y
wiltonii	6	small shrub	compact	medium, brown ind	w, p
'Apricot Fantasy'	6	small shrub	rounded	medium	y/p bicolor
'Bellringer'	7	small shrub	compact	medium	w
'Brown Eyes'	5	medium shrub	compact	medium	p
'Catawbiense Album'	4	medium shrub	rounded	medium	w
'Grace Seabrook'	6	small shrub	spreading	medium, light ind	r
'Hallelujah'	5	small shrub	rounded	coarse	r
'Hélène Schiffner'	6	small shrub	upright	medium, red stems	w

				p/o bicolor
'Lem's Cameo'	7	medium shrub	rounded	medium, glossy	r
'Noyo Chief'	9	medium shrub	rounded	medium, glossy	
'Purple Splendour'	6	medium shrub	compact	coarse	v
'Scintillation'	5	medium shrub	rounded	medium, glossy	p
'Trude Webster'	6	medium shrub	rounded	medium	p

Abbreviations: ind = indumentum, gc = ground cover, p = pink, r = red, w = white, v = violet, o = orange, y = yellow. See List of Tables for sizes.

Table 2. Evergreen rhododendrons with narrow leaves (lanceolate)

	USDA hardiness zone	Plant size in ten years	Plant form	Foliage texture	Flower color
aberconwayi	9	small shrub	upright	medium	w
augustinii	6	medium shrub	compact, upright	fine	v
cinnabarinum	7	medium shrub	upright	medium, shaggy bark	y, o
elegantulum	7	small shrub	compact	medium, red-brown ind	p
griersonianum	8	small shrub	spreading	medium	r
hyperythrum	5	small shrub	compact	medium	w, p
insigne	7	small shrub	compact	medium, glossy	p
roxieanum var. *oreonastes*	6	small shrub	compact	medium, red-brown ind	w
rubiginosum	7	medium shrub	open, upright	medium	p, v
strigillosum	7	small shrub	rounded	medium, bristly	r
yakushimanum	4	dwarf shrub	rounded	medium, brown, white ind	w, p
yunnanense	7	medium shrub	upright	fine	w, p

Abbreviations: ind = indumentum, gc = ground cover, p = pink, r = red, w = white, v = violet, o = orange, y = yellow.
See List of Tables for sizes.

Table 3. Evergreen rhododendrons with egg-shaped or oval leaves (obovate or orbicular)

	USDA hardi-ness zone	Plant size in ten years	Plant form	Foliage texture	Flower color
clementinae	6	small shrub	rounded	medium, brown ind	w, p
orbiculare	7	small shrub	rounded	medium, round	p
oreotrephes	7	medium shrub	upright	medium, bluish	p
thomsonii	7	medium shrub	upright	medium, red bark	r
williamsianum	6	gc	rounded, spreading	fine, bronze new growth	p

Abbreviations: ind = indumentum, gc = ground cover, p = pink, r = red, w = white, v = violet, o = orange, y = yellow. See List of Tables for sizes.

Table 4. Deciduous rhododendrons

	USDA hardiness zone	Plant size in ten years	Plant form	Foliage texture	Flower color
albrechtii	5	small shrub	upright	fine, at branch ends	p
austrinum	5	medium shrub	upright	fine	y, o, r
calendulaceum	4	medium shrub	upright, spreading	fine	y, o
cumberlandense	5	small shrub	upright	fine	o, r
luteum	5	small shrub	upright	fine	y
macrosepalum	8	small shrub	rounded	fine, linear	r-v
mucronulatum	5	medium shrub	open	medium	p, v
occidentale	6	medium shrub	upright	medium	w, p
periclymenoides	5	medium shrub	upright	fine	w, p
prunifolium	5	small shrub	upright	fine	o, r
quinquefolium	6	dwarf shrub	compact	fine	w
schlippenbachii	4	small shrub	open, upright	fine	p, w

Abbreviations: ind = indumentum, gc = ground cover, p = pink, r = red, w = white, v = violet, o = orange, y = yellow. See List of Tables for sizes.

short thin lines burst like firecrackers; in *R. strigillosum*, new growth makes red, stubby lines" (personal communication).

FLOWER COLOR

The effective use of color in the garden can be mystifying. Even the casual observer of color knows that all reds are not equal—or blues or yellows or greens. Trial and error will lead to pleasing color combinations, but this method often grows into frustration. A better approach is to develop a keener awareness of the qualities of color as we see them. Hue, value, and chroma are the three primary elements that define a color. And the effects of light and simultaneous contrast on those elements also influence a color scheme.

Hue is probably the easiest color concept to understand. It refers to the most commonly noted attribute of color, its redness, blueness, and so on. The term *hue* refers to only this one quality of color. A color wheel shows hues on the color spectrum, including mixtures of the primary hues red, blue, and yellow, which create the secondary hues violet, orange, and green. Further gradations between the hues yield more hues, for instance yellow and orange will make yellow-orange, and red and orange will make red-orange. Analogous hues are those adjacent on the color wheel, and complementary hues are those opposite on the color wheel (Plate 10).

In hue combinations, the high contrast of complementary hues creates excitement, but too much can result in chaos. The low contrast of analogous hues is soothing, but too much can be boring. The flowers of *Rhododendron augustinii* are in the blue-violet range, and the flowers of *R. lutescens* are yellow to yellow-orange. These nearly opposite hues would offer high contrast. The hues of many bicolor rhododendron hybrids, such as *Rhododendron* 'Lem's Cameo' with its luscious oranges, creams, and pinks, offer opportunities for unusual combinations (Plate 11).

Groups of analogous hues arouse various emotional reactions in viewers. The warm hues of red, orange, and yellow are aggressive and demand attention. The cool violet and blue hues are more calm and agreeable, easily stepping to the background of a planting. The green of foliage and the hues it adds to a com-

41

bination can often be overlooked in planning, but the many variations of green comprise most of the garden and affect the success of flower color combinations. Foliage hues arouse different reactions in viewers just as flower hues do; yellow-green is warmest and blue-green is coolest.

The value of a color is another concept that helps in understanding successful combinations. Value refers to the light or dark quality caused by the addition of white or black to a hue. The addition of white makes a light value, resulting in pastels or tints, and the addition of black results in shades of dark value. In rhododendron flower color, pastels are most common, but the whole range of value can be found, from the dark *Rhododendron* 'Purple Splendour' to the pastel 'Loderi Venus'. In fact, the white in pastel flowers of different hues can unify them in a planting, as black can unify dark shades.

The additional color concept of chroma, or saturation, refers to the intensity or purity of a color. Chroma describes the amount of gray added to a hue. Saturated colors of high chroma are intense and pure, and low chroma colors appear hazy or diluted. The vireya rhododendron flower colors are known for their high intensity, or high chroma. The vireyas are a subtropical group of rhododendrons native to Southeast Asia, Malaysia, and New Guinea, where they grow epiphytically, high in the jungle canopy. Their flower colors tend to be pure, even dazzling. For instance, *Rhododendron zoelleri* bears yellow and orange flowers so intense they seem to jump out to meet the eye. Chroma does not necessarily correspond to the brightness of a color, however. Even at their most saturated, some hues are brighter than others. Yellow and red are almost always brighter than blue and violet, and tints may appear brighter than pure hues because of their high, light-reflecting white content. Distance changes the chroma of a color by graying hues that are far away. Gardeners can use this natural tendency to add depth to a garden. Place colors of lowest saturation—those with the most gray—in the back of a planting, and colors of highest saturation—those with the least gray—in front.

In the garden many colors fill our field of vision with their combinations of hues, values, and chromas. The colors influence each other and our perceptions of them through a principle known as simultaneous contrast. Hues tend to move away—as they are positioned on the color wheel—from the hues around them. For instance, an orange flower will appear more yellow against a background of red, and more red against a background of yellow. Color values also move away from surrounding values: a tint will appear lighter against a dark background, and the same flower will appear darker against a light background. Chroma, too, will appear to increase against a background of low chroma and decrease against a background of high chroma; in other words, a more saturated color makes a less saturated color seem even more diluted, and vice versa.

Light also greatly influences the perception of color. As the lighting changes through the hours, days, and seasons, colors change too. Low light brightens cool greens and blues, while darkening warm reds and yellows. Bright light brings out the warm reds and yellows, while making pastels disappear. Colors high in value, such as the pastels, and colors of high chroma, such as the vireyas, will look brighter in low light than colors of low value and low chroma. The direction of the light also influences color, whether it passes through a flower from behind or reflects off the surface. Back lighting tends to emphasize the color variation within a flower more than front lighting.

Woody Ching of Bellingham, Washington, is a member of the American Rhododendron Society who has been interested in color all his adult life. He believes the direction and intensity of light are often neglected when placing rhododendrons in the garden. Ching's favorite example showing the importance of light and placement in the garden is the hybrid *Rhododendron* 'Hydon Dawn'. It bears pink flowers with frilled edges and a dark pink, brown-spotted throat. In direct frontal light 'Hydon Dawn' is a nearly uniform bright pink and is not dramatic. But to 'Hydon Dawn' in back light, no other rhododendron in direct light can compare. For Ching, 'Hydon Dawn' should never be placed in the garden where it is seldom back lighted.

A combination of factors causes the dramatic affect of back light on *Rhododendron* 'Hydon Dawn'. Ching explains that when strong white light, such as direct sunlight, strikes the back sides of the petals of a flower, some light is absorbed and some passes through. At the same time, secondary light sources illuminate the flower, such as rays reflecting from the sky and rays reflecting from objects in front of the flower. These secondary light sources are weak in intensity, so they have a graying effect on the color inside the blossom. The transmitted light is much more intense than the secondary reflected light, and the brighter, back-lighted petals illuminate the other petals. Adding further complexity to the situation is the substance of the flower petals. A petal is thinner at its edges than it is at its point of attachment to the stem. Thus, more light passes through the periphery of a flower than near the center, which contributes to the subtle gradation of color from light pink to darker pink at the center of a blossom.

Ching continues to be intrigued by the process of back lighting. Does the pink color of the bright, back-lighted petals intensify the pink color of the other petals because of the pink-colored light striking a surface that is also pink? Do the inside surfaces of the other petals become a deeper pink than the inside surfaces of the back-lighted petals? The pink light on the pink surface does seem to have a cumulative effect. Back light increases the contrast of pinks within the blossom, which also increases the simultaneous contrast.

The master of color quality in the garden, Gertrude Jekyll, in *Color Schemes for the Flower Garden* (1908) describes two plantings of rhododendrons at Munstead Wood: "The rhododendrons . . . are carefully grouped for colour—pink, white, rose and red of the best qualities are in the sunniest part, while, kept well apart from them, near the tall chestnuts and rejoicing in their partial shade, are the purple colourings, of as pure and cool a purple as may be found among carefully selected *ponticum* seedlings and the few named kinds that associate well with them." Jekyll relied on hues adjacent on the spectrum for her pink, rose, and red planting, and she used the single hue purple, or violet, for the other planting.

Create Movement

Without forsaking the principle of site unity and its primary support, plant harmony, gardeners need to build movement into their designs. Think of the stage set of a play. Rich, unified, and well-designed though it may be, it is not enough alone to sustain the interest of the audience and prevent their descent into boredom. Action needs to take place in the garden, just as in a play, in order for it to be attractive—something needs to happen. Both theater and garden audiences should be drawn from scene to scene by the ever-present question: what will happen next? Events should occur before us as we walk through a garden, each contributing to the satisfaction of viewing the whole production. And just like a one-act play, even a small garden can have movement.

Varying the different parts of the garden, giving each its distinct character, creates movement. Just as a play would not present the same characters saying the same things in the same positions in every scene, a garden should not tediously duplicate the same plants over and over. Garden designers often think in terms of garden rooms, in which plants can be grouped for bloom time, cultural preference, color, history, provenance, and all sorts of reasons. Once viewers realize that one room of the garden is different from the others, they will feel compelled to move along to see what is next.

Rhododendrons can play a vital part in a garden's movement through architectural uses. So many can fill this role because of the presence they exude. Like a poised and confident person, a rhododendron commands notice by its very bearing. Rhododendrons can separate one section of the garden from another or form corridors or frames. In a small garden, a single plant of *Rhododendron* 'Noyo Chief', for example, with its glossy, deep green foliage, could serve as a striking room divider.

To help create movement in the garden, think of space as a positive element in the same way as mass, not as a negative element that needs to be filled. Space has a shape and size through which we move our bodies and our sight. Chapter 3 discusses in greater detail the use of space in design. As your garden grows, the mass will tend to encroach upon the space. Consequently,

45

the space must be continually defined, often with pruning tools, including heavy equipment for moving whole plants. Space is a precious garden element required for movement; protect it with vigilance.

Movement in time is another way to stir up excitement. The changing seasons change the garden, creating anticipation for the upcoming act. Rhododendrons can be players in all acts of the garden production if properly choreographed. The early spring bloomers of February and March add the first fresh color, followed by the drama of their April, May, and June performances. In summer their architectural abilities support other plants taking center stage. By fall the foliage color of deciduous azaleas complements the fall colors of other trees and shrubs in the garden. And in winter, the strong presence of the evergreen rhododendrons helps give shape to the garden, contrasting with the leafless silhouettes of deciduous trees and shrubs. Mai Arbegast, a Berkeley, California, landscape architect, says, "What makes a garden? Change. That is the magic of a garden" (personal communication). She emphasizes that gardens change not only from season to season but from year to year and that when planting, think of what the garden will look like in five or ten years.

A great advantage gained from putting movement into garden design is the dramatic and surprising effects that develop. Just as a striking plot twist or unexpected revelation in the theater captivates the audience, so will striking plantings or surprise views entertain visitors to your garden. Many rhododendrons are particularly suited to creating dramatic events in the garden, some by the overwhelming presence of their size and bearing, others by their vivid flower colors, and still others by their striking foliage textures. The key is to choose a variety bred for the role you give it and to stage it properly. Large single specimens of *Rhododendron* 'Cynthia', clothed from top to bottom in luscious pink flowers, make bold spring statements on many front lawns of North America. This cultivar needs space to perform so as not to overwhelm the house or other plants. *Rhododendron* 'Scintillation' or the old hybrids 'Purpureum Elegans' and 'Roseum Elegans' can fill similar roles. In smaller spaces, single specimens can serve as sentinels at the entry to a garden room or as focal points within the rooms. A single specimen can be the focus at the end of a straight corridor, much like a piece of sculpture, and if it is potted, it can be moved for constant attention during blooming or the emergence of striking new foliage. Rhododendrons grafted as standards can make dramatic, formal statements. Surprise views of rhododendrons can add drama to the garden—try hiding a planting around a bend in a path or using rhododendrons to frame a sudden distant view.

Drama and movement can come from a bank of large rhododendrons of heroic bearing lining a driveway or marking a property line. Such is the use of a collection of *Rhododendron griffithianum* crosses by J. Freeman Stephens along the driveway of Pat and Judy Stephens's home near Bellingham, Washington. In May, the large trusses of these shrubs create a wall of pink profusion to guide visitors up the driveway.

Unexpected spots of color can add excitement to a green palette. Many vireyas fill this role dazzlingly. In their native habitat they are seen only from the distance as bright spots of color amid the jungle green. The oranges and yellows are particularly striking and seem especially appropriate for Southern California landscapes, which can accommodate hot colors, and tender species, so well. Mai Arbegast uses vireyas as spot color. Mitch Mitchell of Volcano, Hawaii, also uses vireyas effectively in his jungle garden, placing them both on the ground and high on branches, mimicking their wild habit. In a predominantly green landscape a single, bold spot of pure, intense color can radiate far beyond the small space it occupies.

Introducing fragrance to the predominantly visual experience of viewing a garden is always a surprise and delight. The genus *Rhododendron* includes many species with flower fragrance, and their progeny often carry on this evocative quality. Place fragrant rhododendrons where their flower scent can easily reach the viewer. For example, a specimen of *Rhododendron* 'Mi Amor' near a deck or patio or in a garden room will transform the space with its sweet scent.

One last suggestion for adding drama to the landscape and garden: respect your own personal taste, including your sense of humor. The charm of a private garden is enhanced by revealing its keeper's personality in surprising ways.

Garden Tours

On a harsh seaside site battered by constant wind, near Halifax, Nova Scotia, Walter Ostrom has built a perfect example of a garden unified by its site. As frequently happens in nature, the cultural demands of the site have imposed an aesthetic unity on those plants that are able to survive.

Wind and bright sun set limits on plant material, but in ingenious ways Ostrom has stretched the limits to incorporate a surprisingly large variety of plants. A constant northeast wind will blow the leaves off tall, elepidote rhododendrons, narrowing Ostrom's choices to low-growing or prostrate plants. Mound-shaped plants with thick leaves, such as *Rhododendron yakushimanum*, can withstand the wet south wind off the ocean well, and the small-leafed lepidotes, those with leaf scales, can withstand the wind from any direction. Other rhododendrons that grow on the site are *R. brachycarpum*, *R. roxieanum* var. *oreonastes*, *R. pachysanthum*, *R. recurvoides*, and deciduous and evergreen azaleas. A windbreak of stewartias (*Stewartia* spp.), snowbells (*Styrax* spp.), and birches (*Betula* spp.) helps temper the wind.

Ostrom drains the boggy areas by laying down boulders and covering them above the high water mark with 6 to 8 inches of sand (15 to 20 centimeters). The sand is then covered with a few inches of planting mix (40 percent coarse sand: 50 percent coarse peat: 10 percent bark). When planting near boulders extending above ground level, Ostrom makes sure the plants' roots reach surrounding soil. On scree, the plants receive enough moisture from the nightly condensation on the rocks. Ostrom never waters the garden—he only mulches—and the usual late-summer drought naturally hardens off the rhododendrons. The low-growing native cranberry (*Vaccinium oxycoccos*) provides a living mulch without blocking the sun. The exposure to sun causes the lepidote rhododendrons to "grow tight like boulders" and other plants to form smaller-than-usual leaves. As all the plants age, they begin to protect each other, forming a unified landscape of low-growing, fine-textured plants.

Suggested Reading

Austin, Sandra. 1998. *Color in Garden Design.* Newtown, Connecticut: Taunton Press.

Birren, Faber. 1961. *Creative Color.* New York: Van Nostrand Reinhold.

Eck, Joe. 1996. *Elements of Design.* New York: Henry Holt.

Garu, Augusto. 1993. *Color Harmonies.* Chicago: University of Chicago Press.

Grant, John A., and Carol L. Grant. 1954. *Garden Design.* Seattle: University of Washington Press.

Jekyll, Gertrude. 1908. *Colour Schemes for the Flower Garden.* Rpt. Suffolk, England: Antique Collectors Club, 1982.

Ziegler, Catherine. 1996. *Harmonious Garden.* Portland, Oregon: Timber Press.

CHAPTER 3

Planning the Landscape

O NCE THE DESIGN concepts of site unity, plant harmony, and movement have established a foundation, your next step is to form a landscaping plan. Put ideas down on paper. For some, taking pencil in hand at this point may be a distasteful detour on a trip that is supposed to be fun, but the effort offers the best method for transforming the garden in your mind into a garden at your doorstep. An alternative, if resources allow, is to hire a professional garden designer, but do not bypass this step.

Taking Inventory of the Site

Until the facts of a site are down on paper, the truth may elude even the most observant gardener. Before making a plan or map, take the time for some careful fact-finding. Rhododendrons have their likes and dislikes, as all plants do. Knowing the site prepares a gardener to cater to them, to make rhododendrons healthy, attractive features in the garden.

Starting with the big picture, consider regional climate and physiography. The site may lie within a coniferous forest region, a mixed forest region, a maritime forest region, or a plains region. Defining the characteristics of the environment will help you join forces with nature, instead of fighting against it, to create a beautiful, satisfying garden.

51

Locate the site within the USDA climate zones, which are based on the range of average annual minimum temperatures. The zone designation can serve as a general guide for avoiding rhododendrons that are unlikely to survive a winter on the site. Further, the site may be in a microclimate within the zone, or microclimates may exist within the site. Both situations offer the chance for growing plants more tender than the zone number would imply. Also helpful to know are the average annual maximum temperatures in the climate zone, as well as the area's yearly rainfall.

To add to the big picture, become familiar with the geology of the site. A U.S. Geological Survey map, or comparable government map in another country, can help you to identify underlying bedrock. The type of soil will be influenced by the rock beneath, and the most natural rock garden structures will be constructed from this local rock. The U.S. Geological Survey is also the source for topographic maps giving a site's elevation. Note the changes in elevation within the site. Since rhododendrons need well-draining soil to flourish, slopes often provide good planting areas for them. In addition, air movement is affected by slopes. The coldest spots are often at the bottom—a rhododendron of borderline hardiness may survive on the side of a slope but succumb to lower temperatures at the bottom. Note other land forms, such as ponds and rock outcrops.

In preparation for mapping the site, measure the boundaries and the major buildings, including the house and outbuildings. Find the location of underground utility lines. Note neighboring land forms and structures that affect the site. Large trees are part of the existing structure, and their canopy dimensions should be measured and noted in the inventory sketch or list. If the site includes a woodland of many trees, measure the woodland boundaries. Fences, too, are structures that should be counted in the inventory.

The structures on a site greatly affect the amount and location of sun and shade and the strength of the wind. Rhododendrons generally like all-day dappled sunlight or six hours of sun and six hours of shade. Too much shade promotes lanky growth and a paucity of flowers, and too much sun can cause leaf burn, although some alpine types can flourish in all-day sun and on windy sites. The inventory should indicate areas open to strong wind and the day's areas of sun and shade, including the northern and southern exposure of the site.

Existing gardens and landscaping on the site are also part of the inventory, whether or not they will be part of the new plan. Remember that rhododendrons can be moved from place to place relatively easily because of their shallow, fibrous root systems, as opposed to tap roots. Gardeners have been known to move tree-sized rhododendrons successfully with a back hoe, even transporting whole collections of hundreds of rhododendrons across state borders to new sites. Though a rhododendron may have outgrown its usefulness in the existing landscape, it can be moved to fit a new plan. Not all shrubs are so accommodating. George Ring of Bent Mountain, Virginia, was reminded of the importance of site inventory when he moved 3000 rhododendrons from his garden in Fairfax, Virginia, to the colder, windier, and sunnier site in Bent Mountain. After evaluating the conditions of the new site, Ring had to understand the cultural requirements of each variety: "Suitability of plant for the intended site should be the highest priority in their selection. . . . Fortunately for gardeners, there is a great diversity in the adaptability of specific rhododendrons and azaleas. Some prefer sun and some prefer part shade. Some can withstand very cold temperatures and others can stand heat. Others can withstand neither cold nor heat" (personal communication). Without first taking inventory of the site, Ring would have had no indication of the most favorable, not to mention the safest, positions for his plants.

Define the style of the site—meaning country, suburban, urban, and so on—even though it may fall somewhere between categories. Such terms refer primarily to the surrounding area, be it open countryside, a quiet residential community, or a bustling city. Categorizing the site as such will help build unity into the landscape design (Plate 12).

Another way to promote site unity in a design is to plant native vegetation. At the inventory stage, note any native plants growing on the site. It is helpful to visit a natural site of similar

Table 5. Sun-tolerant rhododendrons

	USDA hardiness zone	Plant size in ten years	Plant form	Foliage texture	Flower color
'Anah Kruschke'	5	medium shrub	compact	medium	v
'Anna Rose Whitney'	6	medium shrub	upright	coarse	p
'Arthur Bedford'	6	medium shrub	upright	medium	v
'Belle Heller'	6	medium shrub	compact	medium	w
'Blue Peter'	6	medium shrub	compact	medium, glossy	v
'Boule de Neige'	4	medium shrub	rounded	medium	w
'Catawbiense Boursault'	5	medium shrub	rounded	medium	v
'Chionoides'	6	small shrub	compact	medium	w
'Cynthia'	5	medium shrub	rounded	medium	p
'Dora Amateis'	5	small shrub	spreading	medium, bronze tone	w
'Fastuosum Flore Pleno'	5	medium shrub	open	medium	v
'Gomer Waterer'	5	medium shrub	upright	medium	w
'Hallelujah'	5	small shrub	rounded	coarse	p
'John Waterer'	5	small shrub	rounded	medium	v
'Nova Zembla'	4	medium shrub	rounded	medium	r
'Old Copper'	6	medium shrub	upright	medium	o
PJM Group	4	small shrub	rounded	medium, fall dark red	v
'Roseum Elegans'	4	medium shrub	rounded	medium	v
'Sappho'	5	medium shrub	open	medium	w
'The Hon. Jean Marie de Montague'	7	medium shrub	spreading	medium	r
Yellow Hammer Group	7	small shrub	upright	fine, light green	y

Abbreviations: ind = indumentum, gc = ground cover, p = pink, r = red, w = white, v = violet, o = orange, y = yellow.
See List of Tables for sizes.

habitat to see which natives grow in the area. Also consider the wildlife occupying or visiting the site.

On a rural site, the inventory will include views into the countryside. Such views can be enhanced by a frame of landscaping (Plate 13). Even a suburban or urban site might have views out to surrounding areas that can be emphasized with landscaping. On the other hand, especially on an urban site, certain views, of adjacent buildings for instance, will be better blocked out with plants or hard structures. All these views are part of the inventory.

SOIL

An inventory of the soil is critical for growing rhododendrons. The four components of soil are minerals, water, air, and organic matter. Generally a good soil contains 48 percent minerals, 25 percent water, 25 percent air, and 2 percent organic matter. The texture of the soil refers to the particle size of its mineral content. Sand is composed of particles 0.05 to 2 millimeters wide, silt of particles of flour size, and clay of microscopic particle size. The soil texture can be tested by taking two cups of soil from the top 6 to 8 inches (15 to 20 centimeters) and placing it in a quart jar. Fill the jar with water, shake it, and let it stand for twenty-four hours. The organic material will float to the top, clay will form the second layer, silt will form the third, and sand will sink to the bottom. Loam is composed of equal amounts of sand, silt, and clay. Sandy loam with a large percentage of organic matter is generally considered ideal for rhododendrons, because of their need for a constant supply of air and moisture. The organic matter in the soil increases the water- and air-holding capacity, supplying nutrients and affecting its acidity. Leaf mold, composted bark, or peat moss will tend to increase acidity.

The soil's draining properties are directly relative to its texture. A quick test for drainage is to dig a hole and fill it with water; if the water remains for more than one or two hours the soil has a high clay content and poor drainage. Under these conditions, rhododendrons will rebel, for they dislike standing water.

I recommend a professional test for soil texture, pH, and nutrient content. Rhododendrons need a soil that is on the acid side, with a pH between 4 and 6, but 5 to 5.5 is ideal. Rhododendrons also need the following major mineral elements in the soil: nitrogen, phosphorus, potassium, calcium, sulfur, and magnesium; and the trace elements manganese, boron, copper, zinc, iron, and molybdenum (Cox 1993). Some gardeners fertilize not at all, while others assiduously apply fertilizer three times a year, before and after flowering and late in the fall. You will have to feel your way, guided by a plant's performance. Complete rhododendron fertilizers or the organic cottonseed meal have proved satisfactory.

Narrowing the Choices

Once the factual inventory of the site is complete, the garden builder must make choices based on landscaping needs, personal taste, and plants' cultural requirements. First consider the more functional needs of the site. Most sites will call for an entryway to the house and a driveway or car park. You may need a children's play area, an outdoor entertaining area, and a garden work area. Structures or views of neighboring buildings may need to be screened. Added fencing may be necessary to keep deer out. The natural environment may require some manipulation, such as putting up a windbreak, providing for overhead shade, or installing an irrigation system.

Also consider personal taste in garden features. Should the site include a woodland garden, rock garden, perennial border, knot garden, island bed, or vast expanse of lawn? Sometimes gardeners run into problems when a site fails to accommodate personal taste. If personal tastes run to sun-loving plants and the site is densely shaded with towering conifers, difficult compromises must be made. Should you cut down the trees or learn to appreciate shade-loving plants? Such conflicts may lead to heart-rending decisions, yet a truly satisfying, harmonious garden will require a coming together of personal tastes and the site.

Some gardeners have preferences for particular types of plants or specific genera or species. For example, one gardener's list might include native plants, species of *Magnolia* and *Sedum*, Japanese maples (*Acer palmatum*), red-flowering plants, and vines. Being true to personal taste, whether orthodox or not, will contribute as much to the style of the garden as the site. Especially for a small garden where space is at a premium, making a list of favorite plants grouped by size will assure their accommodation in the planting plan.

Gardeners with preferences for rhododendrons must find or create a location, such as a woodland, rock garden, or border, in which the plants will thrive. If rhododendrons are to play minor or supporting roles rather than leading roles, they still will need garden environments that nurture them. In spite of the diversity within the genus, all rhododendrons share a few basic cultural requirements, and, like most human beings, they perform best when their basic needs are filled. When placing rhododendrons in the landscape, respect these requirements and be rewarded with plants that need relatively little care. But placing them where they do not belong and neglecting their basic needs will guarantee a bad actor in the garden.

The light requirements of rhododendrons vary with climate and variety and run the gamut from full sun to full shade. Generally, the larger the leaf the more shade is needed. A rule of thumb is to give a rhododendron as much sunlight as it can tolerate without scorching its leaves, for too much shade results in lanky growth and poor flowering. A good source for finding a specific plant's sun tolerance and cold hardiness is *Greer's Guidebook to Available Rhododendrons* (Greer 1996).

The importance of a constant supply of moisture and air in the soil cannot be over-emphasized; irrigation plus the addition of organic matter to the soil may be needed. Three choices for irrigation systems are available to gardeners. Impact sprinklers offer high water volume. A successful alternative is a micro-sprinkler that releases a fine mist, duplicating the mist of the high mountains where many Asian species grow in the wild. With this system, flowers are undamaged, and the water settles gently and evenly on the ground without creating standing pools. Another good system is drip irrigation, in which water is released slowly to the roots of individual plants.

A word of caution about planting rhododendrons from containers. The soil mix in which the plant is growing will be different from garden soil, and because of this difference water has a difficult time moving by capillary action from the garden soil to the container soil. The result is that no water reaches the rootball and the plant dies of thirst. Even water from overhead sprinkling may only reach outside the rootball of the plant. Consequently, water newly planted, especially spring-planted rhododendrons weekly for six months to make sure the rootball remains moist so that it can begin to spread its rootlets into the garden soil.

Mulches are of great value in rhododendron plantings. They help conserve the moisture at the surface of the soil where it is available for the fibrous root system of rhododendrons. Mulches also enhance soil tilth and its ability to provide oxygen. Mulches also provide nutrients. Bark and conifer needles are most commonly used, but many other organic materials will suffice. Once the plant is established, the need for irrigation will decrease. Some gardeners do not water their established rhododendrons at all, allowing them to go dormant during extended drought instead of forcing growth.

Knowing something about the susceptibility of different plants to the various pests and diseases will help gardeners narrow their choices. Knowing about the possible treatments and plants' responses to treatment will also help. Rhododendrons are relatively pest and disease free if provided their basic cultural needs; many gardeners grow them successfully without any application of chemicals. Mixed plantings tend to be more free of disease than monocultures. For the ecologically minded gardener, a system of Integrated Pest Management (IPM) is the best solution. Once you are willing to tolerate a low level of damage—perhaps the hardest part of this method—various IPM techniques can keep damage at a tolerable level. A key step is identifying the enemy so control can be pest specific, as opposed to a random application of chemicals.

Among the most troublesome and disfiguring rhododendron pests is the root weevil. It makes nasty notches on the edges of leaves, and its larvae eat the plants' roots. Beneficial nematodes have been found to control it. Aphids can be controlled through benign insecticidal soaps, and caterpillars can be checked with the biological control *Bacillus thuringiensis*. Honey fungus (*Armillaria*), which characteristically lives in dead tree stumps, can send parasitic rhizomes out to the living roots of rhododendrons. A short-term solution is to protect plants with an underground collar of plastic. In hot climates where the fungus *Phytophthora* can cause root rot and damage to rhododendrons, some gardeners have controlled the fungus by planting the shrubs in raised beds with 50 percent or more fine pine bark mixed with sandy loam.

Drawing the Plan on Paper

With a list of landscape needs and horticultural choices in hand, draw the site. Planning the landscape with paper and pencil is key to developing the best possible design. You can hire a professional landscape designer to make the drawings and help devise the plan. On the other hand, many books instruct the amateur in basic tools of the trade. An excellent book aimed at the professional and serious amateur designer is John Brookes's *Book of Garden Design* (1991). Several simplified techniques, however, will accomplish the job.

First, make a map of the site drawn to scale, with accurate measurements of the boundaries, the house and outbuildings, and other permanent structural elements, such as large trees, fences, and hedges. Remember to indicate north. The most accurate method for keeping everything in scale is to use graph paper on which each square represents 1 foot or 1 meter, or any single unit of measurement. This map will serve as a master plan that can be covered with tracing paper for drawing experimental designs, which can be modified or discarded as the design develops.

MASS AND SPACE

Now comes the first step into the unknown, where the imagination is given free play. This step can be difficult or strange for

59

many gardeners, for it requires forgetting about plants. Instead of thinking about where to place that gorgeous *Rhododendron calophytum* specimen or that superb collection of *R. yakushimanum* hybrids, think in terms of mass formed by solid objects and of open space through which you move. Laura D. Eisener, a landscape architect from Saugus, Massachusetts, who specializes in rhododendrons, uses mass as a tool for creating space. For her, "Most important are the shape and size of the space" (personal communication). Eye-level photographs of the site, preferably black and white, can be helpful aids for visualizing the three-dimensional nature of mass and space.

Because pleasing proportion between mass and space is key to a good design, Brookes's book suggests making a grid to use when drawing new designs. Take the dimensions of a major feature of the house, such as a dominant window or ell, and use it as the basic unit of the grid. Based on this grid, the landscape features will develop in proportion to the house. You now have a master plan on one sheet of paper and a grid on another.

On clean tracing paper placed over the master plan, shade in the areas of mass that were drawn on the master plan, the permanent structures and existing plantings. An abstract drawing of the present site will emerge as a series of shapes delineating both mass and space. Then putting the grid under the drawing of shaded-in mass, begin sketching new, pleasing shapes, whether they be straight edged or curved, basing the dimensions on the grid unit or multiples of it and incorporating the existing mass. Remember to think in terms of the shapes of both mass and space. Eisener warns, "A successful design depends on proper scale and proportion of all the mass elements."

Think also of linking the shapes for movement through the landscape. A variety of space shapes will create interest and draw the viewer on from one landscape feature to another (Plate 14). Two basic space shapes are corridors, approximately more than twice as long as wide, and nodes, of more equal width and length. As Eisener explains, "Corridors are meant to move along. Examples might be a walkway, roadway, or narrow side yard. Corridors are not very restful. To break a corridor up into a node, or resting space, you would need to change the proportions. Either

By creating a narrow space, paths entice viewers from one garden
section to another. Place large rhododendrons far enough away from
the path to allow for growth without encroaching on the walking space.

widen the corridor, or divide it into two smaller spaces. Corridors and nodes can be either large or small—it is the relative proportions that make the difference" (personal communication).

Space can be either open or enclosed. Open space in the
landscape evokes feelings of freedom and unlimited possibility.
It is large in relation to the heights of boundaries, or it may have
no boundaries at all, such as a space that leads to a limitless view
of the countryside, the sea, or the sky (Plate 15). Open space was
a landscape feature in the eighteenth-century English style pro-
moted by Capability Brown, where views of the countryside were
enhanced through grand expanses of lawn and meadow. Such
designs were also inspired by the native sites of alpine rhododendrons under miles of sky, bounded only by distant moun-

tains. Both country sites and suburban sites with views lend themselves to the use of open space. Or, if a suburban site is large enough, open spaces can be incorporated into the design where the space itself makes an attractive view. The Olmsted firm often used open space in this manner at the end of the nineteenth century. Their shrub borders contained large expanses of lawn, as at the Edward B. Dunn Garden in Seattle.

Enclosed space in the landscape evokes an entirely different feeling than open space, one of intimacy and security. An enclosed space is smaller, of more human dimension, and with higher boundaries relative to the space. It has a three-dimensional quality to it, like a room. Eisener uses garden rooms in many of her designs: "The walls could be house walls, trees, shrubs, or fences; floors could be lawn, grasses, wood, paths, ground cover, or brick." She reminds gardeners to observe proper scale and proportion, explaining that "the enclosing elements will influence how you view a space. Enclosing plants with low branches can make a space seem more cramped, while plants with higher branches open up a space. . . . A ceiling of leaves may actually make a space seem bigger. The enclosing masses can be made up of plants or other elements. The tighter the group of plants, the more solid the walls seem and the more impact on the landscape they have" (personal communication).

Shrub-sized rhododendrons can be perfect for enclosing a space, but beware of enclosing a small space with too many shrub-sized rhododendrons. Landscape architect Nan Fairbrother in *The Nature of Landscape Design* (1974) points out that shrubs occupy the same layer in space that we humans do. We are shrub-layer height, and standing next to a shrub has a very different psychological effect than standing next to a tree or a herbaceous perennial. Fairbrother writes, "Surrounded by shrubs of eye level or higher, we can neither move nor see, and shrubs therefore are more claustrophobic than trees."

Once the shapes of mass and space are drawn on paper, your thoughts can turn to the landscape features of the plan. At this point, you can return, perhaps with relief, to the consideration of plants, specifically the use of rhododendrons in the plan. Now, horticulture is added to the art of design.

Today's landscape designers often use the term *framework* to indicate both boundary enclosures and structures within the garden. Traditionally walls, fences, and hedges have provided enclosures. The choice of framework will be governed by the style of the landscaping—and, of course, cost. A mixture of two or three types of enclosure may suit the design.

Draw the outline of the framework on the tracing paper that holds the abstract drawing of existing and new shapes. If the whole site is to be designed as a garden, the whole site will need to be enclosed, for a garden in the classic sense is a place enclosed and separate from the world outside it. The entire site may be enclosed with the hard structures of a fence or wall or the soft structures of plantings at the boundaries. If only a portion of the site is to be designed as a garden only that portion will need to be enclosed, leaving the remainder to flow into the environment beyond the site. In a suburban site, the front yard might flow into the neighboring front yard with only the back yard enclosed. An urban site might be entirely enclosed. For a country site, only a small portion may be enclosed, so that the majority of its boundaries merge with adjoining woodland or field. When a site has a view, it might be framed to focus the eye outward. For greatest satisfaction, however, you should plan at least some amount of enclosed space to lend intimacy and a feeling of refuge to the landscape.

Although large-leafed rhododendrons generally do not lend themselves to the making of formal hedges, which are usually clipped into geometric shapes for the formal garden, several rhododendrons are amenable to such uses because of their upright form, fine foliage, and multi-stemmed branching. *Rhododendron lutescens*, for example, bears its bright yellow flowers along the branches as well as at branch ends and can be clipped without losing its flowers.

Many rhododendrons are suitable for informal hedges, which are left unsheared and free growing. A selection from the hardy *Rhododendron* PJM Group will offer foliage from the ground up—dark red in winter—and in spring will cover itself with bright pink flowers. Informal hedges can also be built of a mixture of plants, including rhododendrons, in which the plants are unified through plant form, foliage texture, or foliage color. For example, glossy foliage connects *Rhododendron* 'Unique', *Camellia* 'Spring Festival', and *Ilex glabra* 'Nigra' in a billowing hedge.

While enclosure defines the boundaries of the garden, interior framework gives architecture to a garden, especially in winter, and has been appropriately described as the "skeleton" or "bones" of a garden. Shrub and tree evergreen rhododendrons can play a key role in the interior framework. Their strong presence in all seasons lends solidity and strength, defining space with steadfast aplomb. Although in bloom rhododendrons may demand the spotlight, during the rest of the year they are willing to play supporting roles to other plants. The key is to prevent them from becoming overbearing actors. If a planting intended to serve as interior framework is to be of shrub-sized rhododendrons exclusively, remember to leave sufficient space around them to avoid the crowded-elevator effect. The gloomy Victorian shrubberies referred to by some garden designers are the result of insufficient adjoining space to offset the light-absorbing green of some rhododendron foliage. Using rhododendrons with glossy leaves, such as *Rhododendron* 'Scintillation', or fine foliage, such as *R. oreotrephes*, can help avoid this effect. Another approach is to plant a mixture of shrubs where lighter textured plants temper the density of the rhododendron foliage and add a variety of shapes; try *Pieris japonica* 'Valley Valentine', with its narrow, glossy leaves, or *Pittosporum eugenioides* with its wavy-edged leaves.

SECTIONS

In listing how you wish to use the site, you already began the task of sectioning the garden: the driveway, the entertainment area, the children's play area, and so on, along with the horticultural choices. Now take the plan of space and mass in hand and section the site according to the chosen uses. With the drawing of space and mass shapes before you, begin putting names on the shapes, taking into account the physical features of slope, exposure, views, soil drainage, and underground utilities. Also take into account the difference between the open and enclosed space on the design plan. Do you want a particular feature, such as the entertainment area, in an enclosed space? Do you want a clipped lawn in an open space where you can stand and look out over a low planting into the neighboring surroundings? Is the whole site to be a garden in the classic sense, or is only part of the site to be developed as a garden?

Designing a garden of rooms, where sections have walls, floors, and possibly ceilings, is a popular approach. Each room can have its own unifying element, such as color, a particular plant genus or family, a pond, or a plant fragrance. The distinctive nature of each room creates interest and anticipation, moving the viewer from one room to the next in a most delightful way. The journey is made even more satisfying if the site dictates the nature of the room. A natural rock outcrop lends itself to a collection of rock garden plants, a shaded area to shade-loving plants, a sunny area to many herbs. To add even more variation the rooms can differ in the degree of formality. A terrace room used for entertainment might be geometric and formal in design with specimen plants in containers set upon a paved surface. Rooms in the strict sense should be enclosed so that the viewers see and experience only one at a time and make a journey of discovery as they move through them. Pay particular attention to the ceiling of a room. Will the sky be the ceiling, or a tree canopy, or a pergola? Each will create a distinct atmosphere, whether open and free or close and intimate (Plate 16).

Gardeners need to take advantage of rhododendrons' diversity. Although those that fit the stereotype—the medium-sized shrub with dark green foliage and pink flowers, such as the East Coast native *Rhododendron maximum*—are beautiful and useful, even the workhorse *R. maximum* has its limits, and overuse leads to boredom. Worse yet is to think that if a rhododendron of this type does not serve the purpose of a particular planting then no rhododendron will. On the contrary, rhododendrons are surprisingly versatile and can enhance many different garden sections, each with its own use or intended horticultural effect.

In the utilitarian sections of the site, for instance, a hedge of

Rhododendron racemosum 'Rock Rose' might separate a driveway from a play area. A sun lover, this upright-growing rhododendron reaches 4 or 5 feet (1.2 to 1.5 meters) and has 2-inch-long leaves (5 centimeters) that are glossy on top and waxy blue-green underneath, erect red stems, and small, perky, clear pink flowers. On a terrace that serves as the entertainment area, tender varieties can be planted in containers. The highly fragrant *Rhododendron* 'Lady Alice Fitzwilliam' languorously adorns itself with lax trusses of wide, funnel-shaped flowers that open from a pink bud and then turn white. The species *R. edgeworthii*, another highly fragrant rhododendron with white flowers, has curiously puckered leaves with a heavy white indumentum on the undersides—a true beauty. These tender plants, if grown in containers, can be moved to a protected area in regions of freezing winter temperatures.

If house foundation plantings are desired, a moderately sized shrub with moderate- to small-sized leaves serves the functions of decorating a foundation and anchoring a house to the site. A suitable hybrid for the U.S. Northwest, which requires hardiness to 10°F (−12°C), would be *Rhododendron* 'Naselle', a rounded, compact grower to only 4 feet (1.2 meters) in ten years, with bright green, 4-inch-long leaves (10 centimeters). Its large flowers change in color from rose to yellow to burnt orange. A hardier plant that reaches only 3 feet (1 meter) in ten years is *Rhododendron* 'Cyprus', an attractive mounding plant, with white flowers and bronze blotch.

In the horticultural sections of the garden, those devoted primarily to the display of plants, the diversity of the genus ably lends itself to an astounding variety of effects. In the mixed border, for instance, the azalea *Rhododendron schlippenbachii*, with its light-textured foliage and elegant pink flowers, comfortably blends with other light-textured shrubs without overpowering them. This species has the added attribute of orange or yellow fall foliage. For the sunny exposures of the rock garden, along with the alpine species such as *R. impeditum*, *R. calostrotum*, and *R. fastigiatum*, I recommend the many hybrids produced by Warren Berg, among them *Rhododendron* 'Patty Bee' with clear yellow flowers and 'Wee Bee' with pink flowers and a red ray through each lobe. The hybrids developed by Peter Cox at Glendoick nursery in Scotland, all named after birds, include *Rhododendron* 'Curlew', with bright yellow flowers, and 'Ptarmigan' with white flowers.

In the dappled shade of the woodland garden, the larger species and hybrids will look at home in the naturalistic setting of trees, shrubs, and ground covers. Their larger size and larger leaves will be balanced by the overhead canopy and companion shrubs. Here the gardener has the greatest choice of rhododendrons, for it is the open woodland of Asia where a great bulk of them grow naturally in the wild. In the woodland, these plants find shelter from wind and a forest floor high in organic matter. The relaxed growth pattern, as opposed to strictly mounding forms, harmonizes with the woodland environment, and the so-called leggy habit of some turns from liability to asset in the natural setting. *Rhododendron calophytum* and *R. sutchuenense*, for instance, with their long, impressive leaves look at home in a way they never would planted beside the doorway of a house. The more tender large-leafed species *R. macabeanum*, *R. sinogrande*, and *R. rex* also require the sheltered environment of the woodland to look their best. The plants of *Rhododendron* Loderi Group, tree-like in habit, also are best suited to the woodland setting.

Planting

Once the sections of the site have been designated on the plan, make a plant list showing where individual plants will go, guided by the design principles of site unity, plant harmony, and movement—and the plant's cultural requirements. The better you know the plants, the easier this task will be. Nevertheless, the learning curve will be high at this stage no matter how much you know. In placing rhododendrons in the landscape, knowledge of the diversity of the genus and its capacity to enhance all sorts of gardening situations is a beginning. Then comes poring over catalogs and books on rhododendrons to find exactly the right plant for the right place. Fortunately, there is ample literature on the subject, and the tables are intended to help with choosing the right plants.

As plants and their locations are chosen, keep in mind the layered dimension of a garden. For textural richness, the ground covers, herbaceous layer, shrub layer, and tree layer should relate to each other harmoniously, both sharing characteristics and offering contrast.

As a general rule, space rhododendrons as follows: shrubs reaching 3 feet (1 meter) in five years plant 2 to 2½ feet (0.6 to 0.8 meters) apart, shrubs reaching 5 feet (1.5 meters) in five years plant 3½ to 4 feet (1.1 to 1.2 meters) apart, and shrubs reaching 7 feet (2.1 meters) in five years plant 5 to 5½ feet (1.5 to 1.7 meters) apart (Clive Justice, personal communication). If a rhododendron outgrows its space, often the best solution is to move it to another location rather than pruning it to reduce its size. However, pruning dead wood, removing spent flowers, and pinching terminal vegetative buds on young plants to encourage side branching can produce bushier, better groomed shrubs. For detailed instructions on pruning rhododendrons see Peter Cox's *Cultivation of Rhododendrons* (1993).

Finally, a garden is always changing, day to day, season to season, year to year. In designing the garden, consider what it will look like in ten years. Rhododendrons along with other plants get taller and wider; others creep imperiously over the ground. The original planting scheme should reflect the essence of a garden: never-ending change.

Garden Tours

Bill and Mary Stipe of Whidbey Island, Washington, have planned and built their garden with particular sensitivity. They judiciously select microclimates for groups of plants and employ ecological cultural techniques in plant care. The center of the site, where the house, greenhouse, vegetable garden, and commercial nursery are located, has been cleared of most large trees, allowing ample sunshine to pervade in the midst of an otherwise very shady native woodland. Consequently a woodland verge has been created that allows for an optimum mix of sun and shade craved by many elepidote rhododendrons. In one spot a relatively shady verge has been planted with *Rhododendron* species of the sections *Grandia* and *Falconeri*, which splendidly exhibit their large leaves against the backdrop of native forest. A sunny slope has been developed into a rock garden with rhododendrons and companions. Another smaller sunny spot has been built as a moraine garden with dwarf rhododendrons and conifers and other companions. Bill Stipe explains his design inspiration: "I look at the landscape and see what it wants to be."

In plant culture, the Stipes adhere to ecological techniques to maintain their garden. Although they have used commercial fertilizers such as ammonium sulfate on the rhododendron beds, as the soil gains the right nutrient balance, they use only organic mulches and composts. Their compost pile is 6 feet high (2 meters) and 30 feet in circumference (9 meters). The naturally acidic soil of pH 4.5 receives some lime, and rock phosphate is added to supplement deficient phosphorous.

The Stipes have used no chemical insecticides. They use beneficial nematodes for root weevil and *Bacillus thuringiensis* for tent caterpillars, although they have used fungicides for powdery mildew. An electric fence, along with hair from their dog, discourages deer, and stumps are removed to deter honey fungus. Watering is minimal, but what watering they do is from untreated well water.

Suggested Reading

Brookes, John. 1991. *Book of Garden Design.* New York: MacMillan.
Cox, Peter. 1993. *Cultivation of Rhododendrons.* London: B. T. Batsford.
Reiley, H. Edward. 1992. *Success with Rhododendrons and Azaleas.* Portland, Oregon: Timber Press.

CHAPTER 4

The Woodland Garden

THE MAJORITY of rhododendrons grow best in the shelter of a woodland setting. With a tree canopy overhead and protection from the sun's hottest rays, not to mention forest duff underfoot offering protection from drought, most species and many hybrids are at home. Many rhododendrons we grow in our gardens are either species or progeny of species that grew wild in the forests of Asia. Ernest H. Wilson found *Rhododendron sutchuenense* in a mixed forest including beeches (*Fagus* spp.), birches (*Betula* spp.), and maples (*Acer* spp.). Sir Joseph Dalton Hooker made some of his greatest finds in the forests of the Sikkim Himalaya: *R. thomsonii, R. hodgsonii, R. grande,* and *R. falconeri.* Peter Cox, plant hunter and nurseryman from Perth, Scotland, notes that many rhododendrons growing without shade in the wild need woodland protection from dehydration and severe cold in climates different from their native environments.

Not only does a woodland provide for the cultural needs of a great many rhododendrons but it provides an aesthetically pleasing setting for the naturalistic growth patterns of many rhododendrons, especially species that resist symmetrical, formal shapes. No wonder the first British rhododendron gardens were woodland gardens, for example Arduaine and Stonefield, for these early collectors were well aware that woodland would offer protection for their prized rhododendrons.

71

Taking Inventory of the Site

Though a basic inventory of any existing woodland should have been made during the initial inventory of the entire site, take a closer look at the nature of the woodland. Consider the size of the woodland. Will it all be developed into a garden, or only a portion of it? Perhaps the outlying areas will be left in their wild state. Interesting features should be recognized, such as rock outcrops, streams, bogs and ponds, and views to outlying countryside. Take into account whether deer are in the area, for deer find many rhododendrons make a fine meal. Another factor to consider is protection from late spring or early fall frosts. On a slope or in a canyon the higher portions are apt to be warmer, while the lower slopes or bottom are apt to be colder and contain frost pockets. In addition, north- or east-facing slopes are better for rhododendrons because the sun's rays hit at a less-direct angle, keeping the ground cooler in summer.

Perhaps most critical in the inventory, however, is the tree canopy, the top layer in the multi-layered woodland. Some trees in the canopy will cast dense shade because their leaves or needles grow close together in one layer on the outside of the tree crown. Such trees are beeches (*Fagus* spp.), maples (*Acer* spp.), oaks (*Quercus* spp.), hickories (*Carya* spp.), spruce (*Picea* spp.), and firs (*Abies* spp.). Woodlands in which these trees predominate, with their crowns overlapping, allow as little as 10 percent of the sun's light to penetrate. Pacific Northwest woodlands with thick stands of Douglas fir (*Pseudotsuga menziesii*) fall into this category. In addition, a thick canopy such as that found in the fir (*Abies* spp.) and hemlock (*Tsuga* spp.) forests of the Northwest can affect the amount of moisture that actually reaches the ground. Much of the precipitation in these woodlands evaporates directly from the canopy.

On the other hand, some trees in the canopy will have crowns of leaves that grow in many layers from the trunk to the outside of the crown, letting in more light. Pines (*Pinus* spp.) tend to fall into this category. These woodlands can let through as much as 50 percent of the light that hits them (Plate 17). As a general rule, rhododendrons suitable for the woodland do not want more than 50 percent shade, whether this be dappled shade or alternating sun and shade. The different areas of a woodland will vary in the amount of light they receive. Glades and woodland perimeters, or verges, will, of course, receive more light than the deepest regions, and depending on the nature of the tree canopy, these outlying areas may be the only ones with sufficient light for rhododendrons. In addition, the intensity of sunlight and amount of cloud cover vary with the climate, making it difficult to apply hard and fast rules for all areas.

The second layer in a woodland is comprised of small trees, the third of shrubs, and the fourth of herbaceous perennials, mosses, and ferns. Note these layers in the inventory, for although they will be enhanced with other natives and exotic plants brought to the site, the essential layered effect of the woodland should be maintained for its richness of texture.

Narrowing the Choices

Those blessed with a woodland of dappled shade, good drainage, sufficient moisture, and the proper pH can plant rhododendrons virtually throughout the site. On a site of this type, the challenge is to create movement and interest by varying one area from another. Natural features such as rock outcrops, streams and ponds, and changes in elevation can serve as guides in creating sections that have unique character. Rhododendron plantings and their shrub and herbaceous companions can be chosen to enhance the natural features. If the climate is agreeable, a protected gully or other benign spot, for instance, could be devoted to the large-leafed rhododendrons, all connected by the gargantuan size of their leaves and tree-like demeanor. The striking *Rhododendron macabeanum, R. rex,* and *R. sinogrande* all display indumentum on their leaves. If natural features are lacking, the rhododendrons themselves, along with their companions, can create the unique character of a section.

In a woodland of dense shade, the planting design for rhododendrons will have to reflect the need most of these plants have for half a day of sunlight. Glades and woodland perimeters

Table 6. Rhododendrons making single- or multi-stemmed trees when mature

	USDA hardiness zone	Plant size in ten years	Plant form	Foliage texture	Flower color
arboreum	7	medium shrub	upright, columnar	medium	r, w, p
calophytum	7	medium shrub	spreading	coarse	w, p
falconeri	8	medium shrub	spreading	coarse, ind, red bark	w, y, p
fulvum	7	small shrub	open, upright	medium	w, p
grande	8	medium shrub	open	coarse, silver ind	y, p
griffithianum	8	medium shrub	upright, open	medium	w, p
hodgsonii	8	medium shrub	rounded	medium, red bark	p, v, r
macabeanum	8	medium shrub	upright	coarse, glossy, ind	y
praestans	8	medium shrub	rounded	coarse, brown ind	w, p
rex	7	medium shrub	upright	coarse, gray ind	w, p
sinogrande	8	medium shrub	rounded	coarse, glossy, ind	w, y
sutchuenense	6	medium shrub	upright	coarse	p, v
'Loderi King George'	7	medium shrub	open	medium	w
'Loderi Pink Diamond'	7	medium shrub	open	medium	p
'Loderi Venus'	7	medium shrub	open	medium	p

Abbreviations: ind = indumentum, gc = ground cover, p = pink, r = red, w = white, v = violet, o = orange, y = yellow.
See List of Tables for sizes.

Table 7. Companion plants: trees

Acer griseum (paperbark maple)	red-brown peeling bark
Acer palmatum (Japanese maple)	rounded form, fall foliage color
Arbutus menziesii (madrona)	red peeling bark
Asimina triloba (paw paw)	drooping leaves, violet flowers, black berries
Betula jacquemontii (birch)	white bark
Cercidiphyllum japonicum (katsura tree)	large tree, yellow or red fall foliage
Cercis canadensis (redbud)	pink flowers
Cornus florida (eastern dogwood)	horizontal branching, red fall foliage, white flowers
Cornus kousa (kousa dogwood)	resistant to dogwood anthracnose, gray and tan bark
Cornus mas (Cornelian cherry)	yellow flowers, round form
Cornus nuttallii (Pacific dogwood)	white flowers, horizontal branching
Cupressus cachmiriana (cypress)	large tree, drooping branchlets, scale-like leaves
Eucryphia lucida	slender form, glossy leaves, white flowers
Franklinia alatamaha (Franklin tree)	upright spreading form, white flowers, fall foliage
Ginkgo biloba (maidenhair tree)	large tree, fan-shaped leaves, yellow fall foliage
Hamamelis virginiana (witch hazel)	flowers after leaf-fall
Ilex opaca (American holly)	pyramidal form, red berries
Magnolia ×soulangiana (saucer magnolia)	deciduous, purple-pink flowers, gray bark
Magnolia stellata (star magnolia)	deciduous, white star-like flowers, gray bark
Magnolia virginiana (sweetbay magnolia)	evergreen in southern U.S., leaf undersides silver, gray bark
Parrotia persica (Persian parrotia)	leaves bronze maturing to green and orange in fall
Sorbus aucuparia (European mountain ash)	orange-red fruit, yellow and red fall foliage
Stewartia pseudocamellia (Japanese stewartia)	peeling bark, bronze leaves, fall color, white flowers
Styrax japonicus (Japanese snowball)	smooth gray bark, white flowers

become the choice spots for planting. Although limiting in some ways, a dense canopy does force the gardener to create sections of woodland that by necessity differ from each other. The rhododendrons at the edge of a dense woodland can be grouped according to form, texture, and color and used as a transition between woodland and lawn or woodland and a herbaceous or mixed border (Plate 18). Ann Lovejoy, a Northwest garden writer and gardener, has used deciduous azaleas along with dogwoods for a natural transition between woods and garden. She finds the fine texture of these shrubs makes the transition "as convincing as possible" (Lovejoy 1997). The same strategy can be used in open glades within the dense woodland or along paths where clearing has let in the sun. Such places offer wonderful opportunities for grouping rhododendrons.

Improving the Site

Although the basic nature of the layered woodland should be respected, you can modify the site or a portion of the site to build the woodland into a true garden and to accommodate more plant varieties, including rhododendrons. Removing dead trees and branches that have fallen to the ground will allow the natural vertical lines of living trees to predominate for the sake of unity. Standing dead trees should also be removed, for they will eventually fall and damage plantings. With dead wood removed, the woodland will already begin to look more garden-like. More than any other type of garden, the woodland garden allows visitors to come inside, to be enclosed by plants on all sides, including the ceiling. Removing dead wood begins to open up the woodland as a place where humans can enter the richly layered environment.

The large trees forming the canopy should remain, but remove those seedlings beneath them that are losing the battle for light and nutrients. These small trees detract from the unified presence of the trunks of the large trees. Of course, keep small trees that lend a particular accent, such as flowers or fall foliage. Depending upon the type of woodland, some plants in the shrub

A woodland verge offers rhododendrons both shade and light and is an ideal spot to plant them.

and herbaceous layers should be removed. In Pacific Northwest woodlands, these layers can be so dense that no room remains for plantings, but keep some of these natives to retain the natural character.

Once the dead wood and extraneous small trees have been cleared out, the woodland will begin to reveal its potential as a garden, and the process of design can begin. Refer to the overall landscape design and make a detailed plan of the woodland area, noting special features and views to outlying countryside. Depending upon the nature of the canopy and the amount of light reaching the woodland floor, sections or rooms can be planned into the woodland. Perhaps a more open area can be developed as a glade so that plants needing more sun, including rhododendrons, can thrive. The "limbing up," or pruning of lower branches on large trees, is a common practice in Pacific Northwest woodlands, allowing more sun to reach the floor without removing the trees.

The making of paths is critical in a woodland garden, for they create movement from one section to another. Generally the paths should follow the contours of the land. If the woodland has changes in elevation, the grade should be gentle enough that the viewer's focus can remain on the plants and views and not on the effort of putting one foot in front of the other. To be able to create interest and movement in the garden, the paths should only allow viewers to see plants close-up and never the whole garden at once. Paths allow for the deliberate focus of viewers' attention, leading from one point of interest to another with purpose.

The construction of paths is both an engineering and artistic feat. The choice of materials suitable for woodland paths is considerable: dirt, grass, moss, bark, stones, gravel, or pine needles. Choose a material that is in keeping with the natural woodland character, is pleasant to walk on, is capable of defining the route, and is easily maintained. Grass, dirt, and moss paths are natural looking, but grass needs mowing and weeding, dirt can become muddy, and moss is easily damaged. The most easily maintained paths for the informal garden are gravel or mulch.

Planting

In general, the formal, symmetrical rhododendron plant forms, such as exhibited by the mounding *Rhododendron yakushimanum* and *R. williamsianum,* are best left for more formal settings in favor of more informal, asymmetrical forms that will harmonize better with the natural woodland setting. The flamboyant colors of many modern hybrids are also often out of character in the woodland environment. But these are only general guides, and your own eye must be the final judge.

The choice, sunny spots of the woodland are where most rhododendrons will thrive, but at least one shade-loving, garden-worthy rhododendron exists in this vast genus for the East Coast of the United States—the eastern native *Rhododendron maximum,* commonly called the rosebay rhododendron. Though dense forest often produces leggy plants of poor form, *R. maximum*—which grows to approximately 15 feet (4.6 meters) and is hardy to −25°F (−30°C)—thrives in shade where its glossy, dark green foliage luxuriates in woodland shadow. Although its white to pink flowers are more prolific in the sun, its foliage is its shining glory, and the plant should be grown in the shade. For an evergreen rhododendron as understory in a dense eastern woodland, it is unsurpassed. Most rhododendrons suitable for the woodland, however, need more sunlight than *R. maximum,* and a dense woodland canopy forces the gardener to find spots where the sun shines part of the day.

THE LARGE PICTURE

In the planting plan, refer to the woodland design plan and its various sections, traveling through them mentally to visualize how they will be viewed—from a distance or close-up. If one section of the woodland garden is to provide a large picture from a distance, such as a view from the house or across an expanse of lawn, massed plantings of larger rhododendrons in the shrub layer should be in scale with the trees that either form a backdrop or intermingle with them. A planting of this kind should include twenty to fifty plants placed 6 to 9 feet apart (2 to 3 meters). The medium to coarse foliage texture of many rhododendrons is well suited to this type of planting and can hold its own in competition with the strong presence of the trees. Hardy standbys for this purpose in northeastern U.S. woodland gardens include *Rhododendron maximum, R. brachycarpum, R. fortunei, Rhododendron* 'Boule de Neige', 'Lee's Dark Purple', 'Catawbense Album', 'Roseum Elegans', and 'Nova Zembla'. In the Pacific Northwest, the list broadens to include *R. calophytum, R. sutchuenense, R. decorum, Rhododendron* 'Grace Seabrook', 'Hallelujah', and 'Trude Webster'. The U.S. Southeast can use *R. catawbiense, R. minus, R. fortunei, Rhododendron* 'Arthur Bedford', 'County of York', and 'Catawbiense Boursault'. In California the list includes *R. aberconwayii, R. ponticum, Rhododendron* 'Purple Splendour', 'Anah Kruschke', and 'Mrs. G. W. Leak'. But this is just a beginning.

A classic use of evergreen azaleas is to mass them in the shrub layer to form a carpet of spring color (Plate 19). Evergreen azalea flower color, however, can be divisive, and great care should be taken to harmonize the colors. Whites can be used to separate clashing colors. Hues in the red to blue sector of the color spectrum should be separated from those in the red to yellow sector. Mass the colors, using three to five or more plants of one color. In the Azalea Woods at Winterthur in Delaware, creator Henry Francis du Pont relied on the Kurume hybrid azaleas developed in Japan, especially those with pastel flowers, to create the woodland carpet. The great range of southeast native deciduous azaleas, massed in the shrub layer at the edge of a woodland, can also make an impact from a distance.

The design technique of layering adds great richness to the woodland garden, with a top layer of tall trees that forms the canopy, a second layer of smaller trees, a shrub layer of rhododendrons and companion shrubs, and a herbaceous perennial or ground cover layer. The possibilities for creating resplendent visual harmonies is almost infinite. A layered woodland offers a full symphony performance. Howard Kline of Leesport, Pennsylvania, has effectively massed rhododendrons with predominantly pastel pink and white flower color under a canopy that offers dappled shade.

Gertrude Jekyll's home garden at Munstead Wood again

Table 8. Evergreen azaleas

	USDA hardiness zone	Plant size in ten years	Plant form	Foliage texture	Flower color
indicum	7	small shrub	compact	fine	r, p
kaempferi	7	small shrub	upright	fine	r, o-r
kiusianum	7	dwarf shrub	spreading	fine	p, v, w
nakaharae	7	gc	prostrate	fine	r
'Alexander'	5	gc	prostrate	fine	r-o
'Caroline Gable'	5	medium shrub	upright	medium	r
'Delaware Valley White'	5	small shrub	rounded	medium	w
'Great Expectations'	6	dwarf shrub	compact	medium	o
'Gumpo'	8	gc	compact	fine	w
'Helen Curtis'	5	small shrub	spreading	medium	w
'Hino-crimson'	6	small shrub	compact	medium	r
'Joseph Hill'	5	gc	mounding	fine	r
'Kazan'	6	gc	compact	fine	r
'Little Gardenia'	6	dwarf shrub	compact	fine	w
'Nancy of Robinhill'	6	dwarf shrub	compact	fine	r/p bicolor

Abbreviations: ind = indumentum, gc = ground cover, p = pink, r = red, w = white, v = violet, o = orange, y = yellow.
See List of Tables for sizes.

offers insight into the most effective techniques for displaying rhododendrons. She planted seventy rhododendrons of ten different varieties 8 feet (2.5 meters) apart at the verge where the lawn and garden joined the woodland. For effectiveness at a distance, she planted them in clumps according to flower color. The clumps of scarlet, rose, and white were placed in relatively sunny spots. The clumps of lilac, purple, and white were planted in light shade. Always concerned with the pictorial effect, Jekyll hoped that the scarlet and rose colors would look richer in the sun and the lilac and purple colors richer in the shade. Holly (*Ilex*) divided the color groups so that the flower colors could not be seen at the same time except from a distance.

One of her favorite lilac-flowered plants was *Rhododendron* 'Album Elegans', a hybrid still available today, which she planted at the back and which grew to "towering masses." Two other of her lilac-flowered rhododendrons that are still available are *Rhododendron* 'Everestianum' and 'Fastuosum Flore Pleno'. Jekyll also used a variety of *R. ponticum* seedlings that she carefully selected on the basis of color. In her group of crimson to pink, the only one available is *Rhododendron* 'John Waterer'. Her beloved 'Bianchi', a pure pink, is no longer available. She also liked 'Sappho', a white with purple blotch that is still available. Since Jekyll's time, however, many improved hybrids in these color groups have been developed.

Jekyll was adamant about separating rhododendrons from the bright, deciduous Ghent azaleas, because she considered their appearances incongruous and impossible to combine for color. She thought the Ghent azalea colors harmonized and, therefore, could be planted together. She orchestrated the colors, though, from white to pale yellow and pink to orange to scarlet. Here again the strongest colors were planted in the most sun (Jekyll 1899).

THE CLOSE-UP VIEW

In the sections of the woodland garden to be viewed at closer range, the planting style changes to draw attention to detail (Plate 20). Along a path, for instance, smaller dwarf rhododendrons will not be lost. If the path passes a bank, the indumentum, the hairy covering, on the leaf underside can be appreciated—the silver of *Rhododendron argyrophyllum*, the dark orange of *R. bureavii*, the gray of *R. insigne*, or the dark brown of *R. tsariense*. Also, along a path the fragrance of the pale pink flowers of *R. fortunei* will not be wasted.

For a more intellectual approach, rhododendron species of a particular subsection of the genus could be grouped together. The academic connection bestowed by taxonomists upon these plants arises from the similarities they often display in visual aspect. For instance, several members of subsection *Taliensia* display thick indumentum, such as *Rhododendron bureavii*, *R. proteoides*, *R. flavorufum*, and *R. taliense*.

In a sunny glade, the red-orange, bell-shaped flowers of *Rhododendron cinnabarinum* will warmly glow in association with other warm-colored flowers. The red flowers of *R. barbatum* and *R. strigillosum* and *Rhododendron* 'Mars', 'Taurus', 'Grace Seabrook', and 'Vulcan' look splendid midst the cool green of the woodland. Several plants of *Rhododendron hodgsonii* could be planted together as a small grove, exhibiting its smooth, reddish bark in striking contrast to its large, shiny green leaves. The key is to vary woodland plantings to create interest and movement.

Companions

THE TREE LAYER

The early collections of rhododendrons in the British Isles were planted in woodlands, but because of a lack of sufficient canopy these woodlands often had to be created from scratch. At Arduaine, James Arthur Campbell planted 2000 Japanese larch (*Larix kaempferi*) for shelter on a bare headland on Loch Melfort. In North America, however, woodland sites usually come ready-made with a whole array of native companions for rhododendrons. If more large trees are to be added, those that are particularly good companions for rhododendrons are pines (*Pinus* spp.), for example *P. strobus*, because of their deep roots and open canopy, and oaks (*Quercus* spp.), for example *Q. garryana*, because of their deep root system.

Small trees add a second layer to the woodland. Magnolias (*Magnolia* spp.), companions to many Asian rhododendrons in the wild, are a natural choice. *Magnolia×soulangiana* is an all-season performer—large pink flowers in spring, large dark green leaves in summer, and smooth gray bark in winter. *Magnolia stellata*, with its star-like white flowers, offers a finer texture. The Japanese maples (*Acer palmatum*), while suitable for many more formal settings, can add a fineness of leaf texture where desired. Many dogwoods (*Cornus* spp.) are a beautiful addition to the woodland because of their horizontal branching, elegant flowers, and fall color. *Cornus kousa* is especially valued for its resistance to dogwood anthracnose. Japanese stewartia (*Stewartia pseudocamellia*) is also an all-season performer, with fresh green leaves in spring, white flowers in summer, colored foliage in fall, and exfoliating bark. Hollies (*Ilex* spp.), of course, will add winter substance to the woodland along with the rhododendrons, and the pyramidal *Ilex opaca* is among the best tree hollies. The attractive, rounded leaves of the eastern redbud (*Cercis canadensis*) will add fall color. The evergreen strawberry tree (*Arbutus unedo*) with its rich, red bark is a stunning addition but thrives best in a Mediterranean-type climate. Smaller conifer cultivars can be found among the genera *Cryptomeria*, *Pinus*, and *Tsuga* to add winter interest to the woodland.

THE SHRUB LAYER

Sharing the same layer as rhododendrons in the woodland are the companion shrubs, so numerous and rich in form, texture, and flower that choice is difficult. The natives, of course, will help anchor the woodland to the site and provide unity. Among choice shrubs to invite are members of the genus *Pieris*, with their mounded forms and drooping panicles of flowers. The many *Camellia* cultivars offer an early flowering season, preceding that of most rhododendrons. The foliage of *Kalmia* species blends beautifully with rhododendrons, and its flowering period comes after the height of rhododendron bloom. The species of *Clethra* flower even later, extending the flowering season into summer. Although it is impossible to mention all the many fine shrub choices, consider the plants of *Hydrangea* because the genus is under-used in the woodland. *Hydrangea quercifolia* is mounding in form with panicles of white flower-like sepals.

THE HERBACEOUS LAYER

The herbaceous layer in the woodland offers yet another palette of plants to harmonize with rhododendrons. First consider the natives of the region. In the Pacific Northwest are deer fern (*Blechnum spicant*) and sword fern (*Polystichum munitum*); several lilies, including the brilliant orange-flowered tiger lily (*Lilium columbianum*); trillium (*Trillium ovatum*) with its prim, white flower; and for wet areas skunk cabbage (*Lysichiton americanum*), magnificent in leaf and startling in flower. In the northeastern U.S. are royal fern (*Osmunda ragalis*); Solomon's seal (*Polygonatum* spp.); and toothwort (*Dentaria laciniata*). In the Midwest are lady's slipper (*Cypripedium reginae*) and various species of *Trillium*. In the Southeast are white wake-robin (*T. grandiflorum*) and Canada violet (*Viola canadensis*). And in the Southwest, mostly limited to California, is giant trillium (*T. chloropetalum*).

Besides natives, enrich the herbaceous layer with plants of the many genera that so ably cohabit with rhododendrons, many from the same native habitats. Among the genus *Primula*, the candelabra primulas (*P. japonica, P. burmanica,* and *P. prolifera*), with flowers in whorls on tall stems, are especially striking massed in a wet area in the woodland. The genus *Hosta* is invaluable for adding a lush foliage carpet to the woodland floor. The variation in foliage color of the many hybrids can be harmonized with rhododendron foliage in ingenious ways. The white margins of *Hosta* 'Francee' will brighten an area planted with rhododendrons of deep green leaf. The blue-green leaves of *Hosta* 'Krossa Regal' will harmonize with the blue-green leaves of *Rhododendron campanulatum* subsp. *aeruginosum.* The genus *Astilbe*, with its feathery foliage and plume-like flowers, offers a wonderful textural contrast to the stolid leaves of many evergreen rhododendrons. *Astilbe* 'Avalanche' with white flowers and *Astilbe* 'Fanal' with bronze foliage and red flowers are especially good. A genus finding favor in many woodland gardens is *Epimedium.* Its heart-shaped, leathery leaves attached to wiry stems are bronze in spring, green in summer, and bronze again in fall. Flowers of red, pink, white, or yellow are borne in airy spikes. No woodland garden should be without the spiked foliage of the genus *Iris*; its strong, vertical lines contrast with the often horizontal lines of rhododendron foliage. Look for the shade-loving types among the beardless irises, which include the native Pacific Coast iris (*I. douglasiana* and *I. innominata*) and the Siberian iris (*I. sibirica*). *Cyclamen coum* and *C. hederifolium* have attractive round leaves arranged in basal clumps and bear white or pink flowers resembling shooting stars.

Among the many creeping perennials for ground cover are carpet bugle (*Ajuga reptans*) which makes a carpet of dark green leaves and bears blue flowers; dead nettle, specifically *Lamium maculatum* 'Beacon Silver' with silver leaves with a green edge; and creeping dogwood (*Cornus canadensis*) bearing leaves in whorls of rich green.

PLANT COMBINATIONS

A white accent against dark green results strikingly from the cold-hardy combination of *Rhododendron ungernii, Viburnum lantana*, and *Hosta undulata*. The leaves of this small, upright-growing rhododendron unfurl with a white indumentum on the upper surface; later they turn dark green and shiny with pale indumentum on the undersides. The mounding viburnum bears small white flowers during the blooming seascn of the rhododendron, which also has white flowers. The hosta leaves are variegated white-on-green.

For a heat-tolerant combination with the unifying characteristic of large leaves, try *Rhododendron fortunei, Clerodendrum trichotomum*, and *Trillium grandiflorum*. In addition, the rhododendron and clerodendrum are both fragrant and carry a reddish cast to various plant parts. The leaves of the fragrant, pink-flowering *R. fortunei* are long (15 inches or 38 centimeters) with a reddish petiole. *Clerodendrum trichotomum*, a small tree from the southeastern U.S., also has large leaves (9 inches or 23 centimeters) and bears fragrant white flowers in July followed by small blue fruits with a reddish calyx. *Trillium grandiflorum*, also a southern native, bears a white flower and large leaves (6 inches or 15 centimeters).

86

Here is a suggestion for a combination with clean and uncluttered lines. The upright-growing leaf habit of *Rhododendron roxieanum* is echoed in the perky, upright needle spires of *Pinus mugo*. The staccato effect of these vertical lines is balanced by the smooth carpet of the moss *Polytrichum commune*. This combination is suitable for northwestern U.S. climates.

Garden Tours

The site Jeanine and Rex Smith chose for their home in Woodinville, Washington, was totally forested with towering, second-growth stands of Douglas fir (*Pseudotsuga menziesii*), western hemlock (*Tsuga heterophylla*), and western red cedar (*Thuja plicata*)—a typical western Washington woodland. After a herculean job of thinning and pruning, the Smiths planted two acres as a woodland garden, using their vast collection of rhododendrons as the main shrub layer. The delightful experience of viewing this garden comes both from the majestic, humbling size of its native trees and from the intimacy of its shrub and herbaceous layers, for the Smiths have managed to let the trees reign while under them creating areas of more human proportion. In addition, the various sections, connected by paths, differ enough from each other to keep the viewer moving, coaxed on by the extraordinary richness of the layered plantings, both native and exotic.

The Smiths have planted small trees to create an additional, lower tree layer, most notably cherries (*Prunus* spp.) and dogwoods (*Cornus* spp.) for spring flowering. A striking stand of birches (*Betula jacquemontii*), with their brilliant white bark and narrow, straight trunks, contrasts with the dark trunks of the natives, lighting up a corner like a sun break on a dark day.

But in the shrub layer of the Smith garden, the rhododendrons are the main event—a message made clear with the bold entrance planting of large hybrids, including the orange-yellow bicolor *Rhododendron* 'Apricot Fantasy' and the red-blotched white flowers of 'Phyllis Korn'. Along the driveway rhododendrons are mixed with other shrubs and ground covers. Here first

87

emerges the Smiths' style of weaving exotic plants and natives—
Oregon grape (*Mahonia aquifolium*), salal (*Gaultheria shallon*),
and many more—among the rhododendrons; this naturalistic
style extends throughout the garden and ties it unquestionably
to the site.

At the same time, specific features claim attention. At the
end of the driveway, against the house, and near the front door
is the striking combination of a Japanese maple (*Acer palmatum*),
lime green in new leaf, and the hybrid *Rhododendron* 'Hotei', with
its yellow trusses, a planting in perfect harmony in early spring.
To one side of the house an expanse of lawn leads down to a
curving mixed border where perennials are backed with rhododendrons, among them several selections from the white-flow-
ering *Rhododendron* Olympic Lady Group, pruned to make room
for perennials at their feet. The rhododendrons are backed, in
turn, by the large native conifers, tying the border to the rest of
the garden. At one end of the mixed border is a small rock garden, open to the sun, where dwarf *R. impeditum*, *R. williamsianum*, and *Rhododendron* 'Maricee' share space among the rocks
with hardy geraniums (*Geranium* spp.), heathers (*Erica*), and
other ericaceous plants.

To the other side of the house, a path leads among the trees,
which are richly underplanted with rhododendrons, other
shrubs, and ground covers. The path continues past the stand of
birch, to the back of the house, where the site slopes down from
the house to the north and affords protection for large-leafed
rhododendrons, including the superb *Rhododendron macabeanum*, among ferns and other woodland ground cover. A deck
offers yet another perspective high above the woodland floor,
with views through the forest trees and over the tops of shrubs.
On the deck, the Smiths have placed bonsai and other container
plants, including *Rhododendron* 'Noyo Brave', extending the
homey comfort of the inside rooms to the outdoors.

In a Pacific Northwest woodland further north near Sumas,
Washington, Lori and Dalen Bayes have built a garden using rhododendrons extensively in the shrub layer under the native tree
canopy, which has been thinned and pruned to add light. The
Bayes also have designed their garden with paths leading from

section to section, each with its own characteristics and plant combinations. In a section of deepest shade, ferns and plants of *Trillium* and *Arisaema* grow at the feet of rhododendrons, and a young collection of large-leafed rhododendrons fills another shady section. In a sunnier area, the mounding *Rhododendron yakushimanum* and *R. pachysanthum* are backed by Japanese maples (*Acer palmatum*). At one spot at the woodland verge, a superb specimen of *R. calophytum* in spring shows its dark red buds against the light green, new leaves of a native vine maple (*Acer circinatum*).

The woodland garden of Dave Hinton near Orono, Ontario, stretches rhododendron cold hardiness to its limit. In the midst of rolling farmland in this harsh climate where temperatures routinely drop to −20°F in winter (−29°C), he has developed a microclimate that supports several of the hardiest rhododendron species plus hybrids he has bred for hardiness. The tree canopy consists of red pine (*Pinus resinosa*) and white spruce (*Picea glauca*), and for additional windbreaks he has planted hedges throughout the property. Paths wind informally through his plantings of *Rhododendron brachycarpum* and *R. smirnowii*, two of the hardiest elepidote rhododendrons; *R. dauricum*, a lepidote species; and the eastern North American native azaleas *R. arborescence*, *R. prunifolium*, and *R. cumberlandense*. Hardy companions, including viburnums (*Viburnum* spp.), peonies (*Paeonia* spp.), and Solomon's seal (*Polygonatum* spp.), enrich the woodland (Plate 21).

George Gray of Williams Bay, Wisconsin, also deals with the rigors of a harsh climate in his woodland garden. The tree canopy primarily consists of red oak (*Quercus rubra*) and white oak (*Q. alba*), but also hickories (*Carya* spp.) and bur oak (*Q. macrocarpa*). He uses strategically placed arborvitae (*Thuja* spp.) for additional protection from wind. The garden, built on a slope, is designed in a semicircle, offering a large-picture view. In addition, grass paths wind among the plantings to give close-up views of individual rhododendrons and companions.

In the Azalea Woods at Winterthur, established by Henry Francis du Pont in 1918, the planting illustrates the classic technique of massing azaleas under a woodland canopy—a technique used in many private woodland gardens today on a smaller scale. Several of Du Pont's methods are particularly instructive: he respected the site of the native oak-and-chestnut woodland and incorporated the garden into the landscape; he enhanced the layered nature of the woodland by adding shrubs and perennials; and he achieved harmony by repeating colors, creating interest through subtle color variation and only occasional color contrast.

Besides dominating the shrub layer with Kurume azaleas, which were brought to the United States from Japan by Ernest H. Wilson, Du Pont added more of the native eastern dogwood (*Cornus florida*) and native Japanese species of *Viburnum*. In the herbaceous layer he added thousands of bluebells (*Endymion* spp.) and other spring bulbs. He developed his color techniques primarily with the Kurume azaleas. He found that in the diffused light on the forest floor the palest colors are luminous and draw viewers into the forest. Using primarily pastels, he planted in large drifts with subtle variation, for instance, a white-striped mauve azalea next to a white azalea with a mauve edge, or a salmon-pink with a blush of white next to a solid salmon-pink. Or to enliven a planting, he might add a single plant of contrasting color, such as one orange azalea in a pink planting. Du Pont's ideas on garden design continue to be instructive in the building of a woodland garden.

In the cold winter and hot summer environment of Urbana, Illinois, Donald Paden has had success with a wide variety of rhododendrons. He has planted a section of his woodland garden with a group of hardy lepidote rhododendrons, *Rhododendron* PJM Group and 'Olga Mezitt', and his own crosses, *R. dauricum* × *R. minus* Carolinianum Group. The site is protected in winter by a yew (*Taxus* sp.) hedge and shaded in summer by a yellow-wood (*Cladrastis lutea*). Pastel pink and white are the dominant flower colors in this planting and in a planting, canopied by a spruce tree (*Picea* sp.), of the deciduous Northern Lights azaleas, bred for extreme cold hardiness at the University of Minnesota Landscape Arboretum. In a section protected from wind by a hedge of Korean box (*Buxus microphylla* var. *koreana*) and shaded in summer by oaks (*Quercus*) are species selections and hybrids of *Rhododendron yakushimanum.* Companion trees in this woodland garden are hollies (*Ilex* spp.), yew (*Taxus* spp.), sour gums (*Nyssa* spp.), Black Hills spruce (*Picea glauca*), other spruce trees (*Picea* spp.), star magnolia (*Magnolia stellata*), large-flowered magnolia (*M. grandiflora*), mimosas (*Mimosa* spp.), and paperbark maple (*Acer griseum*). In the herbaceous layer are peonies (*Paeonia* spp.), hostas (*Hosta* spp.), and sweet woodruff (*Galium odoratum*).

Suggested Reading

Gillmore, Robert. 1996. *Woodland Garden.* Dallas: Taylor.

Greer, Harold E. 1996. *Greer's Guidebook to Available Rhododendrons.* Eugene, Oregon: Offshoot Publications.

Jekyll, Gertrude. 1899. *Wood and Garden.* Rpt. Suffolk, England: Antique Collectors Club, 1981.

CHAPTER 5

The Rock Garden

T HE "RIOT OF COLOR" that plant hunter Reginald Farrer found in the alpine meadows of the Mekong-Salween Divide soon found its way to the cultivated rock gardens of the West. So too did George Forrest's dwarf rhododendrons from Yunnan travel to rock gardens far from their Asian homeland. As plant hunters scoured the wild regions of western China and the Himalayas in search of new plants, they introduced many species of rhododendrons including the low-growing, tiny-leafed, high-altitude rhododendrons that thrived in short summers under bright sun and long winters under heavy snow. Prize among them were the creeping *Rhododendron forrestii* with its flamboyant red flowers, *R. impeditum* with its muted gray-green foliage, and the mounding *R. pemakoense*.

Even before the great influx of Asian species, however, rhododendrons had found their way into the rock gardens of Europe. *Rhododendron ferrugineum* grew wild in the Pyrenees and Alps and was introduced to Britain sometime before 1740. *Rhododendron hirsutum*, also a native of the Alps, came to Britain even earlier in 1656. The compact *R. myrtifolium* came to Britain in 1846 from Eastern Europe. In fact, the "Alpine garden" arose as the name for a specific type of rock garden in Britain devoted to plants from the European Alps.

The rock garden as a garden style in Britain has its origins in that curious garden phenomenon the grotto, where rocks and waterfalls were staged to romanticize the forces of nature, exemplifying the picturesque landscape design. The Victorian rockeries and ferneries were also precursors of the modern rock garden. English garden writer J. C. Loudon was the first to describe a "real" rock garden in 1838, where alpine plants are grown among rocks. Since then, the rock garden as a distinct garden design feature has engendered enough enthusiasm in gardeners to develop a whole range of rock garden styles to fit specific climates, sites, and plant groups, with enthusiasm left over to form rock garden societies and a hefty body of literature.

Where, then, does the alpine rhododendron fit into this garden design feature? Before this question can be answered, we must examine the plant's wild habitat. In nature, underlying bedrock occasionally protrudes above the soil and, in time, erodes through the action of wind and water, forming a highly porous soil which collects in the rock's crevices. Plant life that can thrive in such meager soil develops to adorn the rocky environment with its foliage and flowers. The alpine rhododendrons of the Alps, western China, the Himalayas, and Japan evolved in such an environment, high in the harsh montane reaches at or above timberline.

Although numerous rock plant communities develop on rock exposures at all altitudes, including sea level, and in all sorts of climates, including the desert, the wild habitat of almost all our alpine rhododendrons is characterized by high altitude, short summers, winter snow cover, and high summer rainfall. Exceptions are *Rhododendron lapponicum* and *R. camtschaticum*, which can occur in extreme northerly regions at lower altitudes in tundra environments. *Rhododendron groenlandicum*, a plant placed in the genus in 1990, occurs from sea level to 6000 feet (1830 meters). Though not strictly alpine, these three species are suitable for the rock garden because of their low-growing habit, and for gardening purposes they are grouped with the alpines.

Taking Inventory of the Site

A rock garden can either be built on natural rock outcroppings or be constructed to resemble such natural formations. Although the rocks may aid in the plants' ability to survive by shading their roots or foliage or fostering free drainage, the function of rocks in the rock garden is primarily aesthetic. Because of their low-growing habit, the alpine rhododendrons are well suited aesthetically for rock gardens because of their similarity in scale to rocks (Plate 22). Together they re-create the enchantment of the alpine setting.

Virtually all plants accustomed to a rocky environment need a fast-draining soil. Although all rhododendrons need good drainage, the alpine rhododendrons are particularly demanding in this respect. However, if all these rhododendrons needed was a fast draining soil and a pleasing rock arrangement to enhance their essential alpine aspect, all would be simple. Unfortunately, even though they can be forgiving of less than an exact replication of conditions in the wild, they rebel at certain demands we gardeners sometimes make. They wither in long, hot summers, especially without cool nights. They want moisture during the summer, and do best in misty days. They require an acid soil and cannot take a shady environment or overhanging branches that drop large leaves on them. Moreover, these mountain natives will not survive extreme winter cold without protection. Seattle rock gardener Arthur Dome is on the mark with his advice: ask not which rhododendrons are good for the rock garden, but which rock gardens are good for rhododendrons (Dome 1996). The more the garden climate differs from rhododendrons' home climate in the wild, the more assiduous must the gardener be in meeting the cultural needs of these plants.

The soil absolutely must be free draining yet constantly moist. A sandy loam rich in organic matter is best, for it provides both drainage and moisture retention. Except for the creeping forms, such as *Rhododendron forrestii* or *R. calostrotum* subsp. *keleticum* Radicans Group which can grow in shallow soil, alpine rhododendrons need soil deep enough to encourage deep root growth.

Pockets or crevices between rocks make good planting spots. However, if the pockets serve as water reservoirs, the soil may have to be mounded up to allow water to drain. Because the soil is so crucial to the success of the rhododendrons, soil often has to be brought in. As in their wild, alpine habitats, mulches aid the rhododendrons by holding moisture about the roots, moderating the soil temperature, and providing nutrients (Plate 23).

Along with other rhododendrons, alpine rhododendrons need an acid soil with a pH from 5 to 5.5 ideally. The nutritional needs of the alpines differ little from other rhododendrons except that an overdose of nitrogen may make them grow straggly.

As in nature, the alpine rhododendrons in the garden have light requirements different from those of their woodland counterparts. Their wild habitat above the tree line tells us they need the direct sunlight of the open meadow midst the mineral landscape of rock and scree. While the task of creating a similar landscape in the rock garden is possible, the re-creation of the high elevation climate from which they came is virtually impossible. Remember that high in the mountains in western China and the Himalayas the summers are short and rainy with cool nights, and the winters bring snow to insulate foliage and roots. Depending upon how drastically the garden climate deviates from the natural habitat of these alpines, you will need to compensate for the differences.

As a general rule, the alpines need as much exposure to sunlight as is possible without burning the foliage. The varying climates of North America will dictate how much exposure to sun these plants will take. In the Pacific Northwest, where the climate most nearly resembles the wild habitat—though with major differences—an eastern or southeastern exposure is considered best, with shade from the hot afternoon sun.

While the alpines need as much light as they can take without burning, they also need shelter from wind. In the wild the alpines find refuge behind rocks and in crevices. They protect each other when they grow in vast expanses close together. If the site is particularly windy, the whole rock garden can be screened from wind by hedges, shrub borders, or fences. And during winter's freezing temperatures and lack of snow cover, the alpines may need protection from the cold. Gardeners have devised many ingenious covers such as baskets, frames covered by branches, and mesh frames filled with leaves.

Gardeners with a natural rock outcrop on the site are blessed indeed. For them, the rock formation itself will provide unity with the rest of the site and the surrounding neighborhood. The outcrop also will dictate to a large degree the kind of rock garden you will build, depending on its exposure to sunlight and shelter from wind. In the absence of a natural rock outcrop, banks or hillsides on the site may provide good drainage and are potential locations for building a rock garden from scratch. Very steep banks may lend themselves to a terraced rock garden. A level site can accommodate a rock garden as long as good drainage is established. A raised bed can be mounded over a base of well-draining material, or a scree bed will assure good drainage on a level site.

Narrowing the Choices

The more the climate deviates from the natural habitat of alpine rhododendrons, the narrower is the range of options for a rock garden that will accommodate them. Judging from gardeners' experiences, the Pacific Northwest climate offers more latitude than other regions. Warmer and drier climates are much less flexible in the rhododendrons they will oblige. On the northern coast of California the longevity of the alpines is shorter. Further down the coast, the evergreen azaleas tend to be more successful in the rock garden. In the Northeast a northern exposure is most effective for reducing excessive summer heat on the rocks and foliage. In the Southeast, growing alpine rhododendrons is difficult at best.

The size of the rock garden will also narrow choices, especially in the style of planting. Large rock gardens can accommodate mass plantings reminiscent of the expansive views of high alpine meadows in western China and the Himalayas, while small rock gardens will draw the viewer closer for more intimate looks at foliage and flower. Very few gardeners, however, will have the luxury of planting on a scale of the Royal Botanic Garden Edinburgh, where the massing of alpine rhododendrons is so expertly done. Scale is the key to achieving unity in the rock garden. The groups of plants and plant size should be in scale with the size of the garden and the rocks.

Improving the Site

If the rock garden is to be built on a natural rock outcrop, well-draining soil may have to be added to nooks and crannies for planting. Take care, however, to avoid planting in spots that collect water rather than allowing it to drain through. The nature of the outcrop itself will guide the design of the garden.

If the rocks are to be placed on an existing large slope—a slope with the proper exposure for alpines in the climate—paths of a moderate grade should be planned for viewing and maintenance. Viewers should be able to see all the plants without stepping off the path into the growing areas. If the slope is steep, terraces can be built to hold the soil in place and keep the plants from sliding down the slope in a heavy rain.

If rocks are to be placed on a level site, the site should be excavated about a foot deep (0.3 meters) and filled with rubble for drainage, sloping the area slightly so that the water drains out. Then the garden soil can be mounded to the height of the desired garden. The shape of the garden should be as natural as possible, built in sweeping curves with the base wider so that it is not top heavy.

The correct placement of rocks has received much attention, and ample literature is available for detailed discussions. To create the most natural-looking rock garden, English garden expert Graham Stuart Thomas advises: "We must imagine that the soil from the hillock, thrust up by the rock outcrop, has been wasted away from the top into the valleys, and that underneath it everywhere is solid rock. This is the fundamental upon which the design of all natural rock gardening rests" (Thomas 1989). Generally accepted techniques for creating a natural-looking rock garden are to place rocks so that strata are parallel, to place flat

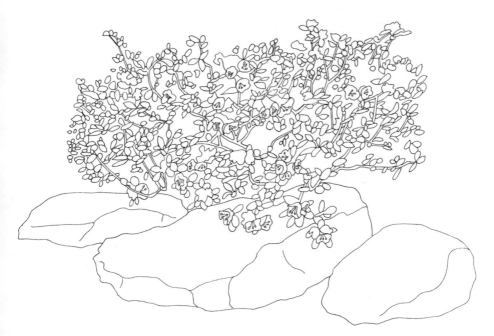

For the most natural-looking rock garden, the rhododendrons should
be in scale with the size of the rocks.

rocks at a tilt and parallel, and to group rocks rather than dotting
them evenly over the site. The rocks should be placed firmly
enough so that standing on them will not dislodge them.

An element of the rock garden, or a feature in itself, is the
scree bed, in nature a mass of rock debris usually at the foot of a
cliff. In the wild, alpine rhododendrons often find the fast draining scree suits their needs nicely, and so they make their homes
in what seems to the human eye the most precarious locations.
In the garden, a scree site must first be excavated about 2 feet
(0.6 meters). Then place 6 inches of rubble (15 centimeters) at
the bottom and cover it with gravel. Spread the soil mixture to
bring the site up to ground level, and place more gravel on top
of the soil. The rock garden at the Rhododendron Species
Botanical Garden in Federal Way, Washington, includes a scree
slope amended with limestone chips to accommodate alpine
companions needing a higher pH than most rhododendrons.

Rhododendron hirsutum, a lime lover, grows directly in the scree bed, which is built at the bottom of the garden.

The most natural-looking rock garden will blend easily into natural garden features at its periphery, such as a woodland or heather bed. Abutting a formal feature, such as a rose garden, will detract from the rock garden's natural character and make it too abrupt, too surprising, too much like a mere pile of rocks.

Planting

The variety of alpine rhododendrons is so rich that numerous designs for planting them in the rock garden are possible, taking advantage of an upright or prostrate habit, a wide range of flower color, fall leaf color, and foliage texture, color, and aroma. A look at their wild habitats gives a clue to two basic designs. The rhododendrons of subsection *Lapponica*, which includes *Rhododendron fastigiatum* and *R. impeditum*, tend to grow in seas of a single species on open, windy mountain sites. Such a sea of *R. impeditum* occurs at Lake Kong Wu, Muli, in southwest Sichuan Province of China. On the other hand, a mixture of alpine species can also grow amid plants of other genera. In the Doshong La area of southeast Tibet, an alpine meadow is home to numerous species of rhododendrons, including *R. forrestii*, *R. cephalanthum*, and *R. aganniphym*, and members of the genera *Cassiope*, *Primula*, and *Bergenia*, which all form a carpet of mixed texture and color united in scale by their shared low-growing habits. While the size of these wild sites cannot be reproduced in the garden, man-made plantings can echo the beauty of such places.

Alpines as a general plant type have varying needs, and you must abandon any fantasy of growing, for example, the exquisite *Rhododendron calostrotum* subsp. *keleticum* Radicans Group midst a group of lovely *Lewisia tweedyi* because their small stature and foliage will complement each other so well. *Rhododendron calostrotum* likes a wet summer, and *Lewisia tweedyi* likes a dry one. The natural habitats of alpines vary so greatly throughout the world, from arid to rain forest, from never freezing to having freezing

Table 9. Rhododendrons with creeping habit

	USDA hardiness zone	Plant size in ten years	Plant form	Foliage texture	Flower color
campylogynum	6	gc	mounding	fine	p, v
camtschaticum	4	gc	compact	fine, deciduous	p
cephalanthum	6	dwarf shrub	spreading	fine, glossy	w, p, y
forrestii	7	gc	mounding	medium, glossy	r
keiskei 'Yaku Fairy'	6	gc	compact	fine	y
lapponicum	4	dwarf shrub	spreading	fine	p, v
nakaharae	6	gc	spreading	medium, glossy	o, r
pemakoense	7	gc	spreading	fine	p, v
pumilum	6	gc	mounding	fine, bluish	p
saluenense	6	dwarf shrub	mounding	fine, glossy	v, r-v
sargentianum	6	gc	compact	fine, glossy	y, w
williamsianum	6	gc	mounding	medium, glossy	p

Abbreviations: ind = indumentum, gc = ground cover, p = pink, r = red, w = white, v = violet, o = orange, y = yellow. See List of Tables for sizes.

temperatures nine months of the year, that it is a wonder any of them will cohabit. When it comes to the rhododendron, however, its many cousins in the Ericaceae offer shared cultural needs and an astounding number of highly garden-worthy plants that can be used in both the mass plantings for structure and the plantings that call for closer views.

THE LARGE PICTURE

Gertrude Jekyll favored the style of massing alpine rhododendrons in the rock garden. She writes: "When the ground is shaped and the rocks placed, the next matter of importance, and that will decide whether the rock garden is to be a thing of some dignity or only the usual rather fussy mixture, is to have a solid planting of suitable small shrubs crowning all the heights. Most important of these will be the alpine rhododendrons; mat in habit, dark of foliage, and on a scale that does not overwhelm the little plant jewels that are to come near them. No shrubs are so suitable for a good part of the main plantings in the higher regions. . . . By using them in bold masses they will give the whole rock garden that feeling of unity and simplicity of design" (Jekyll 1901).

The rock garden at the Royal Botanic Garden Edinburgh masses alpine rhododendrons, notably *Rhododendron fastigiatum* and *R. impeditum,* in its splendid island beds. At Glendoick in Scotland, nurseryman and plant hunter Peter Cox, disliking the isolated specimen in the garden, displays an undulating ground cover of the alpines he has seen growing in groups in the wild.

Most rock gardens will lack the room for planting grand sweeps of one species, but a similar effect can be created by planting a small group of one species so that it merges with a group of another species of similar habit. Such is the style used in the rock garden at the Rhododendron Species Botanical Garden. A particularly attractive planting of *Rhododendron calostrotum* adorns an upper ledge of the garden, growing in a most natural way over and between the rocks.

Another superb alpine species useful for massing—and for many other garden functions as well—grows in the wild on the misty mountaintop of the 6000-foot (1830-meter) island of Yakushima in southern Japan: the magnificent *Rhododendron yakushi-*

manum. Although taller (up to 2½ feet or 0.8 meters) than many alpines mentioned, these plants offer foliage in contrast to the typically small leaves of many alpines and can greatly enhance the larger rock garden. The dramatic foliage show begins with new growth covered in thick, white indumentum. As the beautiful, recurved leaves grow, the upper leaf surface gradually sheds its woolly coat revealing a shiny green, while the leaf undersides develop a tawny indumentum thick and fur-like to the touch. At the Rhododendron Species Botanical Garden, this species is strikingly mass planted just above the rock garden.

Mass plantings of rhododendrons in the rock garden, even if the "mass" is only a small group, will connect the planting to the wild alpine reaches where these plants flourish. These plantings will also give structure and height along with the larger rocks in contrast to the lower growing inhabitants of the rock garden. In the words of Gertrude Jekyll, they will lend dignity.

THE CLOSE-UP VIEW

Plant hunter Reginald Farrer was also an avid rock gardener. He warned against the "currant in the pudding" effect in rock garden design where miniature plants are evenly spaced over a hillock of evenly spaced rocks. Because of their diminutive stature, these gems seem to suggest a planting design that dots them uniformly over the ground, but in truth, such a planting design will result in a most unnatural-looking garden. Using a framework of alpine shrubs is the first step in avoiding such a mistake. The smaller alpines, which call for a close-up look, can also be planted in groups based on cultural needs and design principles. With their fine-textured foliage and bright, showy flowers, the smallest alpine rhododendrons are perfectly suited for such close-up views, nestled between or trailing over the rocks.

Among the smallest alpine rhododendrons and one highly prized for the rock garden is *Rhododendron calostrotum* subsp. *keleticum* Radicans Group. This creeping shrub with tiny, dark green leaves bears single, violet flowers above its foliage. A closely related species of the same subsection *Saluenensia* is *R. saluenense*. Another low-growing shrub of creeping habit, it bears violet flowers and bristly new growth. *Rhododendron pemakoense* forms compact, low mounds of dark green, scaly leaves and bears pink funnel-shaped flowers. Another of the very dwarf alpine rhododendrons is *R. keiskei* 'Yaku Fairy' from the mountains of Japan, which forms a low, dense mound and covers itself with yellow flowers in the spring. Warren Berg used *R. keiskei* to produce *Rhododendron* 'Patty Bee' with yellow flowers and 'Ginny Gee' with white and pink flowers, two hybrids highly suitable for the rock garden. Peter Cox also used *R. keiskei* to produce the low-growing *Rhododendron* 'Wren'. Another creeping species is *R. forrestii*, with its small, round, shiny, dark green leaves, bearing single, red flowers. This beauty, however, needs careful placement—in the open but facing away from direct sunlight. *Rhododendron hippophaeoides* is one alpine that does well in the southern United States. Two excellent low-growing Japanese azalea species for the rock garden are *R. kiusianum*, compact with small, sometimes deciduous leaves and flowering in a variety of colors, and *R. nakaharae*, another creeper, with outstanding forms selected by Polly Hill of Martha's Vineyard, Massachusetts, notably *R. nakaharae* 'Mt. Seven Star'. *Rhododendron cephalanthum*, along with others of section *Pogonanthum*, offers highly aromatic foliage.

Rock garden rhododendrons of small shrub size, which may or may not be alpines in the strict sense, add height to the planting. Among the many choices are compact forms of *Rhododendron racemosum* with its delicate pink flowers; *R. roxieanum* var. *oreonastes* with its distinctively narrow leaves; compact forms of *R. pseudochrysanthum* from Taiwan with its leathery leaves; the cliff dweller from Sichuan, China, *R. williamsianum*, and any number of its hybrids; and the delicately flowered *R. primuliflorum*. An additional attribute of many alpine rhododendrons is that their evergreen foliage takes on a red hue in the fall.

Companions

Rhododendrons come from a large, companionable family, the Ericaceae. In the rock garden that is suitable for rhododendrons, most other rock garden members of the Ericaceae will also live happily in the moist, acid soil protected from the hottest rays of the sun. The approximately 1900 species are mostly shrubs, representing some of the truly great genera of garden plants—among them *Andromeda, Calluna, Cassiope, Erica, Gaultheria, Kalmia, Phyllodoce, Pieris,* and *Vaccinium.*

A number of choice rock garden plants come from the genus *Cassiope,* which occurs naturally from the Arctic Circle to the mountains of California, northern Asia, and northern Europe. Its evergreen leaves grow in scales along its branchlets, and it bears white, bell-like flowers. Height ranges from 1 to 15 inches (2.5 to 38 centimeters). *Cassiope lycopodioides* is mat forming with gray-green leaves and is considered a more adaptable member of the genus. Members of the genus *Phyllodoce* vary from 4 to 18 inches high (10 to 46 centimeters), with needle-like, dark green foliage and flowers in a range of colors. *Phyllodoce empetriformis,* bearing pink bell-shaped flowers, is considered a good rock garden plant. The genus *Gaultheria* offers a number of superb plants for the rock garden, including *G. adenothrix,* with dark green foliage and white blossoms; *G. nummularioides,* a prostrate form; and *G. procumbens,* the native wintergreen. *Kalmiopsis leachiana,* a native of the Siskiyou Mountains of southwest Oregon, though difficult to grow, is a jewel for the rock garden with its thick, dark green leaves and pink flowers. Many dwarf forms of the genus *Vaccinium* make excellent companions, among them *V. macrocarpon* 'Hamilton', which grows to only about 4 inches (10 centimeters) and bears pink flowers.

The genera *Erica* and *Calluna,* native to the British Isles and commonly called heaths or heathers, are best given their own space rather than to be interspersed among the rhododendrons, for they will eventually conquer the non-combative rhododendrons and take over the territory. A heather bed would blend well as a feature adjacent to the rock garden, as both are natural in form.

Among the many herbaceous perennials that make good companions for rhododendrons in the rock garden, because of both their cultural requirements and their growing habit, are species of *Primula, Aquilegia, Gentiana,* and *Erythronium. Primula denticulata* is a native of the Himalayan alpine meadows and so is supremely appropriate. *Aquilegia alpina* is native to the European

Alps. Most species of *Gentiana,* known for the purity of their blue flowers, are alpine and require conditions similar to rhododendrons. Most members of the genus *Erythronium* are native to the western United States and require constant moisture, as do rhododendrons. The genus *Saxifraga* offers some good candidates, including *S. rosacea,* whose foliage turns red in the fall in the Northwest, and *S. umbrosa* with pink flowers on red stalks. To give alpine rhododendrons the best possible chance to thrive, keep the soil around their roots free of competition from other plants, placing their herbaceous companions between them rather than under them.

Mosses add a natural yet groomed appearance to the rock garden and contribute humidity to the surrounding air, an undeniable asset for rhododendrons. Among the many mosses to consider are the hairy cap moss (*Pogonatum contortum*), *Polytrichum piliferum,* and *Atrichum undulatum.* And since the rock garden suitable for rhododendrons is protected from the sun's hottest rays, many ferns will thrive there without overwhelming rhododendrons. Among the best is the exquisite maidenhair (*Adiantum pedatum*). Dwarf conifers, too, can enhance a rock garden, giving contrast in plant form and texture. Try the prickly bun of *Abies koreana* 'Starkers Dwarf' or the slender, upright *Chamaecyparis obtusa* 'Meroke'.

PLANT COMBINATIONS

United by their dark green foliage and ground-hugging habit yet differing from each other in foliage texture are *Rhododendron keiskei* 'Yaku Fairy' with a matte leaf surface, *Vaccinium vitis-idaea* with a shiny leaf surface, and *Pogonatum contortum* with a velvety texture. The combination will demand that the viewer look closely at the detail.

Three rhododendrons from subsection *Lapponica, Rhododendron fastigiatum, R. impeditum,* and *R. intricatum,* planted in merging groups will all exhibit the same mounding habit with slightly different leaf color and texture and with flowers in varying hues of violet blooming at the same time. Viewed from a distance, this combination will be a small version of the wild rhododendron sea.

The hybrid *Rhododendron* 'Wee Bee' planted with *Gaultheria adenothrix* and a mat of *Saxifraga umbrosa* will be united by their low stature. The white and red flowers of 'Wee Bee', the white flowers and red calyces of *G. adenothrix* and the white flowers and red stems of *S. umbrosa* will also unite them—if these three early bloomers see fit to bloom at the same time as they are supposed to do!

Garden Tours

A treasure of a rock garden on a steep, protected but open, east-facing slope near Lake Washington in Seattle belongs to Arthur Dome, whose impeccable gardening judgment has led him to the Ericaceae (Plate 24). Here among rocks and along terraces, ericaceous genera predominate: the alpine species and dwarf hybrids of *Rhododendron, Phyllodoce, Cassiope, Erica, Calluna, Vaccinium, Gaultheria, Arctostaphylos, Arbutus,* and more. This garden bears witness to the fact that success is, in part, the product of choosing the right plants for the site. This site, protected from wind, limited by the steep slope to half-day morning sun, and blessed by good drainage, begged for a garden of alpines that eschewed hot, all-day sun.

Arthur Dome's initial interest in heathers led him inevitably to other ericaceous plants. A trip to Yunnan Province in China and Japan to see these plants in the wild helped fire his horticultural interests. In the course of developing the garden, he removed large shrubs "that did not interest me" and added some 30 yards of top soil (27.5 meters) with cedar compost and recycled lawn waste from the city of Seattle to create a friable, lime-free soil. He placed granite rock in natural arrangements and rebuilt the original retaining walls into terraces with more natural lines. Only the dry northwestern summer, which keeps the site from being perfect for alpine plants, makes irrigation necessary. Also, in winter some of the plants are covered with evergreen boughs to protect them from the sun—when it occasionally shines.

Another Seattle rock garden, this one facing west and open

to the warmer afternoon sun, belongs to Chip Muller. On a clear day, the Olympic Mountains to the west show their eternal snow from this small urban garden of alpines and other small plants. On plant explorations in Asia, Muller has seen many of his plants in the wild.

When he began his garden in 1983, he first removed all the turf from the small, sloping front yard and added a soil mix rich in organic matter and amended with chipped rock. For the large rocks he used a hard limestone. He then sat down with his library of books on rhododendrons and made a list of all the rhododendrons he could find that would grow less than 3 feet (1 meter) in ten years and were native to open sites, hillsides, and cliffs. Muller found that his warm, west-facing site narrowed the list for him. Among rhododendrons that tend to do well in his garden are species from the subsections *Lapponica* and *Saluenensia* and the section *Pogonanthum*, but also thriving are *Rhododendron glaucophyllum, R. haematodes, R. fragariflorum, R. forrestii, R. pachysanthum, R. racemosum* 'Rock Rose', *R. dauricum, R. mucronulatum, R. tsariense*, and many more.

Companion genera to these alpine rhododendrons also need moist soil year-round: *Calluna, Erica, Vaccinium*, and *Arctostaphylos* (which can take some dryness in summer), and the herbaceous *Saxifraga, Gentiana, Bergenia, Primula*. Combinations also include *Armeria meritima*, numerous bulbs, and several small trees. This is not a garden for those alpines that like dry soil in the summer. Micro sprinklers water one-half hour every morning in the summer before the sun comes up, and at the end of summer another half hour at the end of the day.

Close-up views are extremely important in this small urban garden. Front steps and a driveway cut through the slope to provide eye-level perspectives on small plants without forcing viewers to their knees. Plants grouped for contrast create interesting pictures throughout the garden. For instance, against a limestone rock, a saxifrage (*Saxifraga* sp.) lifts its red-violet flowers high enough to show behind *Rhododendron calostrotum* 'Gigha' covered in violet flowers. Around the corner, the pasque flower (*Anemone pulsatilla*) shows its dark red blooms against the same rock.

Further north, Glen Patterson of West Vancouver, British Columbia, has built his rock garden on a massive natural outcrop majestically overlooking English Bay. Because of its unusually large size, the garden can accommodate a collection of trees and herbaceous plants along with Patterson's many alpine rhododendrons. Outstanding in this garden are the crevice plantings of rhododendrons and other alpines, the single accents he achieves, such as one brightly blooming azalea amid the rocks, and the pruned conifers that give a mountaintop feeling to the garden.

The garden developed by Jane Kerr Platt in Portland, Oregon, is a private one well maintained by its late namesake's husband, John Platt. It includes a rock garden that rises from an expanse of lawn in the skillfully integrated design. Backed by a superb mixed border of trees, shrubs, and ground covers, the rock garden is a unit unto itself characterized by low-growing plants among the rocks, yet it is connected to the garden as a whole by the layering technique found throughout the site (Plate 25). In the rock garden, a few low-growing conifers and alpine rhododendrons make the top layer: *Rhododendron* 'Curlew', 'Patty Bee', *R. yakushimanum*, and *R. impeditum*. The next layer includes many bulbs, which make a spring show when the rhododendrons are also blooming. Herbaceous perennials contribute to this second layer, including plants of *Erythronium* with their lily-shaped flowers, species of *Anemone*, low-growing species of *Allium*, and a striking dark red rhubarb (*Rheum rhabarbarum*). (The related alpine rhubarb, *R. nobile*, grows in Tibet at 13,000 feet, or 3965 meters.) The lowest layer of the rock garden is predominantly moss, an important ingredient that ties the parts together like a soft, green carpet.

Jean and Frank Furman of Bridgewater, New Jersey, have built three rock gardens to display their collection of dwarf azaleas and rhododendrons. Their current favorite is a small, sunny rock garden, which is 85 square feet (25.5 square meters) of kidney-shaped, rock-bordered, raised bed (Plate 26). The native clay soil is mixed one to one with sand to provide drainage. In addition, a mixture of peat and sand is used for backfill when planting. The bed faces southwest, receives a small amount of

109

morning shade, is backed by a larger bed of rhododendrons, azaleas, and bulbs, and is protected from wind by woodland trees. The bed contains dwarf and small-shrub-sized rhododendrons, including *Rhododendron mucronulatum* 'Crater's Edge' (unregistered name); *Rhododendron* 'April Rose', an *R. fastigiatum* hybrid; a dwarf form of *R. mucronulatum*; and three dwarf *R. keiskei* hybrids. Dwarf azaleas also fill the planting, including *Rhododendron* 'Kermesinum Rosé' (unregistered name), *R. nakaharae*, and five *R. kiusianum* hybrids. Shrub companions are *Juniperus horizontalis* 'Gray Forest', *J. communis* 'Compressa', *Chamaecyparis obtusa* 'Nana', *C. pisifera* 'Squarrosa Intermedia', *Vaccinium macrocarpon* 'Hamilton', and a dwarf variegated species of *Buxus*. Among the many herbaceous companions are *Armeria juniperifolia*, *Penstemon davidsonii*, *Phlox subulata*, and *Veronica repens*.

Suggested Reading

Greer, Harold E. 1996. *Greer's Guidebook to Available Rhododendrons*. Eugene, Oregon: Offshoot Publications.

Schenk, George. 1997. *Moss Gardening*. Portland, Oregon: Timber Press.

Thomas, Graham Stuart. 1989. *Rock Garden and its Plants*. Portland, Oregon: Sagapress/Timber Press.

CHAPTER 6

The Mixed Border

L OOK TO the mixed border to free rhododendrons from their sometimes stodgy, traditional roles in garden design and to give them the new life they deserve. For too long rhododendrons have been frozen into the design clichés of foundation plantings, isolated in packs in island beds, or worse still, allowed to smother their less robust neighbors until they dominate in a pure but dull monoculture. In a mixed border, rhododendrons can regain their individuality and become contributing members in a diverse society of plants, each contributing in its own way to the health and beauty of the garden. With trees overhead, deciduous shrubs at their sides, and herbaceous perennials at their feet, rhododendrons serve as one genus among many in garden design.

Although the mixed border is the fashion for today's garden, it has, of course, existed all along—or at least since the late nineteenth century when William Robinson revolted against the stylized Victorian garden and reintroduced the natural or wild garden. From Robinson gardeners learned how plants grew in the wild and how to place them next to companions of similar needs, allowing them to grow together naturally. Gertrude Jekyll, inspired by Robinson, brought the border concept to new heights, and even she, who relied heavily on herbaceous perennials in her borders, used small trees and shrubs along with perennials, biennials, annuals, and bulbs.

111

In the mixed border, rhododendrons share the space with other genera, lending architectural support and contributing to harmonies of form, foliage, and color.

The mixed border as a garden design feature differs from the woodland and rock garden features primarily in the way it is viewed—it is a picture painted with plants. In addition, a mixed border has a backdrop, such as a fence or hedge, that supports it visually, much like the backdrop on a stage (Plate 27). The mixed border offers the opportunity to grow a wide variety of plants—trees, shrubs, herbaceous perennials, biennials, annuals, ground covers, vines, and bulbs—in a concentrated area, orchestrating dramatic seasonal change.

Taking Inventory of the Site

First, to determine how to use a mixed border in the overall design of your garden, look at the property from a new perspective. Instead of standing at the perimeter looking into the site in the role of a passerby, stand in the house or on the deck and look out. *You* are meant to be the prime observer, not the casual motorist driving by, and *you* will most often observe it and enjoy it from your living areas, both inside and out. Although some landscape designers prefer to plan features that are most easily viewed from the street, today's homeowners tend to want to view their gardens from the living quarters. The location of the border should allow the seasonal drama of the mixed border to be savored in privacy.

The property may be an empty canvas on which everything will be built and planted from scratch, but most likely it will already contain living and inert features. The embryo of a mixed border may be waiting for discovery. Look for dominant features that could back up or anchor a border—trees, fences, hedges, or perhaps a planting of rhododendrons. Often these dominant features are waiting at the edge of a property, placement appropriate but not essential for the mixed border. Such backdrops often take longest to establish, so using those that already exist will greatly advance the progress of the planting.

A border has a front and a back, and its exposure to sun will influence the choice of plants. If the border location is shaded by trees, consider the type of shade. Dappled shade will allow a greater choice of plants; deep shade will impose limits. Also note the type of soil. Fortunately, along with the rhododendrons, most plants in the mixed border will want a well-draining soil. Plants' needs, however, may diverge over the pH level, which should be tested at the border location.

Narrowing the Choices

Compared to the woodland or rock garden, the mixed border is undemanding of the site. No woods, no natural rock outcrop are needed, just a flat piece of ground that can, preferably, be seen from the living area. Depending upon the climate, a mixed border that includes rhododendrons with large evergreen leaves will require some shade. Dappled shade from large, adjacent trees or from smaller trees and shrubs within the border can provide the necessary environment. The exposure to sunlight can also be tempered by the directional orientation of the border. Rhododendrons, however, vary considerably in their light requirements, offering some selection no matter the exposure to sun. Rhododendrons in a mixed border will also need protection from the wind. The location itself or an existing backdrop may provide a safe refuge.

Improving the Site

To include rhododendrons in the garden the soil will need to be free draining, continually moist, and between 4 and 6 in pH. However, the soil can be varied to accommodate different groups of plants with diverse soil needs. For optimum health of soil and plants, the whole bed, rather than the individual planting holes, should be prepared before planting. Either incorporate amendments deep in the existing soil or add a foot (0.3 meters) of new, good soil and amendments to the surface. Mulch can be added yearly to keep the soil in good health.

The plant material of the mixed border offers a full cast of trees, shrubs, herbaceous perennials, biennials, bulbs, annuals, and ground covers, all combining for a layered effect. But this lively bunch needs a backdrop or frame to unite and contain the action-packed scenes the plants produce. The frame is at the border's back, and although it may not receive the applause that other more visually exciting elements will receive, it is crucial to the border's success. The choice of frame will depend on the style of the house and surroundings—urban, country, suburban, and so on—and could be a fence, wall, or hedge, for example. Hedges, of course, take time to establish. Many mixed borders situated at the edge of woodlands use the woodland itself as a frame.

The great versatility of rhododendrons shows itself from the start in the design of the mixed border. For an informal hedge, rhododendrons could be the sole component, growing unpruned, or they could be combined with other shrubs for a mixed hedge. Some rhododendrons can be pruned for a formal hedge (see Chapter 10). One great advantage to using evergreen rhododendrons for the frame is that they will hold steadfast through the vagaries of the seasons, while the leaf assets of their deciduous neighbors come and go. If you use rhododendrons for the frame, choose the species or hybrids that are proven performers in the region.

Planting

The glory of the mixed border arises from the richness of its multi-layered planting scheme, where plants of widely varying genera bring out the best in each other as they change through the seasons. It is here in the mixed border that rhododendrons are asked to relate most intimately with plants of other genera. Directing such a performance can be daunting, but fortunately plants can always be moved—or scrapped.

THE LARGE PICTURE

While the frame encloses the mixed border and lends unity, a backbone of small trees will lend height and contribute to unity, serving as the top layer in this multi-layered garden feature. The trees can stand on their own or be woven into a hedge. If the trees are native to the region, they can tie the border to the surrounding landscape.

The choice of trees is virtually endless even within the limits of climate and site. Personal tastes here can dictate the choices. Rhododendron lovers have a selection of many plants of the genus that are, in fact, trees. Among the tallest tree rhododendrons is *Rhododendron arboreum,* up to 30 feet high (9 meters) with tough, dark green, shiny leaves that have whitish indumentum on the undersides. The flowers come in blood-red, white, and pink. On the tender side, this plant is a favorite among Northern Californians. *Rhododendron sutchuenense,* a majestic and hardy beauty, has leaves up to 1 foot long (0.3 meters) and pale purple or pink flowers. Like the other tree rhododendrons with large leaves, it needs protection from winds that may damage its leaves. The smooth, plum-colored bark of *R. barbatum* is a treasured asset of this rhododendron, which can grow 30 feet tall (9 meters) in the garden. Add its bright scarlet blooms and a star is born for the mixed border. Other tree rhododendrons of varying hardiness include *R. falconeri, R. fulvum, R. grande, R. hodgsonii, R. macabeanum,* and *R. rex.*

Although not as tall, *Rhododendron catawbiense,* a native of the eastern United States, can grow up to 10 feet (3.1 meters) and be treated like a tree in climates where other tree rhododendrons are too tender. Deciduous azalea *R. prunifolium* can grow to 15 feet or more (4.6 meters) and is a tree-like choice open to gardeners in its native region of the southeastern United States, where some tree rhododendrons will not thrive. An asset is the late bloom of its orange to red flowers.

Many hybrids may be more amenable to particular climates than the species themselves. A splendid group of hybrids was developed by Sir Edmund Loder in England in the early 1900s. Results of his crossing of *Rhododendron fortunei* and *R. griffithianum* are *Rhododendron* 'Loderi King George', 'Loderi Pink Diamond', and 'Loderi Venus'—all fragrant with voluptuous blossoms beyond compare.

Often tree rhododendrons can be pruned, if necessary, to reveal splendid bark and trunk outlines. Do not forget that rhododendrons are amenable to transplanting, and even very large tree rhododendrons can be successfully relocated to new homes. Although groups of these large rhododendrons take up more space than many modern gardens can give, a single specimen can lift the mixed border a cut above the ordinary.

THE CLOSE-UP VIEW

After building the frame of the mixed border and planting the backbone of trees, the next step in orchestrating the border is to fill in the shrub layer. The border requires an intermediate step to lead the eye from the 20-foot (6.1-meter) or taller trees to the lower growing, softer layer of perennials, annuals, and bulbs. This intermediate step relates the trees to the smaller plants—a step that occurs naturally in the wild. Here in this shrub layer is where rhododendrons shine. This intermediate level allows rhododendrons in their incredible variety of plant form, foliage texture, and color to perform in roles made for them, masterfully playing their parts to perfection for the success of the whole show (Plate 28).

The remarkable variety in the genus *Rhododendron* begins with plant forms that repeat and contrast among themselves and their companions to achieve plant harmony. Among upright-growing shrubs are three species of subsection *Triflora, R. augustinii, R. yunnanense,* and *R. lutescens.* Many deciduous azaleas have an upright-growing form, including the West Coast native *R. occidentale* and many of its hybrids. The charming deciduous azalea from Japan *R. albrechtii* is an upright-growing shrub with deep pink blooms adorning the dark branches before or during leafing out. Another upright-growing native from Japan and an early bloomer is *R. mucronulatum,* also deciduous and bearing its pink blooms on bare branches. A star among the uprights is another deciduous azalea from the Far East, *R. schlippenbachii,* which bears star-like white to pink flowers. The evergreen *R. racemosum* is an upright grower with glossy round leaves and flowers of white or pink; *R. racemosum* 'Rock Rose' is one of its better forms.

In contrast to the upright plants is the spreading form, which lends a horizontal accent to the border, such as the evergreen or semi-evergreen azalea *Rhododendron kiusianum.* The many ground-hugging alpine rhododendrons also assume a spreading form as they grow. *Rhododendron nakaharae,* for instance, grows by creeping close to the ground.

The mounding plant form is among the most useful and striking of rhododendron plant forms. *Rhododendron yakushimanum* and many of its hybrids are among the favorites, forming tidy mounds of foliage. *Rhododendron keiskei* 'Yaku Fairy' grows in a compact mound about 1 foot high (0.3 meters). *Rhododendron* 'Unique' is an old hybrid from before 1934 that grows in a tight mound to 4 feet (1.2 meters). Two species from Taiwan, *R. pseudochrysanthum* and *R. pachysanthum,* form beautiful compact mounds of foliage and are becoming popular among gardeners. Other distinctly mound-shaped rhododendrons include *R. campanulatum, R. williamsianum,* and *R. orbiculare.* A rare species, *R. proteoides,* is also now available for those willing to seek it out. It forms a low mound about 1 foot high (0.3 meters).

Rhododendrons offer a range of leaf sizes, as well, varying from the minuscule ½-inch-long (1.3-centimeter) leaf of *Rhododendron calostrotum* subsp. *keleticum* Radicans Group to the giant 18-inch-long (46-centimeter) leaf of *R. praestans*. In-between lies a continuum of sizes for an incredible choice of foliage texture from fine to medium to coarse.

The shape of rhododendron leaves and their great variety of forms and sizes offer endless opportunities for creating harmony in the border. The paddle-shaped leaf form of many large-leafed species and hybrids can lend a lugubrious effect, especially if the leaves hang downward as with *Rhododendron rex* or *R. macabeanum*. The narrow, needle-shaped, upright-growing leaves of *R. roxieanum* var. *oreonastes* tend to perk up a spot in the border, while the small heart-shaped leaves of *R. williamsianum* lend airiness, as do many other small-leafed varieties.

The surface of the leaves also contributes to foliage texture, from the light-reflecting, glossy leaves of *Rhododendron macabeanum*, *R. degronianum*, *R. clementinae*, *R. dauricum*, or *R. anhweiense* to the light-absorbing, matte surface textures of *R. fortunei*. Of subsection *Maddenia*, *R. nuttallii* and *R. edgeworthii* have a puckered texture to their leaves. Others are bristly or hairy. Still others have furry indumentum of white, orange, or brown.

The color of rhododendron leaves also runs a wide gamut from the light green of *Rhododendron auriculatum* to the dark green of the splendid *R. bureavii* with its thick orange indumentum. Some foliage carries a blue cast. The new foliage appearing after flowering, often staccato in effect, adds another dimension in foliage texture and can be as dramatic as a second flowering, for example, the bright red new foliage of *R. nuttallii*.

And do not forget to consider the choices among rhododendron flowers—the crowning glory of the genus. Beginning with their decorative buds and ending with the full-blown blossoms, rhododendrons outshine all else. To be sure, plant form and foliage texture do year-round duty in the mixed border, and in our right minds we place these first when selecting a plant. But the flowers carry great influence and can dazzle us into selecting on their basis alone. The mixed border, more easily than the woodland or rock garden, can utilize the showy flowers

118

of many hybrids through harmony with non-rhododendron companions. But if a plant is selected on flower alone, place it in the border where its form and foliage texture are not essential. Do not force it into a part it is unable to play.

The orchestration of flower color in the mixed border is limitless. To start simply with the repetition of one color from one rhododendron cultivar, plant the compact, yellow-flowering *Rhododendron* 'Princess Anne' in a group of three in one or more spots. Its uniformly yellow flowers will make a strong, lively statement in spring, and in the fall, its bronze foliage will harmonize nicely with other fall colors. A color scheme where rhododendron flower hues are adjacent on the color spectrum, or analogous, would be to combine the red-violet *Rhododendron* 'Purple Lace', violet 'Blue Boy', and blue-violet 'Purple Splendour'. All three flower colors are in dark shades, all have dome-shaped trusses, and all grow to approximately 5 feet in height (1.5 meters). The contrasting, primary hues of yellow and blue could be expressed in rhododendrons by *R. augustinii* 'Barto Blue'— one of the closest to a true blue in the genus—and its close relative *R. lutescens*. Both species bear flowers of the same wide funnel shape and with the same prominent stamens. Subtle color harmonies could begin with a bicolor, such as the yellow and orange *Rhododendron* 'Ring of Fire', adding other rhododendrons or companions with yellow or orange flowers. Complex harmonies such as this are particularly suited to the mixed border.

Companions

In this book the word *companion* refers to non-rhododendrons, but the term falls short in defining accurately the role these plants play in the mixed border. The mixed border is the most democratic of regimes, and in theory the role of each plant is equal to every other, with something of interest always happening somewhere, even in winter. Rhododendrons are as much companions to other plants as other plants are to them. The companions described below and included in the tables are plants that grow happily near rhododendrons because of shared

119

cultural needs. A large mixed border can include groups of plants with different needs.

Trees form the backbone of the mixed border, and numerous splendid species make good companions for rhododendrons. The deciduous, delicately leafed Japanese maple in its many forms, such as *Acer palmatum* 'Atropurpureum' and 'Dissectum', offer lightness and airiness in contrast to the substantial quality of many rhododendrons. The eastern dogwood (*Cornus florida*), the Pacific dogwood (*Cornus nuttallii*), and the dogwood native to Japan and Korea (*Cornus kousa*), all deciduous, have many attributes complementary to rhododendrons: delicate, horizontal limb structure especially attractive in winter, white flowers showing before leaves, and fall foliage color. With a spring show of their own, the flowers of many species and hybrids of *Magnolia* are precursors to the height of the rhododendron bloom season. The gray, winter silhouettes of the deciduous magnolias contrast nicely with evergreen shrubs and trees in the border. A more companionable small tree than the deciduous Japanese stewartia (*Stewartia pseudocamellia*) would be hard to find. Its all-season performance includes light green leaves in the spring, camellia-like flowers in the summer, colored foliage in the fall, and attractive branch pattern in the winter. The evergreen conifers, of which many dwarf cultivars have been developed, offer plant forms in contrast to the dome shape of many rhododendrons. In the winter, the rhododendrons and conifers will be the main contributors of substance to the border.

Companionable plants that can occupy the same layer as rhododendrons offer a challenging number of choices, beginning with the many members of the Ericaceae. Especially suitable for the mixed border are the many new *Kalmia latifolia* cultivars, which follow the rhododendron bloom season with their intricately patterned flowers, yet all year they and rhododendrons harmonize through their glossy, evergreen foliage. Many cultivars of *Pieris* exhibit changing foliage color and drooping clusters of flower buds in the winter. They also harmonize with rhododendrons in foliage and form throughout the year. The ericaceous genus *Vaccinium* includes the domesticated blueberry (*V. corymbosum*), whose fall red foliage and red stems provide winter color in the border. And the deciduous species of *Enki-anthus* can provide good fall color.

Outside the Ericaceae, companionable plants that can provide evergreen foliage in the shrub layer of the mixed border are the many species of *Ilex, Camellia, Daphne,* and *Mahonia.* Among good deciduous shrub companions are species of *Fuchsia,* where climate allows, *Clethra,* which bloom late in the summer, and *Hydrangea,* which also bloom in the summer. An

Table 10. Companion plants: shrubs

Abies koreana 'Starkers Dwarf' (Korean fir)	dwarf conifer, 2- by 3-foot bun (0.6 by 1 meter)
Abies nordmanniana 'Golden Spreader' (Nordmann fir)	dwarf conifer with gold foliage
Actinidia kolomikta	vine, white- and pink-blotched foliage
Andromeda polifolia (bog rosemary)	ground cover, spreading, leathery leaves, pink flowers
Arbutus unedo (strawberry tree)	red bark, white flowers
Camellia japonica (common camellia)	evergreen glossy foliage
Ceanothus pumilus (Siskiyou-mat)	ground cover, mat forming, white to blue flowers
Cedrus deodara 'Prostrata' (deodar)	dwarf conifer, ground cover, low lying
Chamaecyparis obtusa 'Meroke' (hinoke cypress)	dwarf conifer, narrow upright
Clethra alnifolia (sweet pepperbush)	rounded form, fragrant white flowers
Deutzia gracilis	mounding form, white flowers
Fargesia murielae (bamboo)	non-rhizomatous, pencil-thin culms
Fuchsia 'Magellenica Alba'	hardy to USDA zone 9, pink flowers
Fuchsia 'Ricartonii'	hardy to USDA zone 9, violet flowers
Hydrangea anomala var. *petiolaris*	vine, white flowers, glossy dark green leaves
Hydrangea macrophylla (big leaf hydrangea)	mounding form, pink or blue flowers in late summer
Mahonia aquifolium (Oregon grape)	evergreen, glossy leaves, yellow flowers, blue berries
Paeonia suffruticosa (tree peony)	lush foliage, variety of flower color
Picea pungens 'Glauca Pendula' (Colorado spruce)	blue, weeping
Viburnum opulus (cranberry)	rounded form, white flowers, red berries

astounding variety of dwarf evergreen conifer shrubs have been developed to add year-round variety of form, foliage texture, and color. For a narrow, upright shrub try *Chamaecyparis obtusa* 'Meroke', or for a spreading ground cover try *Abies nordmanniana* 'Golden Spreader'.

Bamboo lends a completely different form and texture to a border for those gardeners willing to seek out the safe kinds that will not take over. The well-mannered, hardy *Sinarundinaria nitida* has culms that mature to purple. Bamboo and rhododendrons are natural partners in the mountains of Asia and can cohabit in the mixed border if refereed.

A shrub that shares the cultural needs of rhododendrons but is infrequently invited to share its company is the tree peony (*Paeonia suffruticosa*) and its cultivars. A tree peony can grow as

Table 11. Companion plants: herbaceous perennials

Ajuga reptans (carpet bugle)	ground cover, varying leaf colors
Anemone pulsatilla (European pasque flower)	alpine, fern-like leaves, purple flowers
Aquilegia alpina (alpine columbine)	alpine, blue flowers
Arisaema triphyllum (jack-in-the-pulpit)	spathe green, purple, or white
Armeria meritima (common thrift)	mounding, grass-like leaves, white to pink flowers
Astilbe (meadow sweet)	plume-like flower clusters, fine foliage
Bergenia crassifolia (winter-blooming bergenia)	large, dark green leaves, pink to purple flowers
Brunnera	heart-shaped dark green leaves
Campanula poscharskyana (bellflower)	ground cover, long heart-shaped leaves
Cardiocrinum giganteum var. *giganteum*	to 12 feet (3.7 meters), flowers white with red or purple
Cornus canadensis (bunchberry)	ground cover, red berries in fall
Corydalis lutea	clumping, gray-green foliage, yellow flowers
Dicentra spectabilis (bleeding heart)	pink heart-shaped flowers
Digitalis (foxglove)	tall spikes of flowers in variety of colors
Epimedium rubrum	leathery leaves bronze in spring on wiry stems

tall as 6 feet (1.8 meters) and blooms in late spring. These patrician natives of China, Bhutan, and Tibet, are century-old garden inhabitants of Japan.

The most rapidly changing layer of the mixed border will be the herbaceous layer, composed of herbaceous perennials, annuals, biennials, and bulbs (Plate 29). Though the trees and shrubs are visible all seasons—even if reduced to a few twigs in winter—the herbaceous layer virtually disappears under the snow or into the ground, at least in the coldest regions. But once the ground warms in spring, the herbaceous layer makes up for lost time, beginning with the spring-blooming bulbs. Some gardeners cringe at the thought of planting tulips and daffodils next to rhododendrons, thinking of them as unnatural companions because of their vastly different regions of origin. But the mixed border

Fritillaria meleagris (snake's-head)	nodding bell-shaped flowers on tall stems
Helleborus orientalis (Lenten rose)	blooms very early in green, purple, or pink
Heuchera (coral bells)	clumbs of round leaves, flowers on wiry stems
Hosta (plantain lily)	lush foliage in variety of colors
Iris ensata (Japanese iris)	sword-shaped leaves, variety of colors
Lamium (dead nettle)	ground cover, heart-shaped leaves, many variegated
Lysichiton americanum (skunk cabbage)	lush foliage with yellow spathe, moist areas
Meconopsis betonicifolia (Himalayan poppy)	blue flowers
Myosotis (forget-me-not)	ground cover, blue flowers
Polemonium caeruleum (Jacob's ladder)	clusters of purple flowers on tall stems
Primula denticulata (primrose)	clusters of red, purple, or white flowers on 1-foot stems (0.3 meters)
Rheum nobile (alpine rhubarb)	broad leathery leaves
Saxifraga rosacea (saxifrage)	alpine, spreading, white flowers on stalks
Viola odorata (sweet violet)	ground cover, flowers violet to white, fragrant

requires only that its inhabitants work together in their given location, which many bulbs and rhododendrons do strikingly.

Numerous bulbs, corms, rhizomes, and tubers grow well with rhododendrons. Both the Asiatic and Oriental lily hybrids make excellent companions, following the rhododendrons with summer bloom on large, strong plants. For a bold statement in the border, try the giant lily (*Cardiocrinum giganteum* var. *giganteum*). It bears 10-inch (25-centimeter) fragrant blooms on stems up to 15 feet tall (4.6 meters). On the smaller side, the rhizomatous trilliums (*Trillium* spp.) can easily find needed shade in the shadows of neighboring rhododendrons. Many beardless species and hybrids of *Iris* need moist, acid soil and will do well as companions, their foliage offering a vertical, spiky texture contrast.

Many herbaceous perennials are friendly to a rhododendron environment. Classic companions are species of *Primula*, bearing their bright, spring blooms along with the early flowering rhododendrons. The candelabra primulas (*P. japonica, P. burmanica,* and *P. prolifera*), native to the Himalayas and other native rhododendron environments, are particularly striking with their flowers born in whorls on long stems. Another native companion is the Himalayan poppy (*Meconopsis betonicifolia*), 2 to 4 feet tall (0.6 to 1.2 meters) with sky-blue flowers. The many cultivars of the genus *Astilbe*, many from the Southern Hemisphere, are useful for the light, airy quality of both their foliage and summer-blooming, plume-like flowers. On the other hand, the glossy, heavy textured foliage of the genus *Bergenia* offers substance near the ground. The same can be said of the many species and hybrids of *Hosta*, which offer an additional range of foliage color from blue-green to yellow-green. Variegated forms can brighten a dark corner of the border. Another moisture-loving perennial useful for its range of foliage color—even chocolate—is coral bells (*Heuchera* spp.). Ferns offer delightful contrasts in plant form and foliage texture, and for a mat-like effect, mosses are indispensable. The rapid changes in the herbaceous layer, from first shoot, to bud, to flower, to seed, can perform against a backdrop of evergreen rhododendrons that shined earlier in the season and now humbly shift to supporting roles.

Table 12. Companion plants: ferns and mosses

Adiantum pedatum (maidenhair fern)	frond in finger-like pattern
Athyrium goeringianum 'Pictum' (Japanese painted fern)	deciduous, red-violet midrib
Blechnum spicant (deer fern)	fronds narrow and glossy
Mnium hornum (moss)	light green in spring, darker in summer
Osmunda ragalis (royal fern)	large, coarse
Polystichum munitum (sword fern)	leathery dark green fronds
Polytrichum commune (moss)	moss used in Japanese gardens
Polytrichum piliferum (moss)	sun-tolerant moss

PLANT COMBINATIONS

An early spring plant combination begins with the silver leaf buds that dot the bare branches of *Stewartia pseudocamellia*. The white of the buds is repeated in the remnants of white indumentum left on the leaves of *Rhododendron yakushimanum* after the winter rains. The white is repeated again in the newly opened white, bell-like flowers of *Erica carnea* 'Springwood White'. The white-on-green color combination is the essence of early spring.

In May the luscious pastel pink of *Rhododendron* 'Scintillation' is echoed at its feet in the pale pink of the May-blooming *Eremurus* 'Oase'. Its lily-like leaves harmonize with the new leaves of several clumps of the emerging *Lilium* 'Black Beauty', an Oriental lily whose eventual height will equal the 5-foot (1.5-meter) 'Scintillation'.

The fine textured, arcing foliage of *Acer palmatum* 'Dissectum' perfectly imitates the narrow, arcing leaves of *Rhododendron macrosepalum* 'Linearifolium', whose pink flowers carry the same graceful shape.

After blooming, *Rhododendron* 'President Roosevelt' (unregistered name) displays its most useful feature—variegated foliage, yellow-green along the midrib. This hue together with the bright yellow-green leaves of *Hosta* 'Solar Flare' brighten a shadowed corner. *Adiantum pedatum* with bright green fronds also adds light to a dark corner.

125

Garden Tours

The Jane Kerr Platt Garden in Portland, Oregon, layers trees, shrubs, and herbaceous plants throughout the garden, but in one particular area rhododendrons are integrated into an extraordinary mixed border with a high holly (*Ilex* sp.) hedge at its back and a rock garden on the slope at its feet. The April day of my visit to the garden brought forth the picture of a *Magnolia stellata* 'Jane Platt', the "mother tree" of the form, under-planted with two mounding *Rhododendron yakushimanum*, fronted by smaller, pink mounds of *Rhododendron* 'Ginny Gee'. The ground between was covered with the white, nodding flowers of *Erythronium* and the pink flowers of *Anemone*. To the right came a Japanese stewartia (*Stewartia pseudocamellia*) with new green leaves behind the bright pink flowers and bare branches of *R. reticulatum*. Further to the right was *R. schlippenbachii* with pale pink flowers. Next came a rich texture of trees, shrubs, and ground covers in varying shades of green, including a tree peony (*Paeonia suffruticosa*), wild ginger (*Asarum* spp.), juniper (*Juniperus* spp.), and Solomon's seal (*Polygonatum* spp.). Brightening the picture were the blooms of a dark pink rhododendron of unknown origin showing from behind bare branches. Again to the right, the blue-violet flowers of *R. augustinii* with its new, light green foliage were displayed against the dark green holly hedge. And finally, at the end of the border, white cherry blossoms of the genus *Prunus* drooped over a splendid specimen of *R. schlippenbachii* in bloom against its own new spring-green foliage and the new bronze foliage of a Japanese maple (*Acer palmatum*), at the foot of which was a dark green, prostrate coast redwood (*Sequoia* sp.). The many ingredients of this border were so composed as to look completely natural. I particularly noticed the ease with which several deciduous Japanese rhododendrons, namely *R. schlippenbachii*, *R. reticulatum*, and *R. quinquefolium*, blended naturally with other genera.

The Edward B. Dunn Garden in Seattle was a private garden designed in 1915 by the Olmsted firm and purchased by the city after the death of Dunn. The layering of trees, shrubs, and herbaceous plants is a technique used throughout the garden, but it is perfected in a formal mixed border edging a large expanse of lawn (Plate 30). The woodland of large trees forms a less distinct frame than the holly hedge in the Platt garden, but it gives a similar richness and complexity of texture. Extensive use of rhododendrons gives the border substance. The lower branches of large, mature rhododendrons have been limbed up in order to treat the plants as small trees. In one spot near the front of the border, several trunks bare of limbs show attractive, peeling bark and reveal other plants behind them.

Rhododendron schlippenbachii again proves amenable to cohabiting with other plants, especially the native conifers Douglas fir (*Pseudotsuga menziesii*) and western hemlock (*Tsuga heterophylla*) in the background. An unnamed, pale pink *R. williamsianum* cross by Dunn sits under a saucer magnolia (*Magnolia* ×*soulangiana*). In mid-April the side-by-side placement of these two voluptuous bloomers is breathtaking. Ground covers fill the lowest level of the mixed border, many blooming in early spring as the herbaceous perennials push up their first shoots. Pink erythronium (*Erythronium* spp.), blue forget-me-nots (*Myosotis* spp.), blue violets (*Viola* spp.), and bluebells (*Endymion* spp.) spread a carpet of delicate spring colors throughout the border.

The Edwards Garden and Rhododendron Woods, a public garden in metropolitan Toronto, displays a horseshoe-shaped mixed border backed by a steep, wooded slope. Two particularly striking combinations are a white beardless iris (*Iris* sp.) with the white, deciduous Knap Hill azalea hybrid *Rhododendron* 'Toucan' and bluebells (*Endymion* spp.) at the feet of the red Knap Hill azalea *Rhododendron* 'Satan' (Plate 31).

Suggested Reading

Dirr, Michael A. 1997. *Dirr's Hardy Trees and Shrubs*. Portland, Oregon: Timber Press.

Garden Club of America. 1996. *Plants That Merit Attention: Volume II—Shrubs*, Eds. Janet Meakin Poor and Nancy Peterson Brewster. Portland, Oregon: Timber Press.

Greer, Harold E. 1996. *Greer's Guidebook to Available Rhododen-drons.* Eugene, Oregon: Offshoot Publications.
Lovejoy, Ann. 1990. *Border in Bloom.* Seattle: Sasquatch Books.
Lovejoy, Ann. 1993. *American Mixed Border.* New York: Macmillan.

In the courtyard at the Jane Kerr Platt Garden in Portland, Oregon, *Cedrus atlantica* 'Glauca Pendula' frames *Rhododendron schlippenbachii*.

Plate 1. In the Dragon Pool area of Yunnan Province, China, at 11,078 feet (3300 meters), *Rhododendron tapetiforme* carpets the alpine meadow. Photo by Arthur Dome.

Plate 2. In the Siskiyou Mountains of southwestern Oregon *Rhododendron occidentale* grows in the wild under a canopy of *Pinus*.

Plate 3. Stonefield in Argyll, Scotland, offers a view from its protected site out to Loch Fyne, framed by *Rhododendron falconeri*.

Plate 4. A mature specimen of *Rhododendron thomsonii*, grown from seed collected by Sir Joseph Dalton Hooker in the Himalayas, graces the garden at Stonefield.

Plate 5. At Brodick on the island of Arran on the west coast of Scotland thrives the hybrid *Rhododendron* 'Conroy', dating from 1937.

Plate 6. At the Meerkerk Rhododendron Gardens on Whidbey Island, Washington, plant harmony is achieved in the companion planting of *Sequoia sempervirens* with the hybrid result of *Rhododendron orbiculare* × *Rhododendron* 'Loderi King George'. The yellow-green veins of the rhododendron harmonize with the branch tips of the sequoia.

Plate 7. At the garden of Glen Patterson in West Vancouver, British Columbia, *Rhododendron macrosepalum* 'Linearifolium' harmonizes with *Acer palmatum* 'Dissectum' through their shared lacy foliage.

Plate 8. In March at the Rhododendron Species Botanical Garden in Federal Way, Washington, a companion planting of *Stewartia pseudocamellia*, *Erica carnea* 'Springwood White', and *Rhododendron yakushimanum* is united by white flecks against green foliage.

Plate 9. At the garden of Herb and Betty Spady near Salem, Oregon, *Rhododendron keiskei* 'Yaku Fairy' exhibits a mounding plant form.

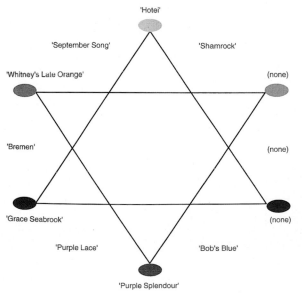

'Hotei'

'September Song'   'Shamrock'

'Whitney's Late Orange'   (none)

'Bremen'   (none)

'Grace Seabrook'   (none)

'Purple Lace'   'Bob's Blue'

'Purple Splendour'

Plate 10. Rhododendron flower hues cover almost the whole spectrum, with wide variation in tints and shades. Illustration by Nicholas Brown.

Plate 11. The hybrid *Rhododendron* 'Lem's Cameo' offers a range of pastels in hues of red and yellow at the garden of Bill and Mary Stipe on Whidbey Island, Washington.

Plate 12. In Cherry Hill, New Jersey, Wing and Pearl Fong have developed their suburban garden in scale with the site, where neither the house nor the garden overpowers the other. Photo by Wing Fong.

Plate 13. On a rural site near Salem, Oregon, Herb and Betty Spady planted an island bed with deciduous azaleas to be viewed from the house. Photo by Herb Spady.

Plate 14. A path at the garden of June Sinclair near Port Ludlow, Washington, creates a narrow, partially enclosed space leading viewers past specimens of *Rhododendron strigillosum, R. wiltonii, R. alutaceum,* and *R. orbiculare* subsp. *cardiobasis*.

Plate 15. The entrance to the garden of J. Powell Huie in Westport Point, Massachusetts, is designed as an open space with a path leading viewers through to a planting of *Rhododendron*, *Hosta*, and *Galium odoratum*. Photo by J. Powell Huie.

Plate 16. At the garden of Frank Fujioka on Whidbey Island, Washington, a room of delicate textures and pastel colors takes shape from *Acer palmatum* 'Beni-tsukasa', *Cercidiphyllum*, and *Rhododendron* 'Primary Pink'.

Plate 17. At the Mendocino Botanical Garden near Fort Bragg, California, the big-leafed *Rhododendron sinogrande* and evergreen azaleas thrive under a canopy of *Pinus muricata* that provides dappled shade.

Plate 18. An open glade viewed from the deck of the garden of Eleanor and Bruce Philp in Fort Bragg, California, offers ample light for rhododendrons and companions at the woodland perimeter.

Plate 19. At Winterthur in Winterthur, Delaware, a massed planting of evergreen azaleas *Rhododendron* 'Snow', 'Arnoldianum', 'Lavender Beauty', and 'Mauve Beauty' creates a carpet of color in the Azalea Woods. *Cornus florida* contributes to the layered effect. Photo by Linda Eirhart.

Plate 20. In May this section in the garden of June Sinclair, near Port Ludlow, Washington, draws the viewer in for a close-up view of the new foliage on *Rhododendron sinogrande*, *R. bureavii*, and *R. pseudochrysanthum*, accentuated by the white tree bark.

Plate 21. Near Orono, Ontario, Dave Hinton uses a rich layer of herbaceous perennials as companions to the hardy *Rhododendron smirnowii*: *Paeonia*, *Hosta*, and *Polygonatum*.

Plate 22. In the rock garden of Frank Fujioka on Whidbey Island, Washington, the dwarf conifers and mounding plant form of the rhododendrons match the scale of the rocks and create unity with the windy, seaside site.

Plate 23. Chip Muller of Seattle has built his urban rock garden on a west-facing slope, first removing the turf and replacing it with soil rich in organic matter and chipped rock. Limestone rock creates an alpine setting.

Plate 24. Arthur Dome of Seattle has built his rock garden on a steep, east-facing site, combining rhododendrons with many ericaceous companions. Photo by Arthur Dome.

Plate 25. At the Jane Kerr Platt Garden in Portland, Oregon, a rock garden is skillfully integrated into the design of the whole garden. The low-growing conifers, ground covers, and rhododendrons are viewed against a mixed border at the rear.

Plate 26. In Bridgewater, New Jersey, Jean and Frank Furman have built a small, sunny rock garden for five dwarf azalea hybrids of *Rhododendron kiusianum*, dwarf conifers *Chamaecyparis obtusa* 'Nana' and *Chamaecyparis pisifera* 'Squarrosa Intermedia', *Iberis, Dianthus, Sempervivum arachnoideum*, and ground covers *Thymus serpyllum, T. serpyllum* 'Minus', and *Antennaria* 'Aprica'. Photo by Jean Furman.

Plate 27. A mixed border at the garden of Wing and Pearl Fong in Cherry Hill, New Jersey, is framed by the house. Small trees, rhododendrons, herbaceous perennials, bulbs, and ground covers create a rich texture. Photo by Wing Fong.

Plate 28. A mixed border at the Mendocino Botanical Garden near Fort Bragg, California, combines *Rhododendron* 'Saffron Queen' and *Pieris forrestii*.

Plate 29. In a mixed border at the Edward B. Dunn Garden in Seattle, rhododendrons are combined with *Pieris*, *Helleborus*, *Meconopsis cambrica*, *Endymion*, and *Chrysanthemum parthenium* for a layered effect.

Plate 30. Rhododendrons, hostas, and ferns create a variety of textures in a shady mixed border at the Edward B. Dunn Garden in Seattle, Washington.

Plate 31. In a mixed border at the Edwards Garden in Toronto, *Iris* and the evergreen azalea *Rhododendron* 'Toucan' connect through their white flowers, yet contrast in foliage texture.

Plate 32. Larry and Alma Allbaugh of Everson, Washington, have designed a bed for their collection of *Rhododendron yakushimanum* hybrids (*Rhododendron* 'Renoir', 'Cupcake', 'King's Ride', 'Mardi Gras', 'Solidarity', 'Amity', 'Canadian Sunset', 'Morgenrot', 'Noyo Brave', 'Wannabee', 'Golfer', 'Cinnamon Bear', 'Laurago', 'Senorita Chere', 'Queen Alice', 'Swen', 'Oliver Twist', 'Centennial Celebration', 'Rosy Dream', 'Bambino', 'Crimson Pippin', and two unnamed crosses), which share a rounded plant habit. As companions, they have selected *Hosta* that also exhibit a rounded form.

Plate 33. Earl Sommerville of Marietta, Georgia, has designed his garden around a collection of native azaleas under a canopy of *Pinus taeda*. Among the focal points is a small waterfall, enhancing the naturalistic setting. Photo by Earl Sommerville.

Plate 34. On a suburban site in Los Angeles, William Moynier has built tidy, brick-edged beds for his collection of vireya rhododendrons, which offer bloom in all seasons. Shown here in bloom are the orange *Rhododendron* 'Cristo Rey' and the pink result of *R. loranthiflorum* × *R. brookeanum*; an evergreen azalea is in the foreground. Photo by William Moynier.

Plate 35. Gordon and Linda Wylie of Eugene, Oregon, have built island beds to set off those rhododendrons in their collection that do not harmonize well with most others. Here, *Rhododendron yakushimanum* hybrids (left) grow under *Tilia cordata* (center). Sharing the mounding form of the hybrids is *Picea abies*. Photo by Gordon Wylie.

Plate 36. Warren Berg of Port Ludlow, Washington, has placed his collection of rhododendrons from subsection *Taliensia* in one bed, joined not only taxonomically but aesthetically through plant form and indumentum on new foliage: *Rhododendron schizopeplum* (left center), *R. roxieanum* (center), *R. pronum* (lower right center), and two plants of *R. proteoides* (bottom).

Plate 37. Bill and Mary Stipe of Whidbey Island, Washington, have enhanced the perimeter of their native woodland with a planting of large-leafed rhododendrons, giving them just the right amount of light to flourish.

Plate 38. Tom Ahern of Bethlehem, Pennsylvania, has enhanced his winter woodland setting with evergreen rhododendrons, which add solidity to a background of deciduous trees. Photo by Tom Ahern.

Plate 39. The West Coast native *Rhododendron macrophyllum* growing wild at a woodland verge near Port Ludlow, Washington, is a good candidate for a native plant garden from Northern California to British Columbia.

Plate 40. At the Edward B. Dunn Garden in Seattle, *Rhododendron occidentale* is encouraged to grow at the verge of a native woodland.

Plate 41. Rex and Jeanine Smith of Woodinville, Washington, encourage native plants to intermingle with their large collection of rhododendrons for a natural, layered effect. The native *Gaultheria shallon* and *Vaccinium parvifolium* add to the shrub layer along with rhododendrons, while the non-native *Galium odoratum* is allowed to cover the ground in a naturalistic way.

Plate 42. In a small space next to St. John's Catholic Church in south San Francisco, Peter Sullivan has built a vireya garden where the hybrid *Rhododendron* 'Lawrence' frames a sculpture. Photo by William Moynier.

Plate 43. In the small courtyard of the Rhododendron Species Botanical Garden in Federal Way, Washington, a potted specimen of *Rhododendron kaempferi* exhibits its simple elegance against a concrete wall.

Plate 44. On a deck overlooking their garden, Rex and Jeanine Smith have created an intimate space through the use of bonsai and other potted plants, backing them with rhododendrons.

Plate 45. At the Baker-McGarva rooftop garden in Vancouver, British Columbia, Susan Baker has used rhododendrons extensively to create a refuge from the city. Photo by Susan Baker.

Plate 46. In the small, urban garden of Chris and Julia Cutler of Seattle, rhododendrons play a supporting role, adding substance and brief spring color to a shady section. Photo by Nicholas Brown.

Plate 47. George Ring of Bent Mountain, Virginia, has designed a foundation planting with an eastern exposure using the deciduous azalea *Rhododendron calendulaceum* and an August Kehr hybrid (*R. maximum* × *R. yakushimanum*). The scale of the planting is appropriate for the house, and the gray color of the house serves as a good background for the plants. Photo by George Ring.

Plate 48. Jim and Suzanne Ramsey of Whidbey Island, Washington, have used *Rhododendron pachysanthum* to fill a niche near an entryway to their house, adding a sign to welcome visitors.

Plate 49. Rose Turner of Fort Bragg, California, espaliered *Rhododendron johnstonianum* against a small lattice and placed it on her patio to enjoy its fragrance.

Plate 50. At the entryway of the Strybing Arboretum in San Francisco, the large-leafed *Rhododendron sinogrande* makes a strong statement in a lushly planted corner. Photo by Kay Anderson.

Plate 51. At Filoli in Woodside, California, the evergreen azalea *Rhododendron* 'Ward's Ruby' is contained by a formal box hedge and framed by *Wisteria*. Photo by Kay Anderson.

CHAPTER 7

The Collector's Garden

T HE INFINITE interest of rhododendrons has turned many
gardeners into avid collectors. Seduced by the lush beauty
of rhododendron flowers and beguiled by the character of their
form and foliage, gardeners begin the accumulation of plants
to satisfy their horticultural appetites. In their pursuit, many find
themselves drawn down new avenues of interest. The collection
of related plants easily leads to a curiosity about rhododendron
taxonomy, or about the history of plant hunting, hybridizing, or
exploring. Beyond sensory delights, gardeners find intellectual
stimulus in this vast genus. They might, indeed, become lost in
the plants, but happily only to find others of similar persuasion.
Once enthusiasts begin a large rhododendron collection, they
encounter a new challenge: how to build a well-designed garden
using their many beloved plants. Rhododendron collections fall
roughly into four groups, determined by the collector's focus
on species, hybrids, geography, or aesthetic appeal. In reality,
however, collections often cross the lines between categories.

Species Collections

Collections of Asian *Rhododendron* species made up those first
great rhododendron gardens of Britain. Seed from the wilds of
the Himalayas and western China flourished in the high rainfall
and protected ravines and shelterbelts on Scotland's moist,

benign west coast. Still growing at Stonefield are mature specimens of Himalayan species that were collected by Sir Joseph Dalton Hooker in the 1850s: *Rhododendron arboreum, R. campanulatum, R. thomsonii, R. cinnabarinum, R. falconeri, R. grande, R. campylocarpum,* and *R. triflorum.* The largest *R. arboreum* is a majestic 42 feet high (12.8 meters). Even at Stonefield, one of the oldest rhododendron gardens, the rhododendrons grow in the good company of a variety of genera of conifer and broadleaf trees—*Pinus, Abies, Larix, Picea, Cupressus, Fagus, Magnolia,* and *Eucalyptus.* And from the start, companion shrubs have both protected and enhanced rhododendron collections. Stonefield shelters rhododendrons from the salt spray with *Griselinia littoralis, Olearia macrodonta,* and *Escallonia macrantha.* Also occupying the shrub layer are *Fuchsia excorticata, Eucryphia glutinosa, Mahonia napaulensis,* and *Cotoneaster frigida.*

The Royal Botanic Garden Edinburgh houses the greatest accumulation of living *Rhododendron* specimens, many of which were collected by plant hunters sent out under its auspices, such as George Forrest. The garden has a complete collection of subsections *Lapponica* and *Saluenensia.* Each subsection is grouped together so that the viewer can compare species within a particular subsection. The meticulously groomed, 3-acre (1.2-hectare) rock garden built of conglomerate boulders and sandstone exhibits alpine *Rhododendron* species, along with small trees, shrubs, and perennials. Viewers can follow paths between the stones and hillocks or walk its edges on well-groomed turf. A woodland garden incorporates the large-leafed rhododendrons with shade-loving perennials, such as plants of *Primula, Lilium,* and *Meconopsis,* growing at their feet. At the edge of the woodland a peat garden built in a series of terraces offers the optimum conditions of coolness and moisture-retentive, acidic soil. An east-facing slope exhibits the azalea collection, a mass of color in May and June and a show of colorful foliage in the fall. Although the scale of this public garden is much grander than private collections, individual collectors can learn much from its organization and features, for it does not look like a monoculture but is integrated into numerous garden habitats.

The Rhododendron Species Botanical Garden in Federal

Way, Washington, is of particular interest for its prime focus on species rhododendrons. A walk through the garden is a walk through the genus. The garden is grouped by subsection, enabling viewers to see the taxonomic connection of one group to another. But the garden is more than a library of plants. Under a native canopy of Douglas fir (*Pseudotsuga menziesii*), western hemlock (*Tsuga heterophylla*), and western red cedar (*Thuja plicata*), limbed high to let in light, the collection is enhanced with companion trees, shrubs, and perennials. A rock garden displays alpine rhododendron species and companions, and a fern collection is being established. In spite of its academic nature, the garden is designed in a naturalistic style of curving beds and paths to show the landscape value of its inhabitants.

Besides being of vital concern to the public arboretums, the taxonomic classification of rhododendrons is of great interest to individual species collectors and adds an intellectual dimension to their gardening. Public arboretums and private collectors alike use the Sleumer/Edinburgh Revision system of classification. With its hierarchy of subgenus, section, and subsection, it provides a tool for some understanding of the phylogeny of this sixty-million-year-old genus.

The current theory of rhododendron evolution is that in the early history of the genus, during the Tertiary period, the then fewer species were more evenly distributed over the Earth because of its more equable climate. With the gradual cooling of the Earth and the onset of glaciation, rhododendrons were restricted to isolated habitats, such as the newly uplifted Tibet-Himalaya region which, with its isolated valleys, fostered the proliferation of species (Irving and Hebda 1993). Current scientific studies of *Rhododendron* DNA are further unraveling the mysteries of the evolutionary development of the genus and its species. In the Western North American Species Project, members of the American Rhododendron Society and the Rhododendron Species Foundation cooperate with scientists at the University of Washington on a project to decipher the phylogeny of *R. macrophyllum*. Such communication and cooperation between the scientific and lay communities can only enhance the private collector's overall gardening experience.

A garden with a species collection can exhibit the distinctive qualities species tend to share with other members within a section or subsection. Members of subsection *Triflora*, which includes *Rhododendron augustinii, R. concinnum, R. keiskei, R. lutescens, R. davidsonianum, R. yunnanense,* and *R. oreotrephes,* bloom with open funnel-shaped corollas in tints of pink, yellow, lavender, and white, all of which have long, upsweeping stamens that give the flowers an ethereal look. Subsection *Taliensia,* which includes *R. bureavii, R. phaeochrysum, R. roxieanum, R. wightii,* and *R. wiltonii,* exhibits a thick, woolly indumentum on the undersides of the leaves. Subsection *Saluenensia* includes only two species, *R. calostrotum* and *R. saluenense.* But *R. calostrotum* has four subspecies, and *R. saluenense* has two; all can be exhibited in a rock garden. These alpine shrubs are distinguished by their open funnel-shaped corollas in colors ranging from red to purple and by the scaly undersides of their leaves. An extremely interesting group of the deciduous azaleas of subgenus *Pentanthera* is section *Sciadorhodion,* which includes *R. schlippenbachii, R. quinquefolium, R. albrechtii,* and *R. pentaphyllum.* Although the distinguishing feature of this section, its non-winged seeds, is not of landscape value, its ten stamens give the flowers an airy quality. The plants of section *Sciadorhodion* share the landscape values of uniquely graceful foliage and flower and striking autumn color.

Grouping rhododendrons based on their taxonomic relationships can be a good idea from a design point of view. The taxonomic ties that bind them together often arise from shared aesthetic characteristics that create unity in a planting. Their differing qualities will create interest along with the harmony of companions.

Hybrid Collections

Occasionally gardeners will become fascinated with the crosses made by a particular hybridizer. Certainly this is true in the rhododendron world, where both public arboretums and private individuals have made collections of certain hybridizers' results. The Arnold Arboretum in Jamaica Plain, Massachusetts, houses

In a rhododendron collector's garden, taxonomically connected species often share similar aesthetic characteristics in form and foliage and can be pleasingly grouped.

a collection of crosses made by Charles O. Dexter of Sandwich, Massachusetts, who used the large-flowered *Rhododendron fortunei* to create many of his hybrids. Among his results are the supremely popular *Rhododendron* 'Scintillation', 'Parker's Pink', and 'Dexter's Champagne'. The collection was planted in the 1950s on Hemlock Hill under a canopy of Canada hemlock (*Tsuga canadensis*). The D. G. Leach Research Station of the Holden Arboretum in Madison, Ohio, houses a collection of David Leach hybrids, among them *Rhododendron* 'Casanova', 'Rio', and 'Burma'. Although this is a working collection that places priority on plant comparisons for breeding purposes, the hemlock (*Tsuga* spp.) canopy creates a sylvan environment. The Washington Park Arboretum in Seattle is developing a collection of crosses by Puget Sound hybridizers, including those by the influential Halfdan Lem, who created *Rhododendron* 'Anna' and 'Lem's Cameo', both used frequently by hybridizers today. The collection is planted on a hillside among magnolias (*Magnolia* spp.) under a native conifer canopy.

The hybrids of Weldon Delp of Harrisville, Pennsylvania, are collected by several East Coast gardeners. Paul James of Franklin County, Virginia, houses a collection of 385 Delp hybrids. They are planted on steep slopes under a light canopy of evergreen and deciduous trees, particularly dogwoods (*Cornus* spp.), and viewers see them from paths that gently lead among the dense plantings. Larry and Alma Allbaugh of Everson, Washington, have collected offspring of *Rhododendron yakushimanum* and planted them together in one slightly sloping bed, backed by their collection of hostas (*Hosta* spp.). Rock steps and mossy rocks around a small pool add texture to the well-framed scene. The rhododendron cultivars are alike in their compact, mounded form. Flower color ranges from pastel pink to dark shades of red. Leaf size and shape vary, but leaf color is uniformly a dark shade of green (Plate 32).

Hybridizers often build collections of their own hybrids and parent plants. These gardens by necessity include beds with rows of seedlings from various crosses, waiting for evaluation from the critical eye of the hybridizer. These beds, however, are always of great interest as a landscape feature in themselves and a part of the garden as a whole.

Frank Fujioka of Whidbey Island, Washington, has created some of the most exciting hybrids to come out of the Pacific Northwest, such as the dark red and white bicolor *Rhododendron* 'Midnight Mystique' and the cream-colored 'Starbright Champagne', with lily-shaped flowers. His garden, on a varied site overlooking Puget Sound, combines his own mature hybrids, parents of his crosses, and a fine collection of Japanese maples (*Acer palmatum*). In the windswept front yard facing the sound, a rock garden displays dwarf rhododendrons, dwarf conifers, hardy geraniums (*Geranium* spp.), and other herbaceous alpines. On the protected slope behind the house, larger rhododendrons, Japanese maples, and conifers are skillfully harmonized; for instance, the early pink leaves of *Acer palmatum* 'Beni tsukasa' nearly repeat the pink of the flowers of *Rhododendron* 'Primary

Pink'. In dramatic contrast to the soft textures of the maples and the sea of pastel rhododendron flowers are several weeping larches (*Larix* spp.). Staked up like standards, their narrow, dark green domes rise above the rhododendrons. On the flat below the slope, Fujioka's many seedlings are planted in rows waiting for evaluation. This collector has managed to make his working garden into a pleasing visual expression.

Geographic Collections

Collectors may focus on a group of rhododendrons native to a particular geographic area. Many gardeners in the southeastern United States collect the native azaleas of the region. One such collector is Earl Sommerville of Marietta, Georgia, who has access to some thirteen native species in his home state and has been collecting them for more than thirty years (Plate 33). His 2-acre (0.8-hectare) garden lies at the base of Kennesaw Mountain, which protects it from severe weather. Of his 3000 plants, Sommerville displays his collection of about 300 native azaleas in an informal woodland setting under a canopy of loblolly pine (*Pinus taeda*). Although recently many diseased pines have been removed, the woodland receives sun from approximately ten in the morning to three in the afternoon.

His collection includes *Rhododendron alabamense, R. austrinum, R. prunifolium, R. periclymenoides, R. calendulaceum, R. cumberlandense, R. flammeum,* and *R. arborescens* and their natural and man-made hybrids. These native deciduous azaleas are interplanted with evergreen rhododendrons and azaleas for their sustaining green foliage through the winter and with camellias (*Camellia* spp.) for flower color in February and March. Japanese maples (*Acer palmatum*) add a further dimension in texture. Peak bloom for the native azaleas comes in mid-April, when these beauties exhibit their fresh, green foliage and the delicacy of their scented flowers. The blooms have long, up-sweeping stamens and stunning color combinations, sometimes within the same flower—white with dark violet, pale pink with yellow, pink with orange, orange with red-orange. To create an informal setting for the collection, Sommerville has built through the garden an 8-foot-wide path (2.5 meters) that curves to reveal slowly what is beyond its bends. A waterfall and a water fountain are prominent focal points year-round. Near the house some of the few formal touches are a bed of evergreen azaleas edged with bricks, a bed of Louisiana irises, and well-groomed turf.

The Callaway Gardens in Pine Mountain, Georgia, include collections of exotic azaleas and rhododendrons, but of prime focus are the azalea natives of the Southeast. Under a canopy of loblolly pine (*Pinus taeda*), the natives and a rich collection of companions thrive in the open shade. This woodland masterpiece is accessible to viewers by wide paths throughout. Of particular importance because of its rarity is the collection of the plumleaf azalea, the Georgia native *Rhododendron prunifolium* with its scented, orange-red flowers that bloom late in the season.

William Moynier of Los Angeles grows a collection of vireyas. These subtropical rhododendron species of section *Vireya*, and their hybrids, are native primarily to Indonesia and Malaysia (Plate 34). Moynier chose this group of rhododendrons because of his warm, dry Southern California climate. His region is generally inhospitable to the Asian native species that need cool, moist growing areas. Vireyas, however, eschew temperatures below freezing and like to dry out briefly between waterings. Although many vireyas are blessed with very attractive foliage, their crowning glory is their bloom—flowers in brilliant, hot hues, pristine whites, and delicate pastels, some rapturously fragrant. The small suburban plot lends itself to the somewhat formal nature of the beds, which are curved, raised, and edged with bricks that match other brickwork on the site. The beds are chock-full of vireyas accompanied by a few low-growing companions, and well-groomed turf contrasts with the lush beds. Since the vireyas bloom in every month of the year and their evergreen foliage is attractive in all seasons, the plantings offer continual interest.

In colder climates, vireya collections can be displayed in pots on a terrace or deck and brought into a cool greenhouse or a suitable indoor location during freezing weather. Using containers for display is especially suited to small gardens.

Table 13. Vireya rhododendron hybrids

	USDA hardiness zone	Plant size in ten years	Plant form	Foliage texture	Flower color
'Aravir'	10	small shrub	compact	glossy	w, fragrant
'Athanasius'	10	small shrub	compact	dark green	o
'Avalon'	10	small shrub	compact	dark green	y, fragrant
'Calavar'	10	small shrub	spreading	dark green	p, fragrant
'Cristo Rey'	10	small shrub	compact	dark green	o/y bicolor
'Jock's Cairn'	10	small shrub	compact	dark green, glossy	y/p bicolor
'Lawrence'	10	medium shrub	spreading	dense with pinching	r
'Ne Plus Ultra'	10	small shrub	spreading	glossy	r
'Pleasant Companion'	10	dwarf shrub	compact	dense	p, fragrant
'Taylori'	10	small shrub	compact	glossy	p

Abbreviations: ind = indumentum, gc = ground cover, p = pink, r = red, w = white, v = violet, o = orange, y = yellow.
See List of Tables for sizes.

Aesthetic Collections

Rhododendron collections can be built around the personal, aesthetic tastes of the collector. Indeed, for most gardeners who grow rhododendrons, aesthetics is the basis of their choice of one rhododendron over another. A particular characteristic of rhododendrons may be attractive, such as yellow flowers, leaf indumentum, or peeling bark, and before realizing it, you have a collection of plants all with this characteristic. The shared characteristic holds the collection together visually in a unified whole.

Rhododendrons might also be part of a collection of plants of different genera that share one or more aesthetic characteristics. A white garden might include *Rhododendron* 'Travis L.', 'Dora Amateis', *R. decorum, R. lindleyi,* or the azalea *Rhododendron* 'Delaware Valley White', all with white flowers. A collection of variegated plants might include the hybrid *Rhododendron* 'President Roosevelt' which is gold along the leaf midrib. A fragrant garden could include *R. decorum, R. occidentale, R. fortunei,* or the hybrid *Rhododendron* 'Fragrantissimum'. A collection of plants with attractive bark could include the species *R. barbatum, R. hodgsonii,* or *R. thomsonii.* The possibilities are endless. This genus of nearly a thousand species and thousands of registered cultivars is so varied in form, texture, and color that a rhododendron will be found to enhance any collection.

Another type of aesthetic collection is one that serves a particular landscape feature, such as a woodland garden or a formal terrace. The landscape feature is top priority, and plants are selected on their contribution to the feature. *Rhododendron calophytum* with its large leaves, might be chosen solely to enhance a dappled clearing in a woodland. And the vireya *Rhododendron* 'Sunny' might be grown in a pot to enhance a terrace. Many landscape architects and garden designers use this approach, starting with the site, adding landscape features next, and installing plants last. The collection of plants is, in this case, a by-product of the site. Faced with the challenge of building a garden *after* the plants are chosen, rhododendron collectors are fortunate compared to many others, for rhododendrons, because of their variety, can be used in many landscape features.

Garden Tours

Gordon and Linda Wylie of Eugene, Oregon, began their garden with the characteristic enthusiasm of true plant collectors. In 1978 they moved into their house on a level, nearly tree-less site. Consequently, they lacked the environment for a classic, informal woodland rhododendron garden. The Wylies first planted sun-tolerant rhododendrons, filling island beds with five plants of the reliable *Rhododendron* 'Unique' and three of the equally reliable 'The Hon. Jean Marie de Montague'. Success with this small collection engendered more enthusiasm. Soon the Wylies' focus turned to choosing rhododendrons whose bloom periods spanned as many months as possible. The same characteristic governed their choice of companion plants, many of which were trees (Plate 35).

The collection expanded with acquisitions of individual specimens from across the spectrum of subgenera: *Rhododendron* (lepidotes), *Hymenanthes* (elepidotes), *Pentanthera* (deciduous azaleas), and *Tsutsutsi* (evergreen azaleas). The Wylies found that plantings of a single subgenus harmonized through form, foliage texture, or flower characteristics shared by the species. They also found that *R. yakushimanum* and its hybrids do not blend well with other rhododendrons and look best singly or in a group of their own.

Both hybrid and species elepidotes comprise the largest portion of the Wylie collection and present the greatest variation in form, texture, and flower color, hence the greatest landscaping challenge. The species are sometimes grouped according to subsection for their taxonomic interest. More often, however, the plants are grouped according to shared characteristics. For instance, in one bed a large *Rhododendron calophytum* is surrounded by species *R. bureavii*, *R. macabeanum*, and *R. fortunei*. The group is unified by large leaves and large plant size.

Both hue and bloom time have been considered to avoid clashing flower colors. One particular planting displays the yellows of *Rhododendron* 'Crest' and 'Cream Pie' (unregistered name), the orange of 'September Song' (unregistered name), and the violet of 'Midnight'. Other plantings express red with

139

yellow hues or multiple tints of pink. The whites tone down bright colors, as expressed in the flowers of *Rhododendron* 'Dora Amateis', 'Gomer Waterer', 'Pawhuska' (unregistered name), and the Loderi grex. Newer hybrids with distinctly different colors in the same flower, such as *Rhododendron* 'Paprika Spiced', 'Ring of Fire', and 'Naselle', are scattered throughout the garden to avoid overwhelming the other flowers.

After experimenting with dwarf elepidotes, the Wylies decided to consolidate a number of them in a small rock garden behind a rock retaining wall, allowing viewers to better observe the unique foliage—and hoped-for flowers—at waist level. The rock garden houses *Rhododendron proteoides, R. pronum*, and several of their hybrids. Because of its unique, puckered foliage, the lepidote *R. edgeworthii* also occupies the rock garden until it outgrows its dwarf stature. Companions in the planting include the native vine maple (*Acer circinatum*), yew (*Taxus* spp.), cammellia (*Camellia sasanqua*), and a mass planting of dwarf narcissus (*Narcissus* spp.).

Companion trees, shrubs, and perennials provide the year-round bloom and textural interest that is possible in the Pacific Northwest. They also prevent the boredom a rhododendron monoculture can create. Companions comprise about one-third of the total number of the Wylies' plants and about 20 percent of the plant volume. Perennial beds offer color after the rhododendrons bloom, and bulbs add to the March and April show. The trees are evenly divided between evergreen and deciduous. The deciduous trees open up the garden in winter and provide structure with their bare limbs. The evergreens sustain a feeling of life and provide background. Among the deciduous trees with colorful, exfoliating bark are paperbark maple (*Acer griseum*), birches (*Betula* spp.) and species of *Stewartia*. For a dogwood, *Cornus kousa* is chosen over *C. florida* or *C. nuttallii* because it is less prone to disease. Deciduous magnolias (*Magnolia* spp.) are chosen over the evergreen type to contrast with the evergreen bulk of the rhododendrons in the winter. The Wylies have found that the challenge for the rhododendron collector is to avoid the look of "just a bunch of green plants when they are out of flower." For this reason they use few camellias (*Camellia* spp.).

Dwarf conifers are planted with the smaller rhododendrons, mostly in raised beds, and pendulous and weeping trees are chosen where their upright counterparts would be too large.

James Powell Huie is another collector of species and hybrid rhododendrons. In Westport Point, Massachusetts, he has built his garden on a sloping, 3-acre (1.2-hectare) site in a mixed woodland of cherry (*Prunus* spp.), juniper (*Juniperus* spp.), oak (*Quercus* spp.), and holly (*Ilex* spp.). He finds the native hollies make particularly good windbreaks. Temperatures routinely drop to 0°F (−18°C) in winter, although his site contains warmer microclimates. He suggests selecting plants that are cold hardy to five degrees colder than the average minimum temperature. His collection includes fifty Dexter hybrids.

The area near Huie's house was designed by a landscape architect in a formal style without large trees or shrubs, but away from the house in the woodland he has built an informal garden for his rhododendron collection. He cleared underbrush and constructed paths that wind naturally like streams among the trees and shrubs. Several paths are wide enough to accommodate a garden tractor, and he has avoided narrow paths between tall rhododendrons. Islands and bays open up viewing areas.

His groups and masses of rhododendrons were planted on the basis of simultaneous bloom time. For Huie, the dead flowers of early bloomers detract from those currently in bloom. Since no rhododendron flower colors clash to his eye, he can ignore differences in color in order to coordinate bloom times. And because of the variety of form and texture within the genus, he finds companion plants other than the canopy of trees unnecessary for creating interest.

Warren Berg of Port Ludlow, Washington, has a collection of Asian species, many of which are grown from seed he himself collected from the wild. Under a native conifer canopy on a protected site that dips down to the waters of Puget Sound, Berg has built a woodland garden around his rhododendron collection. Paths lead among the plantings which are loosely organized according to sections and subsections. Of particular interest to him is subsection *Taliensia*, but he has many prized specimens of

141

little-grown species and his own well-known hybrids. A highlight for any visiting rhododendron aficionado is a breathtaking planting of *Rhododendron roxieanum, R. schizopeplum* (also known as *R. aganniphum* var. *flavorufum*), *R. pronum,* and *R. proteoides,* all having a woolly indumentum (Plate 36).

Suggested Reading

Cox, Peter A., and Kenneth N. E. Cox. 1997. *Encyclopedia of Rhododendron Species.* Perth, Scotland: Glendoick.

Druse, Ken. 1996. *Collector's Garden.* New York: Clarkson Potter.

Galle, Fred. 1987. *Azaleas.* Portland, Oregon: Timber Press.

Royal Horticultural Society. 1998. *Rhododendron Handbook.* London: Royal Horticultural Society.

Salley, Homer, and Harold Greer. 1992. *Rhododendron Hybrids.* 2d ed. Portland, Oregon: Timber Press.

CHAPTER 8

The Native Plant Garden

FOLLOWING NATURE as "head gardener" leads to gardens unified with their environment. Instead of cultivated islands struggling against nature's impending takeover, many of today's gardens happily coexist and even consort with the former enemy. Awareness of the fragile side of the natural environment and a need for at least a hint of nature in everyday life have inspired many to create wild gardens where native plants are the focus, either in a section of the site or in the garden as a whole. These gardeners who attempt to cooperate with nature make their leading landscape principle that of site unity.

Reliance on native plants comes naturally in a wild garden, for they have proven their ability to survive without human aid in a habitat sustained mainly by what nature provides. The choice of exotic plants is, therefore, determined by their ability to thrive along with the natives without chemicals or supplemental water. Make careful study of a plant's wild habitat before choosing a garden site for it.

The design features of the native plant garden are dictated by nature, by climate and microclimate, topography, soil, and rainfall. More than any other type of garden, the native plant garden must be connected to the environment through its design. From a practical standpoint, the garden design should enhance the plants' ability to thrive without harm to the environment. Aesthetically, the design will express an appealing naturalism through bold, cohesive group plantings. The exotic plants chosen for the design must harmonize with the site and, in form, texture, or color, with the native plants.

The history of using native plants in American gardens began with the gardens of Thomas Jefferson and George Washington. The nineteenth-century American designer Andrew Jackson Downing encouraged the public to take an interest in the natural environment as they built their homes and gardens outside urban environments. Later in the century the influential Frederick Law Olmsted Sr. stressed naturalized designs and grew many native plants including *Rhododendron maximum* at his home at Fairsted. Following the spirit of Olmsted into the first half of the twentieth century, the midwestern designer Jens Jensen created private gardens and public parks that related directly to the surrounding prairie region by incorporating native plants. In light of this history, the current style of native plant gardening, encouraged by the ecological movement, was an inevitability.

But how can rhododendrons be used in the design of native plant gardens? Although the principles governing the native plant garden are essentially the same as govern other garden features, in the native plant garden even greater attention must be given to the principle of site unity. Knowledge of and respect for the site are paramount.

Taking Inventory of the Site

The site inventory is little different for the native plant garden than for any other garden. More than any other garden, this type relies heavily on nature's gifts—or lack of them. Therefore, concentrate on the ecological facts of the site. Define the characteristics of the site location within the region and the USDA climate zone. Gather facts about the geology, hydrology, and soil of the site.

An inventory of native plants already on the site, if any, will heighten awareness and understanding of the immediate natural environment. Having native rhododendrons growing wild on the site is highly unlikely, but native trees, shrubs, and herbaceous perennials are more common. Before ripping out plants that do not measure up to an aesthetic standard, find out if they are native. Having native status can make up for a plant's lack of individual eye appeal by helping connect the site to the natural environment. Scouting the neighborhood vacant lots and roadside ditches to see what grows wild, whether the site be a suburban or rural one, will help identify the natives on the site. In the Pacific Northwest a single specimen of Douglas fir (*Pseudotsuga menziesii*), or in the Southeast a tulip tree (*Liriodendron tulipifera*), will anchor a site to its environment. Native shrubs and perennials will perform the same task, though less dramatically.

Narrowing the Choices

The native evergreen *Rhododendron maximum* and *R. macrophyllum* grow wild in sites that provide partial shade and protection from the wind. Such environments most often develop in nature at the edges or in clearings of a woodland. The evergreen *R. catawbiense* grows on the summits and sides of mountains, often in the open, and *R. minus* grows wild in a variety of habitats in the Southeast from the mountains to the plains. The native eastern deciduous azalea *R. calendulaceum* grows in woods and on cliffs and hillsides. *Rhododendron canadense*, native from Labrador to New Jersey, grows along stream banks and swamps and in moist woods. The native North American species inhabit a variety of sites, and one or more may find a happy home in your garden.

Improving the Site

Although a natural garden will require less maintenance than other types of gardens, site improvement can enhance what nature already provides. In a woodland, chances are some pruning will be needed to create sunny clearings for rhododendrons. If rhododendrons will be planted in the verge or in a nearby rock garden, prune overhanging tree limbs that will interfere with their growth. In the coniferous woodlands of the Pacific Northwest, it is common practice to limb up trees throughout the garden area to let in the sun. If no woodland exists, trees can be planted, of course, with at least some natives to connect the garden to the natural environment.

If a house and garden will be built on a natural, undisturbed site, measures can be taken to preserve as many landscape features and native plants as possible. A procedure for construction termed the "building envelope" confines contractors to only a small zone around the house for the workers and construction equipment (Wasowski 1997). The natural area beyond is temporarily fenced off, protecting it from construction disturbances.

Planting

In designing a native plant garden, keep in mind two habitats: the native habitat of each plant you wish to bring to the garden and the native habitat of the garden site and its surrounding environment. The more similar are the habitats, the healthier the plants will be. Note also how the plant you wish to bring into the garden is grouped with others of the same or different species in the wild. Current masters of wild garden design are the Dutch, one of whom is Piet Oudolf, a professional garden designer who works in terms of plant associations rather than single plants, creating bold swaths in overall harmony with the scale of the landscape. In the wild garden, Oudolf encourages self seeding and retains non-invasive natives so that established native plant and wildlife associations are not destroyed. Wild garden design also builds on layers of plants, similar to the layers in natural habitats but enhanced with non-natives (Plate 37, Plate 38).

The use of rhododendrons in wild garden design presents an inviting challenge. The most innovative professional designers use primarily herbaceous perennials to achieve their goals for wild gardening, but the same principles can be applied to other plant types as well. Twenty-four species of rhododendrons are indigenous to North America, including the hardy workhorse shrubs *Rhododendron maximum* and *R. catawbiense*, the beautiful native azaleas of the Southeast, and the West Coast fragrant beauty *R. occidentale*. For those fortunate enough to live in a region of eastern North America where the hardy *R. maximum* grows wild (from Nova Scotia to Georgia), this rhododendron can add mightily to the native plant garden. Its natural habitat is deciduous or coniferous forests, often in dense shade. Its large size—up to 15 feet (4.6 meters)—makes it good in the understory of the eastern woodland garden. Its most useful attribute is its liking for shade, where its large, dark green leaves develop their best color and its pale pink flowers blend naturally into a woodland setting.

Another hardy East Coast elepidote native *Rhododendron catawbiense* grows in the wild on the open summits and sides of mountains in North Carolina and Virginia. An excellent place to see it in the wild is on Roan Mountain, North Carolina, where it grows en masse under the open sky. This, too, is a large plant, up to 6 feet tall (2 meters), but dome-shaped in form with pink to violet flowers. Its greatest attribute in the landscape is its ruggedness; if planted in a large body the plants protect both each other and less robust plants. Good selections from this species are *Rhododendron* 'Catawbiense Grandiflorum' and 'Catawbiense Album' with white flowers.

The lepidote *Rhododendron minus* is native to the Southeast, with *R. minus* var. *chapmanii* occurring as far south as Florida. In North Carolina, South Carolina, Georgia, Alabama, and Tennessee the species grows in woodlands, slopes, and plains; *R. minus* var. *chapmanii* grows on sandy coastal plains in pine forests among palmettos (*Sabal* spp.). *Rhododendron minus* tends toward compactness, reaching a height of about 4 feet (1.2 meters), but can also be straggly in form. Its delicate, relatively small flowers range from pink to pale violet to white. Its greatest landscape value in the native plant garden is that it is both cold and heat hardy and, therefore, a rare evergreen rhododendron naturally adapted to the climate of the Southeast.

The low-growing lepidote *Rhododendron lapponicum* grows wild in Canada's northern reaches and, in fact, occurs in the entire northern polar region. The dwarf forms from the Arctic Circle that grow over permafrost are difficult to grow in the garden, but the less difficult plants of *R. lapponicum* Parvifolium Group from Japan can substitute. The small, scaly leaves turn bronze in winter, and the early-blooming flowers range from pink to pale violet. The rock garden is its natural home, especially if placed where winters are long and cold.

The East Coast and parts of the Midwest and Southwest are gifted with an extraordinary array of native deciduous azaleas, from Newfoundland to Florida to Texas. All the species briefly described below are members of section *Pentanthera* except for two, *R. canadense* and *R. vaseyi*, which belong to section *Rhodora.* Those in section *Pentanthera* are characterized by their funnel-shaped corollas and upsweeping styles that extend beyond the corollas, lending a charming, airy quality. Those in section *Rhodora* bear two-lipped corollas. Flower colors include white, yellow, orange, red, pink, and violet. In form they range from spreading to upright with heights from 3 to 6 feet in cultivation (1 to 2 meters). Many are fragrant and offer fall foliage color.

Rhododendron alabamense bears a white, scented flower with a yellow blotch. It grows wild in Alabama and adjacent states, generally in dry woods and rocky hillsides. *Rhododendron arborescens* also bears a scented, white flower but with a red style and shiny foliage. It occurs from Pennsylvania to Georgia and Alabama in moist woods and beside streams. *Rhododendron atlanticum,* another white-flowered native, is found on the Atlantic coastal plain from Pennsylvania to Georgia, often growing in acid sands as an understory in pine forests. It is low growing (to less than 3 feet or 1 meter), and its scented flowers emerge before the leaves.

Rhododendron austrinum bears yellow to orange flowers with a dark pink tube and orange blotch. It occurs in woods and beside streams in the Florida panhandle, Alabama, Georgia, and Mississippi. *Rhododendron calendulaceum* bears red to orange flowers and is found in woodlands in mountainous areas of Georgia, North Carolina, and Tennessee. *Rhododendron cumberlandense,* with its orange to red flowers on a low-growing plant, is found at high elevations in woods and along ridges in Kentucky, Virginia, Tennessee, Georgia, Alabama, and North Carolina. Bearing fragrant orange to red flowers, *R. flammeum* occurs in open woods and on ridges in the lower Piedmont, Georgia, and South Carolina. *Rhododendron prunifolium*, occurring only in Georgia and Alabama, bears orange to red flowers.

Rhododendron canadense bears small violet flowers on a small, upright plant and is found from Labrador to New Jersey in swamps and moist woods. *Rhododendron canescens* bears pink flowers and occurs in moist woods and along streams on the coastal plains from North Carolina to Florida and west to Texas and Oklahoma. *Rhododendron periclymenoides*, pink flowering and fragrant, has a wide distribution from the Atlantic coastal area inland to the Appalachians and from Vermont to Georgia and Alabama in both moist and dry woods. *Rhododendron prinophyllum*, another pink, fragrant, East Coast native, has wide distribution, from Quebec to Virginia, Arkansas, and Oklahoma. *Rhododendron vaseyi*, bearing white to pink flowers with green throats, is found only in North Carolina in moist ravines and swamps. *Rhododendron viscosum*, bearing white to pink to violet flowers, is widely distributed from Maine to Florida and west to Texas and Oklahoma.

The west coast of North America is home to seven native rhododendrons. The only native elepidote, *Rhododendron macrophyllum*, occurs from Northern California to British Columbia and is usually found at forest margins (Plate 39). Flower color ranges from violet to pink to white. Growing upright to 5 feet (1.5 meters), this rhododendron is properly placed in woodland clearings or verges in the native plant garden.

The deciduous azalea *Rhododendron occidentale* must be planted in native plant gardens located in its growing region— from Oregon to Southern California—for its horticultural values are outstanding: beautiful flowers, fragrance, and fall foliage color. Its flower color varies from white, to white flushed pink, to pink, often with a yellow blotch and red buds. Many fine selected clones are available. It is tall, growing up to 5 feet in cultivation (1.5 meters), and occurs in a variety of locations, from near swampy sites to dry hillsides and even at sites with a high pH of 7.2 to 8.6. In the garden landscape, it looks splendid planted in masses in the open woodland, interspersed with evergreen rhododendrons.

149

A pine branch mingles with the flowers and foliage of the West Coast native azalea *Rhododendron occidentale* where it grows in the wild in the Siskiyou Mountains of Oregon.

The West Coast native azalea *Rhododendron albiflorum* dwells in the mountains and is difficult to grow in the !owland garden, except for the most determined gardener. The charming *R. camtschaticum* from Alaska, a dwarf shrub to 1 foot (0.3 meters), is garden worthy with its hairy leaves, bright pink flowers, and fall foliage color. It is best put to use in the rock garden.

Three former members of genus *Ledum* are now classified within genus *Rhododendron*. They are North American natives *R. groenlandicum*, *R. neoglandulosum*, and *R. tomentosum* subsp. *subarctica*. These lepidotes of the northern regions bear aromatic, hairy leaves and many-flowered, white inflorescences. They range in size from dwarf to prostrate and are candidates for the rock garden.

Companions

Native companions are natural partners for the indigenous North American rhododendrons. I strongly suggest a visit to a wild site where rhododendrons grow to see for yourself their native companions. *Rhododendron maximum* grows in coniferous or deciduous forest, often in dense shade. Near Gregory Bald in North Carolina it grows under a canopy of hemlocks (*Tsuga* spp.) and tulip tree (*Liriodendron tulipifera*). A frequent shrub companion is mountain laurel (*Kalmia latifolia*), another East Coast native. With evergreen foliage and a height of 8 to 10 feet (2.5 to 3.1 meters), it extends the bloom season with dainty flower clusters of pink, red, or white, some with delightfully intricate patterns. Mountain laurel is also a shrub companion to *R. catawbiense.*

Table 14. Native North American companions: small trees

Asimina triloba (paw paw)	Northeast to South
Carpinus caroliniana (American hornbeam)	Southeast
Cornus florida (eastern dogwood)	Northeast to Southeast
Cornus nuttallii (Pacific dogwood)	West Coast
Franklinia alatamaha (Franklin tree)	Southeast
Magnolia grandiflora (southern magnolia)	Southeast
Magnolia virginiana (sweet bay)	coastal Southeast
Stewartia malacodendron (silky camellia)	Southeast
Stewartia ovata (mountain camellia)	Southeast
Styrax americanus (mock orange)	Southeast

Since the habitat of the many eastern native azaleas ranges widely, a wide range of natives make suitable companions. In the northern coniferous forest region of eastern Canada and New England, *Rhododendron canadense* and *R. groenlandicum* combine with bunchberry (*Cornus canadensis*). Further south, in the eastern deciduous forests from southern New England to northern Georgia and Alabama, good companion trees include eastern dogwood (*Cornus florida*) and tulip tree (*Liriodendron tulipifera*); shrubs include mountain laurel (*Kalmia latifolia*), American elderberry (*Sambucus canadensis*), and maple-leaved viburnum (*Viburnum acerifolium*); herbaceous companions include wild ginger (*Asarum canadense*), bleeding heart (*Dicentra eximia*), and white wake-robin (*Trillium grandiflorum*). On Gregory Bald where *R. calendulaceum, R. arborescens, R. cumberlandense,* and *R. viscosum* are found, nearby companions are serviceberries (*Amelanchier* spp.). The southeastern mixed forest region occurring on the upland Piedmont is home to the companionable natives southern magnolia (*Magnolia grandiflora*), loblolly pine (*Pinus taeda*) and heart-leaf (*Asarum virginica*). Along the eastern coastal plain, where *Rhododendron canescens, R. viscosum,* and *R. prunifolium* occur, also native are sweet bay (*Magnolia virginiana*), the sweet pepperbush (*Clethra alnifolia*), and the herbaceous jack-in-the-pulpit (*Arisaema triphyllum*).

In Florida, *Rhododendron minus* var. *chapmanii* grows under pines among the native palmettos (*Sabal* spp.). And far away on the Alaskan west coast, *R. lapponicum* and *R. camtschaticum* mix with low-growing species of *Cassiope, Vaccinium,* and *Loiseleuria,* and mosses and creeping willows (*Salix repens*).

Table 15. Native North American companions: shrubs

Amelanchier (service berry)	Southeast
Cassiope	Northwest to Alaska
Clethra alnifolia (pepperbush)	coastal Southeast
Corylus cornuta (hazelnut)	Northwest
Fothergilla gardenii (witch alder)	Southeast
Gaultheria shallon (salal)	Northwest
Holodiscus discolor (ocean spray)	Northwest
Hydrangea quercifolia (oakleaf hydrangea)	Southeast
Kalmia latifolia (mountain laurel)	East Coast
Loiseleuria (alpine azalea)	Far North
Mahonia aquifolium (Oregon grape)	Northwest
Philadelphus lewisii (mock orange)	Northwest
Sabal (palmetto)	Florida
Sambucus canadensis (American elderberry)	Northeast to Southeast
Vaccinium angustifolium (lowbush blueberry)	Northeast
Vaccinium parvifolium (red huckleberry)	Northwest
Viburnum acerifolium (mapleleaf viburnum)	Northeast to Southeast

Rhododendron macrophyllum grows naturally at forest edges and clearings in the Pacific Northwest from British Columbia to Northern California under a canopy of Douglas fir (*Pseudotsuga menziesii*), western hemlock (*Tsuga heterophylla*), western red cedar (*Thuja plicata*), and coast redwood (*Sequoia sempervirens*). The rhododendron shares the rich shrub layer with salal (*Gaultheria shallon*), Oregon grape (*Mahonia aquifolium*), and sword fern (*Polystichum munitum*) among many others.

The western azalea *Rhododendron occidentale* occurs in a variety of habitats in Oregon and California. In the Siskiyou Mountains of southern Oregon, it grows in the open stands of Jeffrey pine (*Pinus jeffreyi*) near a bog with the reptilian-looking pitcher plant (*Darlingtonia californica*) nearby. In Northern California, it grows under coast redwood (*Sequoia sempervirens*) with redwood sorrel (*Oxalis oregona*), and wild ginger (*Asarum caudatum*).

The Ericaceae, to which the genus *Rhododendron* belongs, is the source of a rich array of botanically related companions, joined not only by taxonomic ties but frequently by cultural needs and aspect. Although ericaceous species—about 1900 in total—are widely distributed throughout the world, new combinations of them are yet to be tried. Introducing them to each

Table 16. Native North American companions: herbaceous perennials

Aquilegia canadensis (wild columbine)	Midwest
Arisaema triphyllum (jack-in-the-pulpit)	coastal Southeast
Asarum canadense (wild ginger)	Northeast to Southeast
Asarum caudatum (wild ginger)	Northern California
Asarum virginica (heart-leaf)	Southeast
Astilbe biternata (false goatsbeard)	Southeast
Cornus canadensis (bunchberry)	Northeast
Darlingtonia californica (pitcher plant)	Northwest
Dicentra eximia (bleeding heart)	Northeast to Southeast
Heuchera americana (rock geranium)	Southeast
Oxalis oregona (redwood sorrel)	Northern California
Smilacina stellata (false Solomon's seal)	Southeast
Trillium grandiflorum (white wake-robin)	Northeast to Southeast
Viola canadensis (tall white viola)	Southeast

other in the native garden can result in wonderful plant relationships that make ecological sense.

A list of ericaceous genera is a list of garden champions. Besides *Rhododendron*, the family includes *Arbutus, Arctostaphylos, Calluna, Cassiope, Daboecia, Enkianthus, Erica, Gaultheria, Kalmia, Kalmiopsis, Leucothoe, Pernettya, Phyllodoce, Pieris*, and *Vaccinium*. All like acid, damp soil, although some, such as plants of *Arbutus* and *Arctostaphylos*, can take drier conditions. Most are evergreen.

Table 17. Native North American ericaceous companions

Arctostaphylos uva-ursi (kinnikinick)	West Coast, ground cover
Cassiope mertensiana (white heather)	West, ground cover
Gaultheria procumbens (wintergreen)	East Coast, ground cover
Gaultheria shallon (salal)	West Coast, ground cover
Kalmia latifolia (mountain laurel)	East, shrub
Kalmiopsis leachiana	Oregon, shrub
Leucothoe axillaris	Southeast, shrub
Leucothoe populifolia	Southeast, shrub
Phyllodoce empetriformis (mountain heather)	West Coast, ground cover
Pieris floribunda (fetterbush)	Southeast, shrub
Pieris phillyreifolia	Southeast, shrub
Vaccinium ovatum (California huckleberry)	West Coast, shrub
Vaccinium macrocarpon (cranberry)	Northeast, ground cover
Vaccinium vitis-idaea (cowberry)	North, ground cover

Madrona (*Arbutus menziesii*) is native to the West Coast from British Columbia to California and grows 50 to 100 feet tall (15.3 to 30.5 meters). Often clinging to cliffs overlooking the ocean, the tree dramatically displays its flaking, red bark and, in spring, its pink or white panicles of blossoms. The smaller *Arbutus unedo* grows to about 12 feet (3.7 meters) and bears orange to red fruit in the fall.

Manzanita (*Arctostaphylos* spp.), also a West Coast native, has leathery leaves suited to drier conditions. The genus includes both evergreen, prostrate shrubs, and small trees. The creeping kinnikinick (*Arctostaphylos uva-ursi*) is useful as a ground cover. Another charming creeper, pine-mat manzanita (*Arctostaphylos nevadensis*) is native to the Siskiyou Mountains of Oregon. Plants of this genus would be appropriate in the rock garden or adjacent to a rhododendron planting where conditions are too dry for rhododendrons.

The heathers and heaths belong to the genera *Calluna* and *Erica*, respectively. *Calluna vulgaris* is the heather of the Scottish highlands. These largely European natives offer many worthy cultivars with bell-shaped flowers varying from white to pink to violet. Although some gardeners sprinkle them among their rhododendrons, they are more effective planted en masse to form a carpet adjacent to rhododendron plantings. This arrangement contrasts the horizontal aspect of the heather carpet with the upright rhododendrons and prevents the *Calluna* and *Erica* from invading the rhododendron roots—a nasty tendency of these two genera. A heather-like genus is the European native *Daboecia*. It includes two species: *D. azorica* with bright rose flowers and *D. cantabrica* with white, pink, or violet flowers. This genus, too, is most suitable for the rock garden.

The genus *Cassiope*, often referred to as a heather and a native of the mountains of the North American West Coast, is a good candidate for the rock garden that receives some shade during the day. Its leaves are scalelike and its flowers white. Similar in aspect but with needlelike leaves is *Phyllodoce*, which blooms in white, yellow, pink, or violet. It too is a native of the mountains of the West Coast and a candidate for the rock garden.

The genus *Enkianthus* includes ten species of deciduous shrubs native to Asia that grow to a height of 8 to 10 feet (2.5 to 3.1 meters). A planting of evergreen rhododendrons benefits from nearby, contrasting deciduous shrubs, especially if they produce colorful foliage in the fall and strong branch silhouettes in winter. *Enkianthus* provides both. The branches of these upright shrubs grow in horizontal layers, bearing red or orange leaves in fall. In spring they bear yellow, red, or white, bell-shaped flowers. *Enkianthus campanulatus*, whose leaves turn yellow, orange, and red in fall, bear light yellow to pink flowers with red veins, and the bark of young growth is red—an added winter bonus.

The genus *Gaultheria* includes some delightful low-growing species good for ground covers and the rock garden. *Gaultheria adenothrix,* with dark green, evergreen foliage, grows about 1 foot (0.3 meters) and produces white, bell-shaped flowers with red calyxes and red fruit. *Gaultheria nummularioides* is prostrate in form, growing about 1 inch tall (2.5 centimeters) and producing pink blossoms and black fruit. The Pacific Northwest native wintergreen (*G. procumbens*) grows 3 to 6 inches (7.6 to 15 centimeters) and bears white flowers and red fruit.

Liking the same light shade as many rhododendrons do, *Kalmiopsis leachiana,* a native of the Siskiyou Mountains of Oregon and the only species in the genus, grows to about 1 foot (0.3 meters) with a 2-foot spread (0.6 meters). It is densely branched, clothed in thick, dark green leaves, and covered in pink flowers.

The genus *Leucothoe* includes a number of evergreen species that will do well in the Southeast. *Leucothoe axillaris,* growing 2 to 4 feet (0.6 to 1.2 meters) high but amenable to pruning, has a spreading form with arching branches and bears white, bell-shaped flowers. Its glossy, leathery leaves turn bronze in winter. *Leucothoe populifolia* grows in the wild from South Carolina to Florida, growing to 5 feet (1.5 meters). It also has an arching habit and bears ivory, fragrant, bell-shaped flowers.

Another genus that grows in drier conditions is the evergreen *Pernettya* with glossy, dark green leaves. *Pernettya mucronata,* reaching to 6 feet (2 meters), bears white flowers and white, pink, or deep violet fruit in fall. The lovely *P. pumila* is a creeping grower to only 4 inches tall (10 centimeters).

The genus *Pieris* offers evergreen rhododendron companions in the 4 to 10-foot range (1.2 to 3.1 meters) and is beautiful in form, foliage, and flower. The new growth is generally bronze, pink, white, or fiery red, depending on the stage and variety, becoming leathery and sometimes glossy when mature. The panicles of flowers bud in winter and open in early spring, before most rhododendrons. *Pieris japonica,* a native of Japan, is an upright, dense, and tiered shrub to 10 feet (3.1 meters) with leaves glossy when mature. Numerous cultivars of this species have been selected. Native to the American Southeast from Virginia to Georgia is *P. floribunda* with upright, white flower clusters and pale green new growth turning glossy, dark green. It grows to 4 feet (1.2 meters) high and wide. Native to western Florida is *P.*

phillyreifolia, growing to 3 feet (1 meter) with arching branches, dark green, glossy leaves, and white, bell-shaped flowers.

The genus *Vaccinium* encompasses some 150 species, deciduous and evergreen, prostrate to 10 feet tall (3.1 meters), and offers interesting companions native to North America. *Vaccinium parvifolium* is the Pacific Northwest native red huckleberry. Numerous North American native blueberries exist, varying in their garden worthiness, including lowbush blueberry (*V. angustifolium*) of eastern Canada and New England. In general, dwarf forms are preferred for the garden. Cranberry (*Vaccinium macrocarpon*) is native from Newfoundland to Minnesota, and its form 'Hamilton' with dark, evergreen foliage and pink flowers reaches only about 4 inches (10 centimeters). Mountain cranberry (*Vaccinium vitis-idaea* var. *minus*) native from Massachusetts to Alaska, also grows to about 4 inches (10 centimeters) with white to pink blossoms and red fruits.

PLANT COMBINATIONS

For a layered effect using northeastern natives, under a canopy of white pine (*Pinus strobus*), plant *Rhododendron maximum* 'Summertime' with white flowers next to *Kalmia latifolia* 'Freckles'. The kalmia bears white flowers with red-violet spots and blooms after the rhododendron. At their feet grow *Cornus canadensis,* with its small, yellow-green flowers surrounded by showy, white bracts in early spring and its red fruit in fall.

For layers of southeastern coastal natives, plant *Magnolia virginiana* with *Rhododendron canescens, Pieris floribunda,* and *Arisaema triphyllum.* The magnolia is a semideciduous tree or shrub, bearing white, fragrant flowers. Its 5-inch-long leaves (13 centimeters) are gray beneath. The deciduous azalea, which can grow to 10 feet (3.1 meters), bears fragrant, white to pink flowers with long tubes and extending stamens. *Pieris floribunda* will sustain the planting in winter with its evergreen foliage. The jack-in-the-pulpit (*A. triphyllum*) will add a lush ground cover in summer.

For a layered planting of Pacific Coast natives, use a canopy of *Pinus jeffreyi* over *Rhododendron occidentale* and *Mahonia aquifolium.* Growing at the edge of the pines, the Oregon grape (*M. aquifolium*) will make an evergreen backdrop for the deciduous azalea, which blooms in delicate pinks and whites and is highly fragrant.

Garden Tours

Many gardens mentioned in previous chapters include native rhododendrons and companions in sections or throughout the garden. For instance, Earl Sommerville of Georgia grows his collection of Southeast native azaleas in a native woodland setting. Jeanine and Rex Smith in Washington display their wide representation of the genus in a native woodland setting, making great use of companion native shrubs such as red huckleberry (*Vaccinium parvifolium*), Oregon grape (*Mahonia aquifolium*), and salal (*Gaultheria shallon*), as well as numerous ferns (Plate 41). And the Edward B. Dunn Garden in Seattle uses the West Coast native azalea *Rhododendron occidentale* at a woodland verge where its delicate white flowers shine like stars against the dark green background (Plate 40).

Suggested Reading

Druse, Ken. 1989. *Natural Garden.* New York: Clarkson Potter.
Kruckeberg, Arthur R. 1982. *Gardening with Native Plants of the Pacific Northwest.* Seattle: University of Washington Press.

CHAPTER 9

The Small Garden

The small, or urban, garden is to the country garden what a sonnet is to a novel. The small garden must tell all in a small space, while the large garden has room to weave its story through many garden features. Although all gardens, whether large, medium, or small, benefit from the same design principles, the small garden requires using them with the greatest precision.

Small gardens are usually, but not always, located in an urban environment with neighbors close by. They provide privacy and a refuge from the sights, sounds, and smells of the city. Although some small gardens will have views of the city or landscape, most will look inward and rely on plants and hard structures for their focus. Many small gardens will consist of only one room and be entirely visible from the house. To deal with the limitation of size, gardeners and garden designers have come up with some sound, innovative solutions in which rhododendrons can play a vital part.

Taking Inventory of the Site

As with any other garden, a site inventory is the first step. Be clear about the goal for the garden—is it meant to be a spot of earth in which to garden and grow plants, a place to entertain, a contemplative refuge, a child's playground, or an outdoor family

Hypertufa troughs and clay pots are used to display rhododendrons and other alpine plants on a deck.

recreation room? Or maybe all it needs to be is a view of living plants from inside the house. Because of its size, every inch of space will be devoted to one intended use.

Gather the same facts as for any site: size, changes in elevation, and soil composition. Pay particular attention to the house when space is limited, since it will be the dominant structure in the garden—consider its color and style and views of the garden site through windows and doors. Also assess the periphery of the site. Is it totally enclosed by high walls, fences, or plants, or does it have an attractive view to beyond the site? Is it open to an unsightly view that needs to be hidden? Whether the garden will rely on a focus within its walls or on a view outside its walls will greatly influence its design. Existing trees, including canopies from off-site trees, and other plants should be noted, along with buildings seen from the site. Pay close attention to the path of sunshine during the day and through the seasons. Small, enclosed urban gardens tend to have a scarcity of sun, and each sun patch will be treasured. Is there a storage facility on the site? Is there access to the street, or will all garden materials have to be carried through the house? Before beginning the garden design, know the site as intimately as you do the kitchen.

Narrowing the Choices

The choices for the small garden are arbitrarily narrowed by site size, house style, amount of direct sunlight, enclosure, and climate. The size of the site will largely determine whether the garden will be one room or more. House style will influence the garden's degree of formality. The amount of sunlight will influence the choice of plants. The enclosure will influence the area of focus, for example, enclosures higher than eye level will force the focus inward. Climate will influence how to build the garden in order to enhance each different season of the year. In spite of these formidable givens, builders of small gardens have many choices to make based on their personal taste. In fact, creativity abounds in small gardens often *because* of the limitations that force unconventional solutions.

Improving the Site

The first step in planning the garden is to think in terms of mass and space as discussed in Chapter 3. In a small garden limit yourself to one or two shapes. If the garden is to be one room, the focus will be directed inward, making shapes of repose more appropriate, such as circles, squares, or hexagons. For more than one room, use long, narrow shapes to create movement from one room to the next.

Many classic garden techniques are useless for building a small garden, especially the reliance on large, curving, naturalistic lines. In a small space, walls or fences at square angles may jut up around the garden site, beyond which buildings may be visible. With a large tree or two in or just outside the site, the effect can be claustrophobic. Though the first impulse might be to scale down shapes and plant sizes in the garden, creating a miniature landscape to offset the overwhelming effect, just the opposite is needed. Strong garden structures and bold, architectural plants are essential for offsetting the intimidating surroundings. Bold yet simple design creates the illusion of spaciousness. Small garden building is not for the meek. Forgo building a complex of garden features or garden rooms for the sake of one or two strong elements.

In an informal garden, design asymmetrically, with shapes that balance rather than mirror each other. Curving shapes will lend a controlled flow that enhances the informality. For a formal garden, use geometrical symmetry with straight lines and plantings well contained in their borders.

Boldly use hard structures to make a framework that draws attention away from the dominating enclosure and creates an inviting space. The materials of the framework and internal space dividers, such as fences, walls, or pergolas, should reflect the style of the house, which is never out of view. Linking the garden to the house, and even its interior, will make a garden appear larger.

Striking yet simple ground surfaces help immeasurably in keeping the eye focused inward on the enclosed small space. Bricks, stone, or concrete pavers laid in attractive designs that complement the house provide sturdy surfaces for foot traffic and garden furniture. Wooden decking can serve the same purpose. A loose surface of gravel or an immaculate plot of grass can visually enhance the garden.

Objects placed within the small garden should also be bold and in harmony with the house style (Plate 42). Garden furniture will likely be dominant and can serve as a focal point. A water feature or containers can pull the eye into the design (Plate 43). Small pots can be grouped to create a larger mass (Plate 44). A raised bed holding a collection of small plants can also appear as a single object.

Planting

The plantings in a small garden will need to be as bold as the hard structures. The amazing genus *Rhododendron* has wealth enough not only to enhance the large, naturalistic woodland garden but also to adorn the small garden, which invariably will provide the partial shade needed in rhododendron culture. The architectural forms, bold textures of foliage, and strong colors of many rhododendrons have often been overlooked in planting small gardens. The journey from vast mountain habitat to the small garden is a long one, but these plants travel well and can become indispensable residents in their new home.

THE INFORMAL STYLE

An informal style arises through an asymmetrical design in which shapes of mass are balanced against each other rather than symmetrically replicated from one side to the other. For instance, a mass of shrubs on one side will balance a pergola on the other. The edges of informal plantings can be more irregular and the plantings less contained, creeping out into the empty space. An informal style can encourage the wild element even in the smallest of gardens.

An informal style in the small garden can be created, in part, by lush, layered plantings of tall shrubs with ground covers spilling over the boundaries. Lushness also gives the illusion of spaciousness. Rhododendrons in this mixed border will best succeed if kept to a select few varieties. In milder climates, the large-leafed types, such as *Rhododendron macabeanum* or *R. rex* subsp. *fictolacteum*, can offer height and bold foliage texture. Height can also be achieved through the use of climbers on the enclosing structure, such as *Clematis montana* 'Tetra Rose' or *Hydrangea anomala* var. *petiolaris*. Or a tall-growing bamboo, such as *Fargesia murielae*, could back up the rhododendron planting, offering a beautiful contrast in foliage, although their invasive roots may have to be contained. The shrubs *Pieris japonica* 'Valley Fire', with its bright red new growth, and *Camellia oleifera* or one of its progeny, with their fragrant winter blooms, would add to the border's lushness. Ferns and mosses could serve as lush ground covers, carrying the eye down to a hard surface where the moss reaches between paving slabs. The flowing effect of less defined edges heightens the informality of the garden.

A tropical-like lushness can be created using several types of large-leafed plants massed together. Many rhododendrons can create this effect in mild climates, such as *Rhododendron sinograde* or *R. rex*, both with glossy leaves. While those in warm climates have a wide choice of large-leafed tropical companions, temperate-climate gardeners can use *Hydrangea quercifolia* 'Snow Queen', with leaves 9 inches long and 6 inches wide (23 by 15 centimeters), or *Fatsia japonica* with fan-like leaves to 16 inches wide (41 centimeters). Tree ferns and hardy palms, such as *Chamaerops humilis*, will contribute to a tropical effect. Large-leafed herbaceous perennials might include *Gunnera manicata*, *Hosta sieboldiana*, or *Bergenia crassifolia*. Planting these large-leafed plants adjacent to the house, in the foreground of the view, with smaller plants farther away, will give the site the illusion of greater depth.

Use plants in pots or other containers, massed together, to soften the hard edges of beds or structures. Rhododendrons do well in containers, and virtually any except the very large can be so planted. Rhododendrons of subsection *Maddenia* are particularly suited to containers in the small garden because of their luscious and frequently fragrant flowers that are best enjoyed up close. Their lack of hardiness, however, will necessitate winter protection in colder climates. Some tend toward straggly form and may have to be staked in the pot. In spite of these deficits, they are worth the trouble. *Rhododendron nuttallii* bears very large, fragrant flowers of creamy white flushed yellow inside and has dark green, puckered leaves up to 1 foot long (0.3 meters). Its red new foliage is a show in itself. *Rhododendron veitchianum* has a large (5-inch or 13-centimeter), fragrant, white flower with a yellow blotch and frilly margins. A choice hybrid within subsection *Maddenia* is *Rhododendron* 'Mi Amor' with fragrant, white flowers up to 6 inches across (15 centimeters). *Rhododendron edgeworthii* of subsection *Edgeworthia* is another tender species of top ranking for pot culture. Its fragrant flowers are white tinged pink, and its leaves are puckered and covered with indumentum.

Another group of rhododendrons excellent for pot culture in the small garden are the species of section *Vireya* and their hybrids. They are even less hardy that those plants of subsections *Maddenia* and *Edgeworthia*, however; in fact, they are unwilling to take any frost at all. If you live in a frost-free climate or have a place to over-winter these plants, they will more than earn their keep, for their exquisite, funnel-shaped flowers are truly unsurpassed in color. Their color quality is pure, often without the tinting effect of white or the shading effect of black, radiating an aura of their native tropics where they grow high in the misty mountains. For instance, *Rhododendron javanicum* and *R. zoelleri* bear orange to yellow flowers, and *R. lochiae* from Australia displays red flowers, all in the brightest of hues and all well suited to cultivation. The increasingly popular vireya hybrids offer even greater color thrills. Among them are *Rhododendron* 'Cristo Rey', a yellow-gold and red-orange bicolor; 'Saint Valentine' with small, bright red flowers; 'Calavar' with flowers of dark pink and cream; and 'Princess Alexandra' with pristine white flowers. The vireyas would make excellent color accents in the tropical-looking planting described above and would have the advantage of continuous bloom. Pot and all could be placed within the bed during frost-free months.

THE FORMAL STYLE

A formal design is often a logical choice for the small garden because of the imposing geometrical nature of the boundary—

walls or fences at right angles enclosing the space—especially if the house style is amenable to formality. The closer the garden design is linked to the house style and interior the larger the garden will appear. Symmetry characterizes the formal style. Its regular outlines and contained plantings guided the design of both the grand French gardens of the seventeenth century and the earlier Italian Renaissance gardens. Formality works nicely in the small garden, because the strong structure needed to sustain formality also is needed to draw attention inward and away from the close boundaries of the small garden.

Rhododendrons can play a surprisingly large role in the plantings of a small, formal garden, especially since many like shade, a common denominator of most of these gardens. In spite of the propensity of some rhododendrons to bring out the wild character of a garden, others can tame it and enhance its civilized character.

Rhododendrons can be used to build formal or semiformal hedges. The rhododendrons of subsection *Triflora*, such as *Rhododendron augustinii* and *R. yunnanense*, will form a clipped or unclipped hedge. Their dense, twiggy, upright growth makes them particularly suitable for clipping into geometrical shapes. The *Rhododendron* PJM Group of hardy lepidote hybrids planted in a row can make an attractive unclipped yet tidy hedge. The foliage is striking in all seasons, with light green, matte foliage in spring, turning shiny green in summer and deepening to mahogany in the fall and winter. The fine texture of the Kurume azaleas, a group of evergreen azaleas bred in Japan more than 300 years ago, make them amenable to shearing into low hedges. Among the many readily available Kurume hybrids for this purpose are *Rhododendron* 'Hino-crimson' (red), 'Blaauw's Pink' (pink), and 'Ward's Ruby' (red). Such hedges can be used to delineate space in the precise manner a formal style requires.

A highly formal plant form is the standard, a stylized shape to which some rhododendrons obligingly conform. The technique involves grafting a dwarf or semidwarf rhododendron on a single-stemmed rootstock such as *Rhododendron* 'Anna Rose Whitney'. Choices for scion are many but include *R. williamsianum*, *R. yakushimanum*, and *Rhododendron* 'Creeping Jenny'. A row of such standards would transform any garden and certainly attract attention inward and away from the boundaries.

Many rhododendrons are of symmetrical form and are well suited to the formal garden. Planted in the ground or in containers, these compact, mounding rhododendrons create a satisfying, formal feeling. Much of the current hybridizing effort is aimed at producing plants of mounding, compact form. Along the way, hybridizers have achieved foliage attractive year-round and flower colors rich in hue. These new hybrids often are better suited to a more formal garden style than a naturalistic one. *Rhododendron* 'Nancy Evans' grows to a rounded 3-foot form (1 meter) in ten years. Its orange-yellow flowers emerge from red buds and then turn a golden yellow while retaining the orange-yellow at the margins. 'Naselle' grows to a rounded 4 feet (1.2 meters) in ten years and bears pink flowers shading to yellow with orange spotting. 'Mindy's Love', another 3-foot shrub (1 meter), bears soft yellow flowers with faint red streaks. 'Midnight Mystique' bears dark-red-edged flowers with white star-like centers.

The above hybrids were developed in the Pacific Northwest and are not necessarily suited to all areas; however, hybridizers in other regions have similar goals as they contend with extremes of heat and cold. *Rhododendron* 'Casanova' was developed in the Midwest. Its pink buds open to yellow flowers, pink on the exterior with an orange flare. Out of the Northeast comes 'Vinecrest', mounding in form with olive-green foliage and yellow flowers with orange rays, emerging from orange-yellow buds. Though these plants may eventually grow too large for the small, formal garden, before they outgrow their usefulness they will give years of pleasure.

Rhododendron yakushimanum is, in many ways, the ultimate rhododendron for the small, formal garden. This species has made the trip to cultivation from its wild mountain home on Yakushima, Japan, with supreme grace. Symmetrical in its mounding, compact form, elegant in its recurved, hairy leaves, and delicate in its white tinged pink flower color, it performs most admirably all year long in the formal garden as a single specimen or as a group. Grown in containers or in the ground, this plant delineates space architecturally and elegantly. Excellent forms are *R. yakushimanum* 'Ken Janeck', 'Koichiro Wada', 'Yaku Angel', 'Mist Maiden', and the Exbury form.

Many wonderful *Rhododendron yakushimanum* hybrids, because of their symmetrical form, perform the same function as their admired parent. *Rhododendron* 'Centennial Celebration' has pale orchid, frilly flowers; 'Yaku Sunrise' has pink flowers darker on the reverse; 'Fantastica' has strong pink flowers fading to white in the throat with green spotting. A number of hybrids are especially outstanding for their foliage. 'Golfer', with recurved leaves like its parent but with silver indumentum on the upper sides of the leaves lasting all year, is a smaller plant than its parent. 'Teddy Bear' has shiny, dark green leaves with reddish indumentum on the undersides.

A collection of dwarf rhododendrons could enhance the small, formal garden if grown in a raised bed that harmonizes in shape and building materials with the rest of the garden. Many diminutive hybrids of fine form, texture, and flower are on the market, including Warren Berg's *Rhododendron* 'Wee Bee' and 'Patty Bee', and Peter Cox's *Rhododendron* 'Wigeon', 'Teal', and 'Ptarmigan'. Also candidates are *Rhododendron* 'Shamrock' with yellow-green flowers, 'Princess Anne' with yellow flowers and bronze winter foliage, and 'Honsu's Baby' with white flowers emerging from pink buds.

THE JAPANESE STYLE

Elements of the Japanese style can be used in the small garden without total commitment to the style or the philosophies that lie behind it. The Japanese style is characterized by restraint, balance, and scale in the use of plants and manmade structures.

The Japanese garden is, above all, an enclosed space of repose away from the cacophonies of everyday life, placing it at once in league with the small, urban garden that aims to be a refuge. Various ways of creating this tranquility in the small garden can be borrowed from the Japanese style. A fence or wall surrounding the garden, separating it from the outside world is only a start. Inside is a representation of the natural world which serves to revive one's spirit. In the environment of the Japanese garden, rocks become mountains and raked sand becomes sea. In spite of the stylized techniques, the goal is to invite the forces of nature in—another approach to infusing the garden with a wild element.

Among the plants meticulously chosen for the role they are to play are the evergreen azaleas, often sheared to represent clouds or receding hills, creating the illusion of distance—a feat fully appreciated by the owner of the small garden. Massed, clipped evergreen azaleas are used for continuity of design against which, for example, a single deciduous, open-branched shrub is placed in contrast. Clipped azaleas can also be used to link the garden to trees visible beyond the garden. Restraint in the use of color is characteristic of the Japanese style, and the vibrant hues of many evergreen azaleas can provide a small spot of bright color that reverberates far beyond its understated use. Seasonal change is emphasized in the Japanese style, and the flowering of the evergreen azaleas celebrates the arrival of spring.

Textural interest is characteristic of the Japanese style, and in the small garden where close-up views of plants are inevitable, texture becomes especially important. For instance, the delicacy of the white flowers and new foliage of *Rhododendron quinque-folium* and the airiness of the exquisite blooms and foliage of *R. schlippenbachii*—both native deciduous azaleas of Japan from section *Sciadorhodion*—are textural wonders excellent for the small garden. The genus, however, abounds in plants of interesting and varying textures.

The Japanese style requires meticulous grooming of plants—an approach suitable for the small garden, in which each plant is always on display and should look its best every day. Skillful pruning enhances form, reveals bark textures, and emphasizes foliage texture. Pruning will also be necessary to keep plants from over-stepping their allotted space as inevitable change occurs.

Finally, seasonal change expressed through the plantings tie the garden to the natural world. Rhododendrons are supremely useful, for they can perform throughout the year with spring flower bloom, summer foliage texture, fall foliage color, and winter silhouettes.

PLANT COMBINATIONS

For a shady corner of the informal garden, preferably near the house in the foreground of the view, a combination of temperate plants creates a tropical effect through their large leaves. *Rhododendron sinogrande*, hardy to 10°F (−12°C), bears the largest leaves of all rhododendrons—up to 30 inches long (75 centimeters)—glossy green on top with silver or fawn indumentum underneath. The new foliage growth is a striking silver. The plant itself can be expected to grow 5 feet (1.5 meters) in ten years. The creamy white to pale yellow flowers are born in ball trusses. The deciduous *Hydrangea anomala* var. *anomala* is a climber, differing from its close relative *H. anomala* var. *petiolaris* by having slightly larger flower heads and orange-red autumn foliage. This vigorous climber bears glossy green, heart-shaped leaves up to 4 inches long (10 centimeters) and white, flat clusters of flowers. It will need support and possible pruning in the small garden. For ground cover, *Bergenia purpurascens* creates a glossy, dark green carpet with its large leaves up to 10 inches long (25 centimeters) that turn dark red in autumn. It bears pink flowers.

For a formal effect in an area with at least partial sun, plant *Clematis montana* 'Tetra Rose' on a fence or lattice as background for a row of *Rhododendron yakushimanum* standards, underplanted with *Tulipa* 'White Parrot' for spring bloom and with the white *Impatiens balsamina* 'Bruno' for summer bloom. Simultaneous bloom comes from the clematis in pink with pale green stamens, the rhododendron in white flushed pink, and the tulip with clear white and occasional green flecks. The summer white flowers of the *Impatiens* will create a carpet beneath the rhododendrons, highlighting their white indumentum.

For a Japanese garden style in a partly shady area, plant *Rhododendron albrechtii* in the foreground. This deciduous rhododendron will display its early spring blossoms, lovely summer foliage, and leafless winter branches most strikingly against the uncluttered backdrop of several plants of the Kurume azalea *Rhododendron* 'Hino-crimson' sheared to mounds. The ground cover moss *Mnium hornum* contributes to the clean effect. *Rhodo-*

170

dendron albrechtii is a very early bloomer, displaying dark pink flowers before or while its leaves unfold. In the Japanese style, these plants are a splash of color midst an otherwise green picture. The bright red flowers of the azalea will appear after the rhododendron is finished blooming. The light green of the moss will darken by summertime.

Garden Tours

Susan Baker of Vancouver, British Columbia, has created a small garden on a rooftop in the midst of a bustling urban environment (Plate 45). Measuring 36 by 16 feet (11 by 4.9 meters), minus a stairwell, the garden provides not only a place to enjoy summer for the Baker family, but also a home for approximately sixty rhododendrons. In order to create a sense of enclosure, hedges contain the floor area and divide it into rooms. A cascade of hanging fuchsias (*Fuchsia* spp.) and pelargoniums (*Pelargonium* spp.) on a pergola rail add further privacy and help screen surrounding buildings. All the plants, of course, are grown in containers. The rhododendrons grow in wooden containers, except for the showy bonsai types, such as *Rhododendron kiusianum*, that grow in clay pots.

Baker chooses the rhododendrons first for their form and texture and second for their flowers. In a few cases, fragrance takes precedence, which puts her to work pruning and shaping the specimen to make it presentable. She has had great success with her tree-sized *Rhododendron* 'Fragrantissimum', a winner of many show prizes. Among the large rhododendrons in this small garden is *R. strigillosum*, chosen for its bristly foliage. The larger rhododendrons in the 5- to 6-foot range (1.5 to 2 meters) have canopies pruned to a maximum of 4 feet wide (1.2 meters). In pruning container-grown rhododendrons, Baker aims for form that is balanced visually, like bonsai, and for the right scale in the context of her garden. Low-growing rhododendrons are ground covers in the whiskey-barrel containers of five dwarf fruit trees. The low canopies of most of the large rhododendrons precludes container companions. But because of the density of rhododendron foliage in the summer, the addition of summer color is essential. Baker has designed monochromatic schemes of closely related colors in deference to the small space. Daylilies (*Hemerocallis* spp.) along with the hanging fuchsias (*Fuchsia* spp.) and pelargoniums (*Pelargonium* spp.) play a key role in the summer color scheme. By August the fruit trees add a festive touch of color against the supporting green of the rhododendrons.

In the narrow urban garden of Chris and Julia Cutler in Seattle, a small number of rhododendrons provide continuity throughout the seasons with their evergreen foliage, starring only briefly for a few weeks in the spring blooming season (Plate 46). Although used in supporting roles, as opposed to the star-performing Japanese maple (*Acer palmatum*) that spans the narrow width of the garden, the rhododendrons earn their keep by providing reliable substance all year, especially in the shadiest section of the site. The Cutler garden, approximately 20 by 70 feet (6.1 by 21.4 meters), is divided into three level terraces descending to the house at the rear of the long, narrow lot. A path down one side of the lot runs straight from the front gate to the front door, but a sense of mystery comes from plantings that partly obscure the sight of the house, such as the lacy canopy of the large Japanese maple.

The front gate opens onto the top terrace, the shadiest portion of the garden, where three rhododendrons stand against the north fence, lending height and structure. At their feet a carpet of woodland plants—hostas (*Hosta* spp.), astilbes (*Astilbe* spp.), dead nettles (*Lamium* spp.), ferns, grasses, and other small woodland plants—spreads out to the path in a tapestry of green. Gold highlights the rich green in *Hosta* 'Little Aureo', a Japanese gold-variegated grass, and in spring, flowers of a yellow rhododendron. This shady terrace feels intimate through the maple (*Acer* spp.) canopy and the hedge-like rhododendrons at the border. Neither gloom nor melancholy pervade the area, because light filters through the delicate foliage of the maple and the rhododendrons are in scale with the garden space. In contrast to the two lower terraces, this terrace is most constant throughout the seasons, with fewer peaks and valleys of performance.

A few steps down and partially hidden by the maple, the second terrace, the sunniest and most cyclical of the three, holds roses and perennials in high contrast to the uppermost terrace. This terrace also is an entity in itself. Further steps lead down to the third terrace, a patio in front of the house for entertaining. Shrubs, including another rhododendron, border the north fence, creating a wall of green. The Cutler garden proves that when rhododendrons are used judiciously they enhance even the smallest garden without imperiously taking over.

Although the full garden of Niki Muller of Portola Valley, California, is not small, the section immediately surrounding the house stands on its own as an example of small garden design. Decks and patios extend the living area outdoors and offer views to the surrounding countryside. The dominant feature in the patio is a large live oak (*Quercus agrifolia*) whose trunk has assumed an almost supine habit but whose wide canopy offers a shady ceiling for plantings beneath it. Among the potted plants on the patio are *Rhododendron* 'Kashu-no-hikari', a white Satsuki azalea with stripes of pink, and the evergreen azalea 'Gay Paree', white with red edges. Other potted plants, including vireya rhododendrons and climbers, create a lush, almost tropical atmosphere. Edging the patio are beds with low-growing plants and small shrubs, contained at the back by a privet (*Ligustrum* spp.) hedge. Adjoining the patio but at a lower level is a swimming pool backed by a hedge of Christmas berry (*Photinia* spp.) interwoven with *Rhododendron* 'Virginia Richards'.

Suggested Reading

Brookes, John. 1969. *Room Outside*. Harmondsworth, England: Penguin Books.

Brookes, John. 1989. *Small Garden Book*. London: Dorling Kindersley.

Page, Gill. 1986. *Town Gardens*. London: Ward, Locke.

CHAPTER 10

Special Features

R HODODENDRONS step naturally into starring roles in the classic woodland and rock gardens. They also agreeably take their place in the mixed border as one shrub among many, and except for a brief spring burst, they humbly defer to other border inhabitants. Even the small garden poses no insurmountable barrier for this vast genus; a perfect solution can always be found among its many members. But even beyond these classic roles, countless other uses await these versatile plants. Special landscape features, such as screens, islands, and ponds, want rhododendrons that comply with a specific landscape need. Other times call for special plant attributes, such as fragrance or fall foliage color. A gardener's imagination in the only limitation.

Hedges

Linear plantings, or hedges, of one or mixed varieties of plants can serve as a backdrop for a border, a screen against unwanted views and intrusions, a delineation of garden areas, or a transition from one garden area to another. Rhododendron hedges, however, do not make windbreaks, as they themselves need protection from the wind.

Rhododendrons with dense, twiggy growth tend to make the

best hedges for clipping into formal shapes. As discussed in Chapter 9, rhododendrons of the subsection *Triflora*, for example *Rhododendron augustinii*, and the numerous evergreen azaleas are amenable to clipping into hedges. Selections from the *Rhododendron* Yellow Hammer Group are good for the formal hedge, as is the evergreen azalea *R. simsii*, which thrives in warm summers.

For unclipped, informal hedges look for vigorously growing types, such as *Rhododendron minus* Carolinianum Group and *R. catawbiense*, both of which have proven useful for single-variety hedges in the southeastern United States. They delineate space with more natural, flowing lines than the clipped hedge. The cultivar *Rhododendron* 'Barto Lavender' with large, wavy leaves is another good choice for the informal hedge because of its vigorous growth habit. Rhododendrons also contribute to hedges of mixed shrubs, along with such appealing companions as *Camellia japonica*, *Gardenia jasminoides*, and *Viburnum japonicum*.

Hedges fill linear space to make a backdrop, a screen, a divider, or a transition. A hedge can be an excellent backdrop to a border, as discussed in Chapter 6. The hedge contains the border just as a stage set contains a theatrical production, heightening the drama playing out in front of it. The hedge as screen may be decorative in foliage and flower, but its main purpose is to hide whatever lies on the other side. Density will be critical for a screen; therefore, choose the most densely growing *Rhododendron* species, such as *R. augustinii*. On the other hand, the hedge that delineates space need not be visually impenetrable. It needs only to separate one space from another. Even a hedge through which you can see, such as a lattice fence, will serve the purpose of marking a property line or separating one garden area from another. Besides stopping the eye as a hedge does for these purposes, hedges can create a corridor or transition from one area to another, pulling the eye—and the foot—along its length to an opening or special sight at the end.

For a hardy hedge with seasonal change in East Coast gardens, I suggest *Rhododendron maximum* and *Cornus alba* 'Gouchaltii'. The dark green foliage of *R. maximum* sustains the bulk all year, and its violet flowers enliven the hedge in spring. Interspersed alongside, the dogwood (*C. alba* 'Gouchaltii') will lighten the look of the rhododendron with its white and light green variegated foliage. And in winter, the dogwood's red stems will lend interest against the dark green leaves of *R. maximum.*

Islands

Island beds in a sea of lawn or other ground cover lend drama and the illusion of space to a garden. They provide a unique way to display rhododendrons and their companions from all angles, like a border viewed from all sides, with the backdrop composed of tall plants in the center. The keys to their success are that their size be in scale with the rest of the garden, that the visual weight of the plantings be balanced with other plantings in the garden, and that some repetition of plant material occur between the island and the rest of the garden. The tracing-paper grid discussed in Chapter 3 can help determine the right scale for the island.

An island design can be unified by a particular color scheme, foliage theme, or plant form, so long as it also connects to the rest of the garden. At the Royal Botanic Garden Edinburgh dwarf varieties are massed on variously shaped islands surrounded by impeccably groomed grass. The island plantings are unified by the dwarf, rounded form of the rhododendrons. The warm yellow and orange colors of many Exbury-Knaphill deciduous azaleas, developed by Lionel de Rothschild of Exbury, could be massed on a large island bed along with companions of compatible flower colors. An island featuring certain species of the subsection *Taliensia* would make a striking island planting, unified by compact form and indumentum on the foliage. Use larger companions to form a backbone, such as *Rhododendron bureavii*, *R. clementinae*, and *R. roxieanum*. Smaller plants for the edges are *R. pronum* and *R. proteoides*.

Evergreen azaleas *Rhododendron* 'Geisha Pink' (unregistered name), 'Rose Greeley', 'Festive', and 'Christmas Cheer' mix well with creeping phlox (*Phlox subulata*) in blue and pink. Stephen Brainerd in a 1994 article in *The Azalean* suggests dividing a

177

circular island bed into two teardrop shapes in a yin-yang position, planting the phlox as ground cover, blue in one section and pink in the other. Over the light blue phlox plant 'Geisha Pink' on the outside and 'Rose Greeley' in the center. Over the pink phlox plant 'Christmas Cheer' on the outside and 'Festive' in the center.

Foundation Plantings

More than any other landscape use, foundation plantings have given rhododendrons a bad name through poor design and maintenance. Homeowners often fail to consider the ultimate size of their chosen variety. More often than not, in ten years the plants have grown above the windowsills. In addition, rhododendrons with heavy leaf texture overpower a small house. Between the overgrown size and heavy texture develops a gothic landscape.

The banking of masses of plants against house foundations has fallen out of vogue among designers. They reason that a garden is meant to be viewed from inside the house, whereas foundation plantings are meant to be viewed from the street, along with the house. The two design concepts are in conflict. In addition, house foundations are no longer considered uniformly ugly, to be covered up as quickly as possible with leaves and flowers. From a practical point of view, any work on a house, such as painting, will be easier without having to maneuver around plants. However, foundation planting can add a decorative touch to a house if done in good taste with respect for the house and the plants (Plate 47). Remember to plant the rhododendrons at least 3 feet (1 meter) from the house and out from under the eaves.

In a foundation planting, the size of the mature plants must be in scale with the house. Numerous hybrid rhododendrons of low stature are on the market. Their approximate height in ten years is given either on the plant tag or in catalogs or plant literature. These small, mounding plants can be placed under windows without threat of impending gloom. Evergreen azaleas are

178

particularly suited for foundation plantings of small houses because of their fine texture. Larger, two-story houses can accommodate larger plants. To add depth to the plantings, curve the bed and plant the rhododendrons in groups.

Rhododendron 'Bow Bells' and *Hydrangea macrophylla* var. *macrophylla* 'Blue Danube' make an excellent combination for a foundation planting. These selections are visually linked by their mounded form, neither growing more than 4 feet (1.2 meters) in ten years. The flowers of 'Bow Bells' begin as deep pink buds that change to light pink as they open. The foliage is jade green. The hydrangea has dark green foliage with blue flowers in summer. The colors of this planting would be best against a house in gray or natural wood siding.

Single-Specimen Accents

Drab entryways, corners, niches, and other small spaces can be turned into a source of delight when decorated with the right plant. The single specimen absolutely must excel in all its attributes of form, foliage, and flower. Many rhododendrons have sufficient year-round charm to hold their own as a single specimen or main accent in a small planting.

Among these star rhododendrons are those chosen by the American Rhododendron Society to receive the Superior Plant Award. *Rhododendron* 'Scintillation', which reaches 5 feet (1.5 meters) in approximately ten years, has deep, shiny green leaves with a wavy texture and bears pastel pink flowers with a flare in the throat. 'Lem's Cameo', which reaches the same height, has deep, shiny green mature foliage and bronze-red new foliage. Its flowers are a striking apricot cream and pink. Numerous other hybrids of recent origin meet the demanding requirements of single specimens, for today's hybridizers are focusing their efforts on producing outstanding characteristics in all the categories of foliage, form, and flower.

Many species also can hold their own as a single specimen for use in small spaces. *Rhododendron schlippenbachii*, with its superb light green summer foliage, bronze fall foliage, and exqui-

Table 18. Rhododendrons suitable as single specimens

	USDA hardiness zone	Plant size in ten years	Plant form	Foliage texture	Flower color
bureavii	6	small shrub	rounded	medium, thick rust ind	w, p
macabeanum	8	medium shrub	upright	coarse, glossy, ind	y
nuttallii	8	medium shrub	open	coarse, wrinkled	large y, w
orbiculare	7	medium shrub	rounded	medium, round	p
pachysanthum	6	dwarf shrub	rounded	medium, silver ind	p, w
proteoides	6	gc	compact	medium, rust ind	w, p
prunifolium	5	small shrub	upright	fine, deciduous	o, r, late
pseudochrysanthum	6	dwarf shrub	compact	medium, glossy	p, w
roxieanum	6	small shrub	compact, upright	narrow, rust ind	w, p
schlippenbachii	4	medium shrub	upright, open	fine, deciduous	p, w
williamsianum	6	gc	mounding	medium, glossy	p
yakushimanum	4	dwarf shrub	mounding	medium, ind	w, p
'Fantastica'	6	small shrub	mounding	medium, dark green	p
'Kashu-no-hikari'	7	dwarf shrub	compact	fine, evergreen azalea	w, p stripes
'Lem's Cameo'	7	medium shrub	rounded	medium, bronze when new	o/p bicolor
'Mi Amor'	8	medium shrub	open	coarse	large w
'Noyo Chief'	9	medium shrub	rounded	medium, glossy	r
'Point Defiance'	6	medium shrub	rounded	coarse	w/p bicolor
'Scintillation'	5	medium shrub	upright	medium, glossy	p
'Songbird'	6	small shrub	compact	fine, glossy	v

'Starbright Champagne'	7	small shrub	rounded	medium	w/y bicolor
'Sunny' (vireya)	10	small shrub	open, rounded	medium, glossy	y/o bicolor
'Unique'	6	small shrub	rounded	medium	p/w bicolor
'Wee Bee'	7	gc	mounded	fine	p, r stripes

Abbreviations: ind = indumentum, gc = ground cover, p = pink, r = red, w = white, v = violet, o = orange, y = yellow. See List of Tables for sizes.

site pink flowers is an excellent plant on its own. Since it is deciduous, back it with an evergreen for winter display of its bare
branches. *Cedrus atlantica* 'Glauca Pendula' is an excellent evergreen companion. Its pendulous branches and blue-green needles perfectly frame the azalea and its delicate spring blooms
and brilliant fall foliage. Another deciduous azalea, the eastern
North American native *R. prunifolium*, with bright green foliage
and late-blooming red flowers, can be grown as a small tree in a
large, shady entryway.

Scale is important in choosing a plant of a size that will neither overwhelm the space nor become lost in it (Plate 48). Frequently, single rhododendron specimens stand in the midst of a
lawn, but from a design point of view, these efforts usually fail
because of inequality of scale. Either the plant is much too small
in proportion to the lawn and house, or it is much too large,
overwhelming both lawn and house. However, with an equal
scale between rhododendron and lawn and house, the design
scheme can succeed.

More appropriate scale for single specimens is available in
many different corners of the garden. Single specimens can be
used as the focal point at the end of a corridor, drawing the eye
forward for a visual reward, just as a piece of garden sculpture
would. Or a single plant can be placed as a signpost to mark a
transition from one garden area to another. A single specimen
can enhance a stairway or deck if planted to be visible through or
over the hard structure. In the garden of Dee and Dick Daneri in
Fortuna, California, the beautiful *Rhododendron* 'Mi Amor' is
planted against the deck so that its large, fragrant flowers reach
above the deck railing. At the garden of Richard and Barbara
Levin in Bellingham, Washington, visitors see a specimen of *Rhododendron* 'Grace Seabrook' through a stair railing as they de-
scend into the garden.

Bonsai, Espalier, and Topiary

By pruning and manipulating growth patterns, gardeners can
train their rhododendrons to perform amazing feats. These

plants can be made to retain their miniature size into maturity (bonsai), to climb walls (espalier), and to assume unnatural shapes (topiary). While some gardeners consider this "plant torture," others find great satisfaction in practicing the garden arts of bonsai, espalier, and topiary.

Bonsai creates the illusion of a mature plant in the wild. It is an excellent way to energize a small space. Display the plants in small areas, such as patios and decks, on structures that bring them near eye level, so viewers can appreciate them close-up. Evergreen azaleas have been used for bonsai for centuries. Two popular species are *Rhododendron nakaharae* and *R. kiusianum*, which is sometimes deciduous. The evergreen Satsuki and Kurume azaleas from Japan are excellent for bonsai because of their small leaves and attractive trunk and branch habit. Numerous cultivars from these groups are on the market, such as the Satsuki *Rhododendron* 'Kazan' and the Kurume *Rhododendron* 'Christmas Cheer'. Other bonsai candidates can be found among the hybrid groups Gable, Glenn Dale, Shammarello, North Tisbury, Linwood, and Robin Hill.

The art of espalier—training a plant to grow against a flat surface by pruning and manipulating its branches—is occasionally practiced on rhododendrons. An espalier displays beautiful foliage and flowers without the distraction of poor form. Especially appropriate for this technique are the members of subsection *Maddenia* and their hybrids, which tend to be rangy in form but superb in leaf texture, flower, and perhaps best of all, fragrance (Plate 49). As gardeners discover the magnificent qualities of the *Maddenia* rhododendrons, the practice of espalier will undoubtedly increase, especially in warmer climates where hard freezes will not damage them.

A good combination for espalier is *Rhododendron johnstonianum* and *Clematis* 'Jackmanii Rubra'. The lanky rhododendron takes new form trained against a lattice frame. And in spring, the glory of its fragrant flowers is well displayed. The clematis intertwines with the rhododendron, coloring the framework with reddish pink flowers in summer.

Topiary is the art of pruning and shaping plants into odd or ornamental shapes. It is rarely practiced with rhododendrons,

183

The art of espalier is especially suited to rhododendrons from subsection *Maddenia* because of their lanky growth habit.

but at least one azalea—*Rhododendron* 'Fielder's White'—has submitted to it at the Marston House Garden in San Diego. With the growing interest in topiary, azaleas and other rhododendrons are bound to contribute to the form.

Containers

Rhododendrons grown in containers can serve as accents on decks, patios, or in borders, or they can be used to build whole gardens (Plate 50). Potted rhododendrons can make an entryway inviting, enhance the coziness of a deck or patio, serve as sentinels to mark transitions between garden areas, or theatrically focus the eye on a center-stage spot. Pot-grown rhododendrons enliven a garden like exclamation points.

With container-grown plants, the pot itself draws attention as any hard structure in the garden does; therefore, find containers that enhance the plant's assets and contribute to the unity of the whole garden. In a full garden of container-grown plants, such as Susan Baker's rooftop garden in Vancouver, British Columbia, the individual containers will be less punctuating and more unifying, making a collection of containers with some common denominator, such as material or shape.

Rhododendrons are highly suitable for pot culture because of their surface-feeding, fibrous root system. Virtually any rhododendron can be grown in a pot, restricted only by its size in maturity. Container culture will fulfill a rhododendron's demands for acidic, well-draining, moist soil—perhaps even better than the ground—so long as the roots are kept cool in summer and protected from prolonged frost in winter. Generally on the West Coast of the United States, container-grown plants may be over-wintered outdoors, but on the East Coast they will have to be protected indoors. Rhododendrons will grow in containers full of many different kinds of media, but a good, basic mix consists of equal parts peat, perlite, and bark. The plants will need a regular regimen of fertilizing.

Scale is most critical in the use of container-grown rhododendrons: the plant and pot must be visually balanced. The symmetrical, mounded shapes of *Rhododendron* 'Nancy Evans', 'Naselle', 'September Song', or 'Dora Amateis', for instance, lend formality, while the asymmetrical forms of the big-leaf rhododendrons and members of subsection *Maddenia* lend informality. Many dwarf cultivars are excellent for containers, such as *Rhododendron* 'Patty Bee', 'Ginny Gee', 'Wee Bee', 'Curlew', and 'Princess Anne'.

Mobility is a great asset of growing rhododendrons in containers. Pot and all can move in and out of the limelight, depending on the plant's performance of the moment. A plant with a single asset of new foliage growth, brilliant flower, or seductive fragrance can take center stage during its peak and then retreat to an inconspicuous location. Placing potted plants in a border is a good way to augment a color scheme at just the right time.

Troughs are a choice of container that add attractive hard

structure to the garden with their weathered, mossy rock surfaces. They also offer a hospitable environment and the perfect frame for displaying the smallest rhododendrons. The alpine rhododendrons that are slow growing, prostrate, and small-leafed are particularly suited to troughs and can be delightfully displayed together or with companions. Among the most diminutive species are *Rhododendron calostrotum* subsp. *keleticum* Radicans Group and *R. forrestii* subsp. *forrestii* Repens Group. Other larger alpine species and cultivars, such as *R. keiskei* 'Yaku Fairy', *R. williamsianum*, *Rhododendron* 'Patty Bee', 'Honsu's Baby', and 'Too Bee', can fill a trough until they outgrow it, when they will easily transplant to the rock garden. Diminutive dwarf conifers and other ericaceous plants, such as *Andromeda polifolia* 'Compacta' and *Arctostaphylos alpina*, make excellent companions in troughs and offer a contrast of texture and form.

Four diminutive evergreen species create a miniature alpine garden when combined in a trough. *Rhododendron impeditum* Litangense Group with violet flowers, *R. keiskei* 'Yaku Fairy' with yellow flowers, *Vaccinium macrocarpon* 'Hamilton' with pink flowers, and *Tsuga canadensis* 'Cloud Prince' in a light blue-green make a quintessential spring color combination.

The traditional alpine trough is made from the porous, volcanic rock called "tufa." The man-made imitation is called a hypertufa trough. It is made from a mixture of peat, cement, and vermiculite to create a light, porous material similar to tufa. The cement may change the soil pH, making acid-loving plants require amendments. The advantages of growing alpines in a trough are cool soil, mobility, and close-up display. Instructions for hypertufa trough construction and the best soil mixes are available from the North American Rock Garden Society.

Troughs not only offer their inhabitants optimum growing environments but they function as landscape accents much like sculpture. The design key to planting the trough is scale. Many rhododendrons and their companions will eventually become too large and will have to be planted elsewhere. Scale is also the key to placing the trough. Like bonsai, the trough needs a small area, such as a deck, terrace, or entryway, where it will not be lost. Groups of troughs should occupy a larger space, as do the grand trough displays at the Royal Botanic Garden Edinburgh and the VanDusen Garden in Vancouver, British Columbia.

Raised Beds

A raised bed of amended soil on top of a well-draining base supplies many assets of a trough. A raised bed is not mobile, of course, but is does provide optimum soil conditions and a visual frame for the planting. Both the display of plants within the bed and the bed itself function as design elements, just as with troughs. The raised bed, however, tends to be larger, supporting many more plants and occupying a larger space in the garden. By definition, a raised bed is built above ground level, with materials such as railroad ties, bricks, or rocks holding the added soil. Any hard, non-alkaline material will make a good frame. Stones or bricks can be cemented together with hypertufa to keep water from draining away too quickly. A recommended size for the bed is 5 by 2 feet (1.5 by 0.6 meters) so all parts are within reach.

A raised bed is a good place for alpine rhododendrons and companions that are particularly demanding in their cultural requirements. Perfect drainage, pH, and nutrition are relatively easy to provide in a raised bed. For rhododendrons and other ericaceous plants, the bed should be in dappled sunlight but open to the sky to keep tree limbs, leaves, and drips from falling on it. The site may also need a windbreak. The materials and the site will dictate the shape of the bed, but two raised beds constructed and planted as mirror images would be appropriate for a formal garden, or one gracefully curving bed would be appropriate for the informal garden. On a small site, it could simply substitute for a classic rock garden.

The peat wall, a British phenomenon not much used in North America, is a variation on the raised bed using blocks of moist peat in place of the hard frame. The peat wall at the Royal Botanic Garden Edinburgh at the foot of a north-facing slope, was built with moist peat blocks dug from a peat bog and constructed much the same as any wall. The space between the peat wall and slope is filled with a mixture of soil and peat. Although most garden sites will best accommodate a raised bed, the peat wall demonstrates how cultural requirements can be the inspiration for new garden features. The peat wall offers a highly controlled soil environment for acid-loving plants where native soils tend to be alkaline.

Water Features

In the wild, rhododendrons grow next to streams, on cliffs drenched with rain, and near ponds. Even bogs are home to *Rhododendron canadense* in Newfoundland and *R. occidentale* in the Siskiyou Mountains of Oregon. Nothing could be more natural than planting rhododendrons near water in the garden. The trick is to plant them in free-draining soil, not soggy soil, for their roots need air.

Many gardeners do indeed place their rhododendrons near water features with good design results. At the Crystal Springs Rhododendron Garden in Portland, Oregon, high above a pond next to a stream rhododendrons grace the bank with their voluptuous blooms. At the Edward B. Dunn Garden in Seattle, a bright red azalea energizes the lush greenery surrounding a small pond. At the Herb and Betty Spady garden near Salem, Oregon, rhododendrons are mirrored in the pond at their feet. An island in that pond is home to an exuberant planting of Exbury-type azaleas. Japanese gardens are rarely without water, since a key ingredient is a reflecting pond for meditation. The sheared azaleas at the edge of a pond at the Nitobe Garden in Vancouver, British Columbia, are doubled in the still water. In the Japanese garden at the Washington Park Arboretum in Seattle, rhododendrons grow right to the edge of a stream, dropping petals onto the surface during bloom season. Water features and rhododendrons bring out the best in each other.

Plantings for Fall Color

In fall, many deciduous azaleas put on a second show of color in their leaves, joining the cast of many other deciduous shrubs and trees for the big fall show. Among the East Coast natives, *Rhododendron calendulaceum*, *R. viscosum*, and *R. vaseyi* add their gold and russet hues to the garden landscape. The crimson fall foliage of the West Coast native azalea, *R. occidentale*, makes a splendid show. Two members of subsection *Sciadorhodion*, *R. quinquefolium* and *R. schlippenbachii*, are fall color contributors, with the latter turning a brilliant orange-red for a stunning spot of color. The fall foliage of azalea *R. luteum* ranges from red to orange to purple. The evergreen foliage of *R. rubiginosum* and *R. dauricum* turns russet in the fall, while the foliage of the *Rhododendron* PJM Group deepens to a rich mahogany. For additional fall color, many other ericaceous plants make good companions, such as *Enkianthus perulatus*, *Vaccinium corymbosum*, and *Leucothoe fontanesiana* 'Scarletta'.

Plantings for Fragrance

The genus *Rhododendron* is bestowed with so many fine garden attributes that fragrance is hardly necessary to place it among the most worthy of all genera. Yet there it is. The sweetly scented *Rhododendron maddenii*, *R. lindleyi*, *R. nuttallii*, and *R. burmanicum*, all of the subsection *Maddenia*, are worth growing for their scent alone. The exquisite white tinged pink flowers of *R. edgeworthii* deliver a fragrance so delicious it should be planted where viewers can get close enough to enjoy it fully. Many East Coast native azaleas are fragrant, and the long blooming season of a collection can perfume a garden well into the summer. The honeysweet scent of azalea *R. luteum* can infuse a whole garden.

The evergreen species *Rhododendron auriculatum*, *R. decorum*, *R. fortunei*, and *R. diaprepes*, and many of their progeny, are fragrant. *Rhododendron* 'Loderi King George' and 'Loderi Venus' and others of the Loderi group are renowned for their heavy fragrance. Many vireyas also are fragrant: *Rhododendron jasmini-*

189

Table 19. Fragrant rhododendrons

	USDA hardiness zone	Plant size in ten years	Plant form	Foliage texture	Flower color
decorum	7	medium shrub	upright, compact	medium	w, p
edgeworthii	8	small shrub	open	medium, wrinkled	w, p
fortunei	5	medium shrub	open, upright	medium	p, w
griffithianum	8	medium shrub	open, upright	medium, light green	w, p
jasminiflorum (vireya)	10	small shrub	spreading	fine	w
lindleyi	9	medium shrub	open, upright	medium	w, p
loranthiflorum (vireya)	10	small shrub	upright	medium, glossy	w
luteum	5	small shrub	open, upright	medium, deciduous	y
nuttallii	8	medium shrub	open	coarse, wrinkled	large y
occidentale	6	medium shrub	upright	medium, deciduous	w, p
periclymenoides	5	medium shrub	upright	fine, deciduous	p, w
viscosum	5	medium shrub	upright	fine, deciduous	w, p
'Aravir' (vireya)	10	small shrub	compact	medium	w
'Else Frye'	8	small shrub	open	medium, glossy	w, p
'Fragrantissimum'	8	small shrub	open	medium	w, p
'Harry Tagg'	5	small shrub	compact	medium	w, y
'Lady Alice Fitzwilliam'	9	medium shrub	open	medium	w
'Marshall Pierce Madison' (vireya)	10	small shrub	upright	coarse	large p
'Mi Amor'	8	medium shrub	open	medium	large w
'Rose Scott'	8	small shrub	open	medium	w, p

Abbreviations: ind = indumentum, gc = ground cover, p = pink, r = red, w = white, v = violet, o = orange, y = yellow. See List of Tables for sizes.

florum, R. loranthiflorum, R. konori, and *R. tuba.* These deserve to be placed within smelling distance for the full benefit of their wonderful scent.

Besides flower fragrance, many rhododendron leaves are pleasantly aromatic and add yet another dimension to the garden. Many members of section *Pogonanthum—Rhododendron anthopogon* subsp. *anthopogon, R. cephalanthum, R. primuliflorum, R. sargentianum,* and *R. trichostomum*—have highly aromatic foliage. The leaves, especially when rubbed or crushed, waft a pungent scent into the air.

Garden Tours

In Orleans, Massachusetts, the Cape Cod Chapter of the American Rhododendron Society built and maintains a rhododendron garden designed in island beds by society member Connie LeClair, a landscape designer. The site is a village green of approximately 1 acre (0.4 hectares), but it appears even larger because of connecting public grounds. The display garden takes up 5950 square feet (546 square meters), in three island beds, one of which is two levels, that together roughly form a circle. The goal in designing the garden was to display a variety of rhododendrons, respecting the design elements of scale, textural contrast, and color harmony. The large-leafed plants form the midrib of the islands with medium- and small-leafed plants on the edges. The color scheme moves around the circle from pink and white into purple, yellow, coral, white, red, white, cream, coral, and back to pink. Spring bloom time was considered to avoid spottiness from lack of bloom in certain places. Three plants of each variety total 131 rhododendrons. Hostas (*Hosta* spp.) and daylilies (*Hemerocallis* spp.) are companion plants.

Filoli, a formal garden in Woodside, California, near San Francisco, offers proof that rhododendrons can be used in many ways besides classic woodland and rock gardens. Near the estate house, the bright red evergreen azalea *Rhododendron* 'Ward's Ruby' accents boxwood hedges framed by the violet flowers of *Wisteria* (Plate 51). In various spots and with various compan-

191

ions, 'Ward's Ruby' punctuates the meticulous landscape with its brilliant flower color. In the walled garden against a warm brick wall, *Rhododendron* 'Fragrantissimum' is trained as an espalier, spreading its fragrant flowers in a splendid display. In a unique, hedge-like planting against another wall, interspersed with shrubby magnolias (*Magnolia* spp.), *Rhododendron* 'Lurline' billows out its pastel pink blossoms in puffy clouds. At the back of the grounds, a collection of large rhododendrons grows in a walled, shady area. The pink-violet flowers of *Rhododendron* 'Mrs. G. W. Leak' arch over the top of the wall in a most inviting way.

In Sebastopol, California, Parker Smith has designed his small garden around seasonally changing flower color combinations. He uses many varieties in the fragrant subsection *Maddenia*. As the flower colors change from the yellows and blue-violets of early spring to the later whites and pinks and red accents, fragrance is an added sensuous delight. Among the fragrant *Maddenia* varieties are the frilly white *Rhododendron* 'Harry Tagg'; the white tinged pink *R. maddenii*; the white *R. ciliicalyx*; the yellow-blotched white *R. cuffeanum*; the yellow-blotched, white tinged pink *R. scopulorum*; and the pale yellow *R. nuttallii*. The later blooming Exbury azaleas extend the season of fragrance into late spring.

Suggested Reading

Challis, Myles. 1988. *Exotic Gardening in Cool Climates.* London: Fourth Estate.

Galle, Fred. 1987. *Azaleas.* Portland, Oregon: Timber Press.

Bibliography

Adler, Judy. 1997. An ecologist's garden. *Pacific Horticulture* 58: 43–48.

Aker, Scott. 1998. IPM: an inside look. *American Gardener* 77: 7–13.

American Rhododendron Society. 1945. Articles of Incorporation of the American Rhododendron Society. In *Rhododendron Yearbook for 1945*. Portland, Oregon: American Rhododendron Society. 125–127.

Ardle, Jon, and Sarah Higgens. 1997. Designing for the new millennium. *Garden* 122: 738–741.

Austin, Sandra. 1998. *Color in Garden Design*. Newtown, Connecticut: Taunton Press.

Bacher, John G. 1945. Rhododendrons for the rockery. In *Rhododendron Yearbook for 1945*. Portland, Oregon: American Rhododendron Society. 50–57.

Bailey, L. H. 1976. *Hortus Third: A Concise Dictionary of Plants Cultivated in the United States and Canada*. Rev. and exp. by staff of Liberty Hyde Bailey Hortorium. New York: Macmillan.

Baker, Susan. 1988. Rooftop living with rhododendrons. *Journal American Rhododendron Society* 42: 201.

Barrett, Clarence. 1997. The rhododendron standard. *Journal American Rhododendron Society* 51: 90–91.

Betts, Edwin M., and Hazelhurst B. Perkins. 1941. *Thomas Jeffer-*

son's Garden at Monticello. Charlottesville: University Press of Virginia.

Beveridge, Charles E., and Paul Rocheleau. 1995. *Frederick Law Olmsted: Designing the American Landscape*. New York: Rizzoli.

Birren, Faber. 1961. *Creative Color*. New York: Van Nostrand Reinhold.

Blake, Felice. 1985. Rhododendrons for foliage effect. *Journal American Rhododendron Society* 39: 2–4.

Brainerd, Stephen S. 1994. Designing with azaleas. *Azalean* 16: 73–74.

Brainerd, Stephen S. 1996. Azaleas by design. *Azalean* 18: 14.

Brookes, John. 1969. *Room Outside*. Harmondsworth, England: Penguin Books.

Brookes, John. 1984. *Garden*. London: Dorling Kindersley.

Brookes, John. 1989. *Small Garden Book*. London: Dorling Kindersley.

Brookes, John. 1991. *Book of Garden Design*. New York: MacMillan.

Brookes, John. 1994. *Garden Design Workbook*. New York: Dorling Kindersley.

Brookes, John. 1998. *Natural Landscapes*. New York: Dorling Kindersley.

Brown, Jane. 1995. *Beatrix: The Gardening Life of Beatrix Jones Farrand*. New York: Viking.

Burrell, C. Colston. 1995. Preface. In *Woodland Gardens, Shade Gets Chic*. Brooklyn Handbook No. 145. Brooklyn, New York: Brooklyn Botanic Garden.

Callaway, Dorothy J. 1994. *World of Magnolias*. Portland: Timber Press.

Cave, Phillip. 1993. *Creating Japanese Gardens*. Boston: Charles E. Tuttle.

Challis, Myles. 1988. *Exotic Gardening in Cool Climates*. London: Fourth Estate.

Chijiiwa, Hideaki. 1987. *Guide to Creative Color Combinations*. Rockport, Massachusetts: Rockport Publishers.

Cook, Alleyne. 1997. Tower Court: a personal account. *Journal American Rhododendron Society* 51: 102–104.

Cowan, J. Macqueen. 1956. Stonefield-Argyll. In *Royal Horticul-*

tural Society Yearbook. London: Rhododendron Horticultural Society. 16–21.

Cox, Peter. 1985. *Smaller Rhododendrons.* Portland, Oregon: Timber Press.

Cox, Peter. 1990. *Larger Rhododendron Species.* Portland, Oregon: Timber Press.

Cox, Peter. 1991. British-American Sichuan expedition, 1990. *Journal American Rhododendron Society* 45: 62–65, 101–104.

Cox, Peter. 1993. *Cultivation of Rhododendrons.* London: B. T. Batsford.

Cox, Peter A., and Kenneth N. E. Cox. 1997. *Encyclopedia of Rhododendron Species.* Perth, Scotland: Glendoick.

Cross, James E. 1980. Some dwarf rhododendrons for the Northeast. *Bulletin of the American Rock Garden Society* 38: 22–27.

Cullen, James. 1996. The importance of the herbarium. In *Rhododendron Story*, Ed. Cynthia Postan. London: Royal Horticultural Society. 38–48.

Davidian, H. H. 1982. *Rhododendron Species Volume I, Lepidotes.* Portland, Oregon: Timber Press.

Davidian, H. H. 1989. *Rhododendron Species Volume II, Elepidotes, Part 1.* Portland, Oregon: Timber Press.

Davidian, H. H. 1992. *Rhododendron Species Volume III, Elepidotes, Part 2.* Portland, Oregon: Timber Press.

Davidian, H. H. 1995. *Rhododendron Species Volume IV, Azaleas.* Portland, Oregon: Timber Press.

Dickey, Page. 1997. *Breaking Ground.* New York: Workman.

Dirr, Michael A. 1997. *Dirr's Hardy Trees and Shrubs.* Portland, Oregon: Timber Press.

Dome, Arthur P. 1992. Ericaceous companion plants. *Journal American Rhododendron Society* 46: 86–89.

Dome, Arthur P. 1995. Cassiopes and phyllodoces: pseudo-heathers of North America. *Rock Garden Quarterly* 53: 17–20.

Dome, Arthur P. 1996. Rhododendrons for the rock garden. *Journal American Rhododendron Society* 50: 122–124.

Drew, Leslie. 1998. Honey fungus: the story of a deadly takeover. *Journal American Rhododendron Society* 52: 44–47.

Druse, Ken. 1989. *Natural Garden.* New York: Clarkson Potter.

Druse, Ken. 1996. *Collector's Garden.* New York: Clarkson Potter.

Eck, Joe. 1996. *Elements of Design.* New York: Henry Holt.

Elliott, Brent. 1996. Rhododendrons in British gardens: a short history. In *Rhododendron Story,* Ed. Cynthia Postan. London: Royal Horticultural Society. 156–186.

Epstein, Harold. 1991. Saga of a woodland garden. *Bulletin of the American Rock Garden Society* 49: 3–10.

Fairbrother, Nan. 1974. *Nature of Landscape Design.* New York: Alfred A. Knopf.

Farrer, Reginald. 1921. *Rainbow Ridge.* Rpt. London: Cadogan Books, 1986.

Flint, Harrison L. 1983. *Landscape Plants for Eastern North America.* New York: Wiley-Interscience.

Galle, Fred. 1987. *Azaleas.* Portland, Oregon: Timber Press.

Garden Club of America. 1996. *Plants That Merit Attention: Volume II—Shrubs,* Eds. Janet Meakin Poor and Nancy Peterson Brewster. Portland, Oregon: Timber Press.

Garu, Augusto. 1993. *Color Harmonies.* Chicago: University of Chicago Press.

Gillmore, Robert. 1996. *Woodland Garden.* Dallas: Taylor.

Grant, John A., and Carol L. Grant. 1954. *Garden Design.* Seattle: University of Washington Press.

Greer, Harold E. 1996. *Greer's Guidebook to Available Rhododendrons.* Eugene, Oregon: Offshoot Publications.

Grese, Robert E. 1992. *Jens Jensen, Maker of Natural Parks and Gardens.* Baltimore: Johns Hopkins Press.

Griswold, Mac. 1996. Fairsted: a landscape as Olmsted's Looking Glass. *Arnoldia* 56: 2–20.

Griswold, Mac, and Eleanor Weller. 1988. *Golden Age of American Gardens.* New York: Harry N. Abrams.

Grossman, Jeannette. 1950. Ground covers for rhododendrons. *Quarterly Bulletin of the American Rhododendron Society* 4: 120–121.

Grossman, Jeanette. 1952. Dwarf species rhododendrons. *Quarterly Bulletin of the American Rhododendron Society* 6: 110–111.

Groszkiewicz, Ted. 1984. Azalea/rhododendron bonsai. *Journal American Rhododendron Society* 38: 113.

Hanger, Francis. 1947. Miniature and alpine rhododendrons.

In *Rhododendron Yearbook for 1947*. Portland, Oregon: American Rhododendron Society. 27–37.

Hansen, Ruth M. 1950. The use of color in rhododendron plantings. *Quarterly Bulletin of the American Rhododendron Society* 4: 105–108.

Hatch, Reuben. 1984. The rock garden and rhododendrons. *Journal American Rhododendron Society* 38: 146.

Hay, Ida. 1995. *Science in the Pleasure Ground*. Boston: Northeastern University Press.

Henny, John. 1995. ARS charter members: John Henny. *Journal American Rhododendron Society* 49: 80.

Hinkley, Dan. 1997. Creating great bones for urban gardens with trees and shrubs for multi-seasonal interest. Lecture presented at the Northwest Horticultural Society Urban Garden Symposium, 24 April 1997 at the Center for Urban Horticulture, University of Washington, Seattle.

Hobhouse, Penelope. 1985. *Color in Your Garden*. Boston: Little, Brown.

Hobhouse, Penelope. 1989. *Borders*. New York: Harper and Row.

Hobhouse, Penelope. 1992. *Gardening Through the Ages*. New York: Simon and Schuster.

Holaday, Joseph A. 1992. The Barto rhododendron nursery. *Journal American Rhododendron Society* 46: 93, 97.

Holmdahl, O. E. 1946. Rhododendrons in the landscape design. In *Rhododendron Yearbook for 1946*. Portland, Oregon: American Rhododendron Society. 43–52.

Hooker, Sir Joseph Dalton. 1905. *Himalayan Journal*. London: Ward, Locke.

Hootman, Steven. 1993. RSF displays new alpine garden. *Journal American Rhododendron Society* 47: 30–31.

Irving, E., and R. Hebda. 1993. Concerning the origin and distribution of rhododendrons. *Journal American Rhododendron Society* 47: 139–146, 157–162.

James, D. W. 1950. Notes on alpine rhododendrons. *Quarterly Bulletin of the American Rhododendron Society* 4: 77–78.

Jekyll, Gertrude. 1899. *Wood and Garden*. Rpt. Suffolk, England: Antique Collectors Club, 1981.

Jekyll, Gertrude. 1901. *Wall, Water and Woodland Gardens.* Rpt. Suffolk, England: Antique Collectors Club, 1982.

Jekyll, Gertrude. 1908. *Colour Schemes for the Flower Garden.* Rpt. Suffolk, England: Antique Collectors Club, 1982.

Jones, Adele. 1995. Happy birthday holiday: a northwestern celebration. *Journal American Rhododendron Society* 49: 30–34, 43–46.

Justice, Clive. 1984. A program to evaluate rhododendrons for landscape purposes. *Journal American Rhododendron Society* 38: 147–150.

Kingdon Ward, Frank. 1913. *Land of the Blue Poppy.* Rpt. London: Minerva Press, 1933.

Kingdon Ward, Frank. 1930. *Plant Hunting on the Edge of the World.* Rpt. London: Cadogan Books, 1985.

Kingsbury, Noël, and Brita von Schoenaich. 1995. Learning from nature. *Garden* 120: 366–369.

Kneller, Marianna. 1995. *Book of Rhododendrons.* Portland, Oregon: Timber Press.

Konrad, Mark. 1992. Designing a classic rhododendron garden. *Journal American Rhododendron Society* 46: 94–96.

Kron, Kathleen A. 1996. Identifying the native azaleas. *Azalean* 18: 72–74.

Kruckeberg, Arthur R. 1982. *Gardening with Native Plants of the Pacific Northwest.* Seattle: University of Washington Press.

Kruckeberg, Arthur R. 1998. The Japanese design connection. *Washington Park Arboretum Bulletin* 60: 14–18.

Lacey, Stephen. 1998. The adventurous gardener. Lecture presented to Whatcom Horticultural Society 25 February 1998 at Whatcom Museum of History and Art, Bellingham, Washington.

Leach, David G. 1961. *Rhododendrons of the World.* New York: Charles Scribner's Sons.

Lilley, S. E. 1972. *Ericaceous and Peat Loving Plants.* London: Alpine Garden Society.

Livingston, Philip A., and Franklin H. West. 1978. *Hybrids and Hybridizers: Rhododendrons and Azaleas for Eastern North America.* Newtown Square, Pennsylvania: Harrowood Books.

Lloyd, Christopher. 1986. *Mixed Border.* RHS Wisley Handbook. London: Cassell Educational.

Lovejoy, Ann. 1990. *Border in Bloom.* Seattle: Sasquatch Books.

Lovejoy, Ann. 1993. *American Mixed Border.* New York: Macmillan.

Lovejoy, Ann. 1997. Gardening from scratch. *Pacific Horticulture* 58: 35–39.

Lyte, Charles. 1983. *Plant Hunters.* London: Orbis.

Magnani, Denise. 1995. *The Winterthur Garden: Henry Francis du Pont's Romance with the Land.* New York: Harry N. Abrams.

Manigault, Edward L. 1953. Native azaleas in naturalistic plantings. *Quarterly Bulletin of the American Rhododendron Society* 7: 164–172.

McHoy, Peter. 1984a. *Garden Construction.* Poole, England: Blandford Press.

McHoy, Peter. 1984b. *Garden Planning and Design.* Poole, England: Blandford Press.

McLellan, George K., and Sandra McDonald. 1996. Magic on the mountain: an azalea heaven on Gregory Bald. *Journal American Rhododendron Society* 50: 90–94.

Meier, Lauren. 1996. Notes on restoring the woody plants at Fairsted. *Arnoldia* 56: 26–31.

Metheny, D. 1991. *Hardy Heather Species.* Seaside, Oregon: Frontier.

Minch, Jean. 1987. Armchair watering. *Journal American Rhododendron Society* 41: 94–95.

Mitchell, R. A. 1997. Vireyas in Hawaii. 1997. *Journal American Rhododendron Society* 51: 122–124.

Mossman, Doris, and Frank Mossman. 1982. *Rhododendron lapponicum* and *Rhododendron camtschaticum* subspecies *glandulosum* in the Nome, Alaska, area. *Journal American Rhododendron Society* 36: 94–95.

Muirhead, G. D. 1951. Trees to associate with rhododendrons. *Quarterly Bulletin of the American Rhododendron Society* 5: 145–151.

Muller, Charles H., and Keith White. 1996. Over the Doshong La. *Journal American Rhododendron Society* 50: 146–153, 160.

Munsell, Albert H. 1929. *Munsell Book of Color.* New Windsor, New York: Macbeth.

Murcott, Richard. 1997. *Journal American Rhododendron Society* 51: 156–157.

Nachman, Rosalie. 1985. Designing shady gardens. *Journal American Rhododendron Society* 39: 10–12.

National Trust for Scotland. 1993. Arduaine Garden. Marketing Division of the National Trust for Scotland. Pamphlet J1468/WWD.250M.

Nosal, Matthew A. 1976. Azaleas in the landscape: using pink to perfection. *Quarterly Bulletin of the American Rhododendron Society* 30: 144–147.

Ogden, Doan R. 1979. Rhododendrons in the landscape. *Quarterly Bulletin of the American Rhododendron Society* 24: 36–38.

Page, Gill. 1986. *Town Gardens.* London: Ward, Locke.

Parks, Joe. 1996. Secrets to beautiful rhododendron garden design. *Journal American Rhododendron Society* 50: 182–184.

Parks, Joe. 1997. Paths for the informal garden. *Journal American Rhododendron Society* 51: 283–286.

Price, Charles, and Glenn Withey. 1997. Mingling, layering and sequencing: getting the most out of limited space. Lecture presented at the Northwest Horticultural Society Urban Garden Symposium, 24 April 1997 at the Center for Urban Horticulture, University of Washington, Seattle.

Reiley, H. Edward. 1992. *Success with Rhododendrons and Azaleas.* Portland, Oregon: Timber Press.

RHS Colour Chart. 1966. Royal Horticultural Society, London.

Ring, George. 1980. Small rhododendrons and azaleas for the mid South. *Bulletin of the American Rock Garden Society* 38: 27–31.

Robertson, Iain M. 1997a. First things first: creating intimacy with garden architecture. Lecture presented at the Northwest Horticultural Society Urban Garden Symposium, 24 April 1997 at the Center for Urban Horticulture, University of Washington, Seattle.

Robertson, Iain M. 1997b. Designing the garden path experience. *Washington Park Arboretum Bulletin* 59: 6–10.

Rock, Joseph F. 1948. Dr. Joseph F. Rock letter. *Quarterly Bulletin of the American Rhododendron Society* 2: 7–8.

Roth, Sally. 1997. *Natural Landscaping.* Emmaus, Pennsylvania: Rodale Press.

Royal Horticultural Society. 1998. *Rhododendron Handbook.* London: Royal Horticultural Society.

Salley, Homer. 1995. The Delp rhododendron hybrids. *Journal American Rhododendron Society* 49: 122–125.

Salley, Homer. 1997. Roan Mountain: its rhododendrons and its festivals. *Journal American Rhododendron Society* 51: 27–29.

Salley, Homer, and Harold Greer. 1992. *Rhododendron Hybrids.* 2d ed. Portland, Oregon: Timber Press.

Schenk, George. 1997. *Moss Gardening.* Portland, Oregon: Timber Press.

Scott, Frank J. 1870. *Victorian Gardens: The Art of Beautifying Suburban Homes, A Victorian Handbook.* New York: D. Appleton.

Sheedy, Betty. 1974. Landscaping—how to if you want to. *Quarterly Bulletin of the American Rhododendron Society* 28: 32.

Skinner, Henry T. 1955. In search of native azaleas. *Morris Arboretum Bulletin* 6: 3–22.

Smith, Cecil. 1952. On selecting a site for a rhododendron garden. *Quarterly Bulletin of the American Rhododendron Society* 6: 43–44.

Smyser, Carol A. 1982. *Nature's Design: A Practical Guide to Natural Landscaping.* Emmaus, Pennsylvania: Rodale Press.

Stockmal, Robert. 1988. Designing with rhododendrons. *Journal American Rhododendron Society* 42: 140–141.

Streatfield, David. 1998. The resonance of Japan in Pacific Northwest gardens. *Washington Park Arboretum Bulletin* 60: 2–5.

Strong, Roy. 1987. *Creating Small Gardens.* New York: Villard Books.

Sunset Western Garden Book. 1988. Menlo Park, California: Lane.

Tait, William. 1997. The Royal Botanic Garden, Edinburgh: a walk by the peat walls. *Hortus* 41: 40–46.

Thomas, Graham Stuart. 1989. *Rock Garden and its Plants.* Portland, Oregon: Sagapress/Timber Press.

Tobex, George B., Jr. 1973. *A History of Landscape Architecture: The Relationship of People to Environment.* New York: American Elsevier.

Toll, Julie. 1995. *Small Garden.* Royal Horticultural Society Collection. London: Conran Octopus.

Tyrrell, C. Gordon. 1969. Companion plants for rhododendrons. *Quarterly Bulletin of the American Rhododendron Society* 23: 158–161.

Wasowski, Andy. 1997. The building envelope. *American Gardener* 76: 26–33.

Whittemore, Ev. 1994. Rock garden design: tips for beginners. *Bulletin of the American Rock Garden Society* 52: 21–24.

Wick, Jock. 1997. The evolution from accessorized yard to intimate garden. Lecture presented at the Northwest Horticultural Society Urban Garden Symposium, 24 April 1997 at the Center for Urban Horticulture, University of Washington, Seattle.

Wilson, Ernest H. 1913. *Naturalist in Western China.* Rpt. London: Cadogan Books, 1986.

Wott, John A. 1998. Beyond the emperor's gates. *Washington Park Arboretum Bulletin* 60: 6–10.

Ziegler, Catherine. 1996. *Harmonious Garden.* Portland, Oregon: Timber Press.

Index of Plants

Abies 72, 130
  A. koreana 'Starkers Dwarf'
    106, 121
  A. nordmanniana 'Golden
    Spreader' 121, 122
Acer 14, 71, 72
  A. circinatum 89, 140
  A. griseum 75, 91, 140
  A. palmatum 57, 75, 84, 88, 89,
    126, 134, 135, 172
  A. palmatum 'Atropureum' 120
  A. palmatum 'Beni-tsukasa' 134,
    Plate 16
  A. palmatum 'Dissectum' 120,
    125
  A. palmatum 'Ever Red' 33
Actinidia kolomikta 121
Acuba 23
Adiantum pedatum 106, 125
Ajuga reptans 86, 122
Allium 109
alpenrose. See *Rhododendron
    hirsutum*
alpine azalea. See *Loiseleuria*
alpine columbine. See *Aquilegia
    alpina*
alpine rhubarb. See *Rheum nobile*

Amelanchier 152
American elderberry. See
    Sambucus canadensis
American holly. See *Ilex opaca*
American hornbeam. See
    Carpinus caroliniana
Andromeda 23, 105
  A. polifolia 121
  A. polifolia 'Compacta' 186
Anemone 109, 126
  A. pulsatilla 108, 122
Aquilegia 105
  A. alpina 105, 122
  A. canadensis 153
arborvitae. See *Thuja*
Arbutus 107, 154
  A. menziesii 75, 154
  A. unedo 84, 121, 154
Arctostaphylos 107, 108, 154
  A. alpina 186
  A. nevadensis 154
  A. uva-ursi 154
Arisaema 89
  A. triphyllum 122, 152, 153,
    157
Armeria juniperifolia 110
  A. meritima 108, 122

Asarum 126
   A. canadense 152
   A. caudatum 153
   A. virginica 152, 153
Asimina triloba 75, 151
Astilbe 85, 122, 124, 172
   A. biternata 153
   A. 'Avalanche' 85
   A. 'Fanal' 85
Athyrium goeringianum 'Pictum'
   125
Atrichum undulatum 106
bamboo. See *Fargesia murielae,*
   Sinarundinaria nitida
beech. See *Fagus*
bellflower. See *Campanula*
   poscharskyana
Bergenia 31, 48, 71, 75, 140
   B. crassifolia 122, 164
   B. purpurascens 170
Betula 31, 48, 71, 75, 140
   B. jacquemontii 75, 87
big leaf hydrangea. See *Hydrangea*
   macrophylla
birch. See *Betula*
bishop pine. See *Pinus muricata*
Black Hills spruce. See *Picea*
   glauca
Blechnum spicant 85, 125
bleeding heart. See *Dicentra*
   spectabilis, Dicentra eximia
bluebell. See *Endymion*
blueberry. See *Vaccinium*
   corymbosum
bog rosemary. See *Andromeda*
   polifolia
Brunnera 122
bunchberry. See *Cornus*
   canadensis
bur oak. See *Quercus macrocarpa*
Buxus 110
   B. microphylla var. *koreana* 90
California huckleberry. See
   Vaccinium ovatum

Calluna 105, 107, 108, 154, 155
   C. vulgaris 155
Camellia 84, 121, 135, 140
   C. japonica 121, 176
   C. oleifera 164
   C. sasanqua 140
   C. 'Spring Festival' 64
Campanula poscharskyana 122
Canada hemlock. See *Tsuga*
   canadensis
Canada violet. See *Viola canadensis*
candelabra primula. See *Primula*
   burmanica, P. japonica, P.
   prolifera
cap moss. See *Pogonatum*
   contortum
Cardiocrinum giganteum var.
   giganteum 122, 124
carpet bugle. See *Ajuga reptans*
Carpinus caroliniana 151
Carya 72, 89
Cassiope 100, 105, 107, 152, 154,
   155
   C. lycopodioides 105
   C. mertensiana 154
Ceanothus pumilus 121
Cedrus atlantica 'Glauca Pendula'
   182
   C. deodara 'Prostrata' 121
Cercidiphyllum Plate 16
   C. japonicum 75
Cercis canadensis 75, 84
Chamaecyparis obtusa 'Meroke'
   106, 121, 122
   C. obtusa 'Nana' 110
   C. pisifera 'Squarrosa
   Intermedia' 110
Chamaerops humilis 164
cherry. See *Prunus*
Christmas berry. See *Photinia*
Cladrastis lutea 90
Clematis 'Jackmanii Rubra' 183
   C. montana 'Tetra Rose' 164,
   170

Clerodendrum trichotomum 86
Clethra 84, 121, 152
   C. alnifolia 121, 152
coast redwood. See *Sequoia sempervirens*
Colorado spruce. See *Picea pungens* 'Glauca Pendula'
columbine. See *Aquilegia*
coral bells. See *Heuchera*
Cornelian cherry. See *Cornus mas*
Cornus 84, 87, 134
   C. alba 'Gouchaltii' 176
   C. canadensis 86, 122, 151, 153, 157
   C. florida 75, 90, 120, 140, 151, Plate 19
   C. kousa 75, 84, 120, 140
   C. mas 75
   C. nuttallii 75, 120, 140, 151
Corydalis lutea 122
Corylus cornuta 152
Cotoneaster frigida 130
cowberry. See *Vaccinium vitis-idaea*
cranberry. See *Vaccinium oxycoccos, Vaccinium macrocarpon, Viburnum opulus*
creeping dogwood. See *Cornus canadensis*
creeping phlox. See *Phlox subulata*
Cryptomeria 84
Cupressus 130
   C. cachmiriana 75
cypress. See *Cupressus*
Cyclamen coum 86
   C. hederifolium 86
Cypripedium reginae 85
Daboecia 154, 155
   D. azorica 155
   D. cantabrica 155
Daphne 121
Darlingtonia californica 153

daylily. See *Hemerocallis*
dead nettle. See *Lamium maculatum* 'Beacon Silver'
deer fern. See *Blechnum spicant*
Dentaria laciniata 85
Deutzia gracilis 121
Diapensia 30
Dicentra eximia 152, 153
   D. spectabilis 122
Digitalis 122
dogwood. See *Cornus*
Douglas fir. See *Pseudotsuga menziesii*
eastern dogwood. See *Cornus florida*
eastern redbud. See *Cercis canadensis*
Endymion 90, 127
Enkianthus 121, 154, 155
   E. campanulatus 155
   E. perulatus 189
Epimedium 85
   E. rubrum 122
Eremus 'Oase' 125
Erica 88, 105, 107, 108, 154, 155
   E. carnea 'Spring Wood White' 125, Plate 8
Erythronium 105, 106, 109, 126, 127
Escallonia macrantha 130
Eucalyptus 130
Eucryphia glutinosa 130
   E. lucida 75
Euonymus 23
European mountain ash. See *Sorbus aucuparia*
European pasque flower. See *Anemone pulsatilla*
Fagus 72
false goatsbeard. See *Astilbe biternata*
false Solomon's seal. See *Smilacina stellata*
Fargesia murielae 121, 164

Fatsia japonica 164
fetterbush. See *Pieris floribunda*
forget-me-not. See *Myosotis*
Fothergilla gardenii 152
foxglove. See *Digitalis*
Franklinia alatamaha 75, 151
Franklin tree. See *Franklinia
    alatamaha*
Fritillaria meleagris 123
Fuchsia 121, 171, 172
    F. excorticata 130
    F. 'Magellenica Alba' 121
    F. 'Ricartonii' 121
Gable azaleas 183
Galium odoratum 91, Plate 41
Gardenia jasminoides 176
Gaultheria 105, 107, 154, 155
    G. adenothrix 105, 107, 155
    G. nummularioides 105, 156
    G. procumbens 105, 154, 156
    G. shallon 88, 152, 153, 154,
        158, Plate 41
Gentiana 105, 106, 108
Ghent azaleas 82
giant trillium. See *Trillium
    chloropetalum*
Ginkgo biloba 75
Glenn Dale azaleas 25, 183
Griselinia littoralis 130
Gunnera manicata 164
hairy cap moss. See *Pogonatum
    contortum*
Hamamelis 25
    H. virginiana 75
hazelnut. See *Corylus cornuta*
heart-leaf. See *Asarum virginica*
Helleborus orientalis 123
Hemerocallis 172, 191
hemlock. See *Tsuga*
Heuchera 123, 124
    H. americana 153
hickory. See *Carya*
Himalayan poppy. See *Meconopsis
    betonicifolia*

Holodiscus discolor 152
Hosta 85, 91, 123, 124, 134, 172,
    191, Plate 21, Plate 32
    H. 'Francee' 85
    H. 'Krossa Regal' 85
    H. 'Little Aureo' 172
    H. sieboldiana 164
    H. 'Solar Flare' 125
    H. undulata 86
Hydrangea 14, 84, 121
    H. anomala var. *anomala* 170
    H. anomala var. *petiolaris* 121,
        164, 170
    H. macrophylla 121
    H. macrophylla var. *macrophylla*
        'Blue Danube' 179
    H. quercifolia 85, 152
    H. quercifolia 'Snow Queen'
        164
Ilex 82, 84, 91, 121, 126, 141
    I. glabra 'Nigra' 64
    I. opaca 75, 84
Impatiens balsamina 'Bruno' 170
Iris 86, 124, 127, Plate 31
    I. douglasiana 86
    I. ensata 123
    I. innominata 86
    I. sibirica 86
jack-in-the-pulpit. See *Arisaema
    triphyllum*
Jacob's ladder. See *Polemonium
    caeruleum*
Japanese iris. See *Iris ensata*
Japanese larch. See *Larix
    kaempferi*
Japanese maple. See *Acer
    palmatum*
Japanese painted fern. See
    Athyrium goeringianum
    'Pictum'
Japanese snowball. See *Styrax
    japonicus*
Japanese stewartia. See *Stewartia
    pseudocamellia*

Jeffrey pine. See *Pinus jeffreyi*
Juniperus 126, 141
  J. communis 'Compressa' 110
  J. horizontalis 'Gray Forest' 110
Kalmia 84, 105, 154
  K. latifolia 120, 151, 152, 154
  K. latifolia 'Freckles' 157
Kalmiopsis 154
  K. leachiana 105, 154, 156
katsura tree. See *Cercidiphyllum japonicum*
kinnikinick. See *Arcotstaphylos uva-ursi*
Knap Hill azaleas. See *Rhododendron* 'Toucan', *R.* 'Satan'
Korean box. See *Buxus microphylla* var. *koreana*
Korean fir. See *Abies koreana* 'Starker's Dwarf'
kousa dogwood. See *Cornus kousa*
Kurume azaleas 80, 90, 166, 170, 183. See also *Rhododendron* 'Christmas Cheer'
lady's slipper. See *Cypripedium reginae*
Lamium 123, 172
  L. maculatum 'Beacon Silver' 86
large-flowered magnolia. See *Magnolia grandiflora*
Larix 130, 135
  L. kaempferi 18, 83
laurel. See *Laurus*
Laurus 23
Ledum 150
Lenten rose. See *Helleborus orientalis*
Leucothoe 154, 156
  L. axillaris 154, 156
  L. fontanesiana 'Scarletta' 189
  L. populifolia 154, 156
Ligustrum 173

Lilium 130
  L. 'Black Beauty' 125
  L. columbianum 85
Linwood azaleas 183
Liriodendron tulipifera 145, 151
loblolly pine. See *Pinus taeda*
Loiseleuria 152
London pride. See *Saxifraga umbrosa*
lowbush blueberry. See *Vaccinium angustifolium*
Lysichiton americanum 85, 123
madrona. See *Arbutus menziesii*
Magnolia 25, 57, 84, 120, 130, 134, 140, 192
  M. grandiflora 91, 151, 152
  M. ×soulangiana 75, 84, 127
  M. stellata 75, 84, 91
  M. stellata 'Jane Platt' 126
  M. virginiana 75, 151, 152, 157
Mahonia 23, 121
  M. aquifolium 88, 121, 152, 153, 157, 158
  M. nepalensis 130
maidenhair fern. See *Adiantum pedatum*
maidenhair tree. See *Ginkgo biloba*
manzanita. See *Arctostaphylos*
maple. See *Acer*
maple-leaf viburnum. See *Viburnum acerifolium*
meadow sweet. See *Astilbe*
Meconopsis 130
  M. betonicifolia 123, 124
Mimosa 91
Mnium hornum 125, 170
mock orange. See *Philadelphus lewisii, Styrax americanus*
moss. See *Mnium hornum, Polytrichum commune, Polytrichum piliferum*
mountain camellia. See *Stewartia ovata*

mountain heather. See *Phyllodoce empetriformis*
mountain laurel. See *Kalmia latifolia*
Myosotis 123, 127
Narcissus 140
Nordman fir. See *Abies nordmanniana* 'Golden Spreader'
North Tisbury azaleas 183
Nyssa 91
oak. See *Quercus*
oakleaf hydrangea. See *Hydrangea quercifolia*
ocean spray. See *Holodiscus discolor*
Olearia macrodonta 130
Oregon grape. See *Mahonia aquifolium*
Osmunda ragalis 85, 125
Oxalis oregona 153
Pacific Coast iris. See *Iris douglasiana, I. innominata*
Pacific dogwood. See *Cornus nuttallii*
Paeonia 89, 91, Plate 21
  P. suffruticosa 121, 122, 126
palm. See *Chamaerops humilis*
palmetto. See *Sabal*
paperbark maple. See *Acer griseum*
Parrotia persica 75
pasque flower. See *Anemone pulsatilla*
paw paw. See *Asimina triloba*
Pelargonium 171, 172
Penstemon davidsonii 110
peony. See *Paeonia*
Pernettya 154, 156
  P. mucronata 156
  P. pumila 156
Persian perrotia. See *Parrotia persica*
Philadelphus lewisii 152

Phlox subulata 110, 177
Photinia 173
Phyllodoce 105, 107, 154, 155
  P. empetriformis 105, 154
Picea 72, 90, 91, 130
  P. abies Plate 35
  P. glauca 89, 91
  P. pungens 'Glauca Pendula' 121
Pieris 84, 105, 120, 154, 156
  P. floribunda 154, 156, 157
  P. forrestii Plate 28
  P. japonica 156
  P. japonica 'Valley of Fire' 164
  P. japonica 'Valley Valentine' 64
  P. phillyreifolia 154, 156
pine. See *Pinus*
pine-mat manzanita. See *Arctostaphylos nevadensis*
Pinus 72, 83, 84, 130, Plate 2
  P. jeffreyi 153, 157
  P. mugo 87
  P. muricata Plate 17
  P. resinosa 89
  P. strobus 83, 157
  P. taeda 135, 136, 152, Plate 33
pitcher plant. See *Darlingtonia californica*
Pittosporum eugenioides 64
plantain lily. See *Hosta*
Pogonatum contortum 106
Polemonium caeruleum 123
Polygonatum 85, 89, 126, Plate 21
Polystichum munitum 85, 125, 153
Polytrichum commune 87, 125
  P. piliferum 106, 125
primrose. See *Primula denticulata*
Primula 14, 15, 30, 85, 100, 105, 108, 124, 130
  P. burmanica 85, 124
  P. denticulata 105, 123
  P. japonica 85, 124
  P. prolifera 85, 124

privet. See *Ligustrum*
Prunus 87, 126, 141
Pseudotsuga menziesii 87, 127, 131, 145, 153
Quercus 72, 83, 90, 141
   Q. agrifolia 173
   Q. alba 89
   Q. garryana 83
   Q. macrocarpa 89
   Q. rubra 89
redbud. See *Cercis canadensis*
red huckleberry. See *Vaccinium parvifolium*
red oak. See *Quercus rubra*
red pine. See *Pinus resinosa*
redwood sorrel. See *Oxalis oregona*
Rheum 15
   R. nobile 109, 123
   R. rhabarbarum 109
Rhododendron
   R. aberconwayii 38, 80
   R. adenopodum 31
   R. aganniphum 100
   R. alabamense 135, 148
   R. albiflorum 150
   R. albrechtii 40, 117, 132, 170
   R. 'Album Elegans' 24, 82
   R. 'Alexander' 81
   R. alutaceum Plate 14
   R. 'Anah Kruschke' 54, 80
   R. anhweiense 118
   R. 'Anna' 133
   R. 'Anna Rose Whitney' 54, 166
   R. anthopogon subsp. *anthopogon* 191
   R. 'Apricot Fantasy' 36, 87
   R. 'April Rose' 110
   R. 'Aravir' 137, 190
   R. arborescens 21, 89, 135, 148, 152
   R. arboreum 16, 19, 30, 74, 115, 130
   R. argyrophyllum 83

R. argyrophyllum subsp. *nankingense* 36
R. 'Arnoldianum' Plate 19
R. 'Arthur Bedford' 54, 80
R. 'Athanasius' 137
R. atlanticum 148
R. augustinii 15, 17, 33, 34, 35, 38, 41, 117, 126, 132, 166, 176
R. auriculatum 118, 189
R. austrinum 40, 135, 148
R. 'Avalon' 137
R. 'Bambino' Plate 32
R. barbatum 21, 36, 83, 115, 138
R. 'Barto Lavender' 176
R. 'Beauty of Littleworth' 21
R. 'Belle Heller' 54
R. 'Bellringer' 36
R. 'Bianchi' 82
R. 'Blaauw's Pink' 166
R. 'Blue Peter' 54
R. 'Bob's Blue' Plate 10
R. 'Boule de Neige' 54, 80
R. 'Bow Bells' 179
R. brachycarpum 36, 48, 80, 89
R. 'Bremen' Plate 10
R. 'Brown Eyes' 36
R. bureavii 36, 83, 118, 132, 139, 177, 180, Plate 20
R. 'Burma' 133
R. burmanicum 189
R. 'Calavar' 137, 165
R. calendulaceum 15, 35, 40, 135, 145, 148, 152, 189, Plate 47
R. calophytum 15, 33, 60, 67, 74, 80, 89, 138, 139
R. calostrotum 66, 102, 132
R. calostrotum 'Gigha' 108
R. calostrotum subsp. *keleticum* Radicans Group 34, 95, 100, 103, 118, 186
R. campanulatum 19, 21, 117, 130

[*Rhododendron*]

R. campanulatum subsp.
  aeruginosum 36, 85
R. campylocarpum 19, 130
R. campylogynum 101
R. camtschaticum 94, 101, 150,
  152
R. canadense 145, 148, 149, 151,
  188
R. 'Canadian Sunset' Plate 32
R. canescens 16, 149, 152, 157
R. 'Caroline' 25
R. 'Caroline Gable' 81
R. 'Casanova' 133, 167
R. catawbiense 16, 21, 24, 80,
  116, 145, 146, 147, 176
R. 'Catawbiense Album' 36, 80
R. 'Catawbiense Boursault' 54,
  80
R. 'Centennial Celebration'
  168, Plate 32
R. cephalanthum 100, 101, 104,
  191
R. chamaethomsonii 30
R. 'Chionoides' 54
R. 'Christmas Cheer' 177, 178
R. ciliicalyx 192
R. cinnabarinum 19, 38, 83, 130
R. 'Cinnamon Bear' Plate 32
R. clementinae 39, 118, 177
R. concinnum 132
R. 'Conroy' Plate 5
R. 'County of York' 80
R. 'Cream Pie' 139
R. 'Creeping Jenny' 166
R. 'Crimson Pippin' Plate 32
R. 'Cristo Rey' 137, 165, Plate
  34
R. cuffeanum 192
R. cumberlandense 40, 89, 135,
  148, 152
R. 'Cupcake' Plate 32
R. 'Curlew' 67, 109, 185
R. 'Cynthia' 20, 26, 46, 54

R. 'Cyprus' 66
R. dauricum 16, 34, 89, 90, 108,
  118, 189
R. davidsonianum 132
R. decorum 80, 138, 189, 190
R. degronianum 118
R. 'Delaware Valley White' 81,
  138
R. 'Dexter's Champagne' 133
R. diaprepes 189
R. 'Dora Amateis' 54, 138, 140,
  180
R. edgeworthii 15, 66, 118, 140,
  165, 189, 190
R. elegantulum 38
R. 'Else Frye' 190
R. 'Everestianum' 82
R. falconeri 17, 19, 71, 74, 116,
  130
R. 'Fantastica' 168, 180
R. fastigiatum 66, 100, 102, 106,
  110
R. 'Fastuosum Flore Pleno' 54,
  82
R. ferrugineum 16, 93
R. 'Festive' 177, 178
R. 'Fielder's White' 184
R. flammeum 135, 148
R. flavorufum 83
R. formosum 19
R. forrestii 15, 17, 30, 33, 93, 95,
  100, 101, 104, 108
R. forrestii subsp. *forrestii*
  Repens Group 186
R. fortunei 17, 36, 80, 83, 86,
  116, 118, 133, 138, 139, 189,
  190
R. fragariflorum 108
R. 'Fragrantissimum' 138, 171,
  190, 192
R. fulvum 74, 116
R. 'Gay Paree' 173
R. 'Geisha Pink' 177, 178
R. 'Giganteum' 24

R. 'Ginny Gee' 104, 126, 185

R. glaucophyllum 108

R. 'Goldbug' 25

R. 'Golfer' 168, Plate 32

R. 'Gomer Waterer' 54, 140

R. 'Grace Seabrook' 36, 80, 83, 182, Plate 10

R. grande 17, 19, 71, 74, 116, 130

R. 'Great Expectations' 81

R. griersonianum 38

R. griffithianum 20, 47, 74, 116, 190

R. groenlandicum 94, 150, 151

R. 'Gumpo' 81

R. haematodes 108

R. 'Hallelujah' 36, 54, 80

R. 'Harry Tagg' 190, 192

R. 'Helen Curtis' 81

R. 'Hélène Schiffner' 36

R. 'Hino-crimson' 81, 166, 170

R. hippophaeoides 104

R. hirsutum 16, 93, 100

R. hodgsonii 17, 71, 74, 83, 116, 138

R. 'Honsu's Baby' 168, 186

R. 'Hotei' 88

R. 'Hydon Dawn' 43

R. hyperythrum 38

R. impeditum 66, 88, 93, 100, 102, 106, 109

R. impeditum Litangense Group 186

R. indicum 81

R. insigne 38, 83

R. intricatum 106

R. jasminiflorum 189, 190

R. javanicum 165

R. 'Jock's Cairn' 137

R. johnstonianum 183, Plate 49

R. 'John Waterer' 54, 82

R. 'Joseph Hill' 81

R. kaempferi 81, Plate 43

R. 'Kashu-no-hikari' 173, 180

R. 'Kazan' 81, 183

R. keiskei 104, 110, 132

R. keiskei 'Yaku Fairy' 101, 104, 106, 117, 186, Plate 9

R. 'Kermesinum Rosé' 110

R. 'King's Ride' Plate 32

R. kiusianum 81, 104, 110, 117, 171, 183

R. konori 191

R. 'Lady Alice Fitzwilliam' 66, 190

R. lapponicum 94, 101, 147, 152

R. lapponicum Parvifolium Group 148

R. 'Laurago' Plate 32

R. 'Lavender Beauty' Plate 19

R. 'Lawrence' 137, Plate 42

R. 'Lee's Dark Purple' 80

R. 'Lem's Cameo' 37, 41, 134, 179, 180, Plate 11

R. lindleyi 138, 189, 190

R. 'Little Gardenia' 81

R. lochiae 165

R. 'Loderi King George' 20, 26, 33, 74, 116, 189

R. 'Loderi Pink Diamond' 74, 116

R. 'Loderi Venus' 20, 26, 42, 74, 116, 189

R. longesquamatum 15

R. loranthiflorum 190, 191

R. 'Lurline' 192

R. luteiflorum 18

R. lutescens 34, 35, 41, 63, 117, 132

R. luteum 40, 189, 190

R. macabeanum 34, 67, 73, 74, 88, 116, 118, 139, 164, 180

R. macrophyllum 131, 145, 149, 153, Plate 39

R. macrosepalum 40

R. macrosepalum 'Linearifolium' 125

R. maculiferum 31

[*Rhododendron*]

R. maddenii 19, 189, 192

R. 'Mardi Gras' Plate 32

R. 'Maricee' 88

R. 'Mars' 83

R. 'Mauve Beauty' Plate 19

R. maximum 16, 21, 23, 24, 36, 65, 79, 80, 144, 145, 146, 147, 151, 176

R. maximum 'Summertime' 157

R. 'Mi Amor' 47, 165, 180, 182, 190

R. 'Midnight' 139

R. 'Midnight Mistique' 134

R. 'Mindy's Love' 167

R. minus 21, 80, 145, 147

R. minus Carolinianum Group 90, 176

R. minus var. *chapmanii* 147, 152

R. 'Morgenrot' Plate 32

R. 'Mrs. G. W. Leak' 80, 192

R. 'Mrs. Milner' 24

R. mucronulatum 40, 108, 110, 117

R. mucronulatum 'Crater's Edge' 110

R. myrtifolium 93

R. nakaharae 81, 101, 104, 110, 117, 183

R. nakaharae 'Mt. Seven Star' 104

R. 'Nancy Evans' 167, 185

R. 'Nancy of Robinhill' 81

R. 'Naselle' 66, 140, 167, 185

R. neoglandulosum 150

R. 'Ne Plus Ultra' 137

R. 'Nova Zembla' 54, 80

R. 'Noyo Brave' 88, Plate 32

R. 'Noyo Chief' 37, 45, 180

R. nuttallii 33, 118, 165, 180, 189, 190, 192

R. occidentale 16, 40, 117, 138, 147, 149, 150, 153, 157, 158, 188, 189, 190, Plate 2, Plate 40

R. 'Olga Mezitt' 90

R. 'Oliver Twist' Plate 32

R. Olympic Lady Group 88

R. orbiculare 34, 39, 117, 180

R. orbiculare subsp. *cardiobasis* Plate 14

R. oreodoxa var. *fargesii* 31

R. oreotrephes 39, 64, 132

R. pachysanthum 48, 89, 108, 117, 180, Plate 48

R. 'Paprika Spiced' 140

R. 'Parker's Pink' 133

R. 'Patty Bee' 66, 104, 109, 168, 185, 186

R. 'Pawhuska' 140

R. pemakoense 93, 101, 103

R. pentaphyllum 132

R. periclymenoides 21, 40, 135, 149, 190

R. phaeochrysum 15, 36, 132

R. 'Phyllis Korn' 87

R. 'Pink Pearl' 20

R. PJM Group 16, 54, 63, 90, 166, 189

R. 'Pleasant Companion' 137

R. 'Point Defiance' 180

R. ponticum 16, 44, 80

R. praestans 18, 74, 118

R. 'President Roosevelt' 125, 138

R. 'Primary Pink' 134, Plate 16

R. primuliflorum 104, 191

R. 'Princess Alexandra' 165

R. 'Princess Anne' 168, 185

R. prinophyllum 149

R. pronum 140, 142, 177, Plate 36

R. proteoides 83, 117, 140, 142, 177, 180, Plate 36

R. prunifolium 15, 40, 89, 116, 135, 136, 149, 152, 180, 182

R. pseudochrysanthum 104, 117, 180, Plate 20

R. 'Ptarmigan' 67, 168

R. pumilum 101

R. 'Purple Lace' Plate 10

R. 'Purple Splendour' 37, 42, 80, Plate 10

R. 'Purpureum Elegans' 46

R. 'Queen Alice' Plate 32

R. quinquefolium 40, 126, 132, 169, 189

R. racemosum 35, 104, 117

R. racemosum 'Rock Rose' 66, 108, 117

R. recurvoides 48

R. 'Renoir' Plate 32

R. reticulatum 126

R. rex 67, 73, 74, 116, 118, 164

R. rex subsp. *fictolacteum* 164

R. 'Ring of Fire' 140

R. 'Rio' 133

R. 'Rose Greeley' 177, 178

R. 'Rose Scott' 190

R. 'Roseum Elegans' 46, 54, 80

R. 'Rosy Dream' Plate 32

R. roxieanum 34, 87, 132, 142, 177, 180, Plate 36

R. roxieanum var. *oreonastes* 38, 48, 118

R. rubiginosum 38, 189

R. 'Saffron Queen' Plate 28

R. 'Saint Valentine' 165

R. saluenense 101, 103, 132

R. 'Sappho' 54, 82

R. sargentianum 101, 191

R. 'Satan' 127

R. schizopeplum 142, Plate 36

R. schlippenbachii 17, 23, 40, 66, 117, 126, 127, 132, 169, 179, 180, 189

R. 'Scintillation' 25, 37, 46, 64, 125, 133, 179, 180

R. scopulorum 192

R. 'Senorita Chere' Plate 32

R. 'September Song' 139, 185, Plate 10

R. 'Shamrock' 168, Plate 10

R. 'Shilsonii' 21

R. simsii 176

R. sinogrande 34, 35, 67, 73, 74, 164, 170, Plate 17, Plate 20, Plate 50

R. smirnowii 36, 89, Plate 21

R. 'Snow' Plate 19

R. 'Solidarity' Plate 32

R. 'Starbright Champagne' 134, 181

R. strigillosum 38, 41, 83, 171, Plate 14

R. 'Sunny' 138, 181

R. sutchuenense 14, 31, 34, 67, 71, 74, 80, 115

R. 'Swen' Plate 32

R. taliense 83

R. tapetiforme Plate 1

R. 'Taurus' 34, 83

R. 'Taylori' 137

R. 'Teal' 168

R. 'Teddy Bear' 168

R. 'The Hon. Jean Marie de Montague' 54, 139

R. thomsonii 17, 19, 21, 39, 71, 130, 138, Plate 4

R. tomentosum subsp. *subarctica* 150

R. 'Too Bee' 186

R. 'Toucan' 127, Plate 31

R. 'Travis L.' 138

R. trichostomum 191

R. triflorum 130

R. 'Trude Webster' 37, 80

R. tsariense 83, 108

R. tuba 191

R. ungernii 36, 86

R. 'Unique' 64, 117, 139, 180

R. vaseyi 148, 149, 189

R. veitchianum 165

R. 'Vinecrest' 167

[*Rhododendron*]
  R. 'Virginia Richards' 173
  R. viscosum 16, 149, 152, 189, 190
  R. 'Vulcan' 83
  R. 'Wannabee' Plate 32
  R. wardii 17, 36
  R. 'Ward's Ruby' 166, 191, 192, Plate 51
  R. 'Wee Bee' 66, 107, 168, 180, 185
  R. 'Whitney's Late Orange' Plate 10
  R. 'Wigeon' 168
  R. wightii 132
  R. williamsianum 17, 33, 39, 79, 88, 101, 104, 117, 118, 127, 166, 180, 186
  R. wiltonii 36, 132, Plate 14
  R. 'Wren' 104
  R. 'Wyanokie' 25
  R. yakushimanum 17, 26, 33, 34, 38, 48, 60, 79, 89, 91, 102, 109, 117, 125, 126, 134, 139, 166, 167, 170, 180, Plate 8
  R. yakushimanum 'Ken Janek' 168
  R. yakushimanum 'Koichiro Wada' 168
  R. yakushimanum 'Mist Maiden' 168
  R. yakushimanum 'Yaku Angel' 168
  R. 'Yaku Sunrise' 168
  R. Yellow Hammer Group 54, 176
  R. yunnanense 34, 35, 38, 117, 132, 166
  R. zoelleri 42, 165
Robin Hill azaleas 183
rock geranium. See *Heuchera americana*
rosebay rhododendron. See *Rhododendron maximum*

royal fern. See *Osmunda ragalis*
Sabal 147, 152
salal. See *Gaultheria shallon*
Salix repens 152
Sambucus canadensis 152
Satsuki azaleas, 173, 183. See also *R.* 'kashu-no-hikari', *R.* 'Kazan'
saucer magnolia. See *Magnolia ×soulangiana*
Saxifraga 15, 105, 108
  S. rosacea 105, 123
  S. umbrosa 105, 107
Sedum 15, 57
Sequoia 126
  S. sempervirens 25, 153, Plate 6
serviceberry. See *Amelanchier*
Shammarello azaleas 183
Siberian iris. See *Iris sibirica*
silky camellia. See *Stewartia malacodendron*
Sinarundinaria nitida 122
Siskiyou-mat. See *Ceanothus pumilus*
skunk cabbage. See *Lysichiton americanum*
Smilacina stellata 153
snake's-head. See *Fritillaria meleagris*
snowbell. See *Styrax*
Solomon's seal. See *Polygonatum*
Sorbus aucuparia 75
sourgum. See *Nyssa*
southern magnolia. See *Magnolia grandiflora*
Spiraea 22
spruce. See *Picea*
star magnolia. See *Magnolia stellata*
Stewartia 48, 140
  S. malacodendron 15
  S. ovata 151
  S. pseudocamellia 75, 84, 120, 125, 126, Plate 8

strawberry tree. See *Arbutus unedo*
Styrax 48
   S. americanus 151
   S. japonicus 75
sweet bay magnolia. See *Magnolia virginiana*
sweet pepperbush. See *Clethra alnifolia*
sweet violet. See *Viola odorata*
sweet woodruff. See *Galium odoratum*
sword fern. See *Polystichum munitum*
Syringa 22
tall white violet. See *Viola canadensis*
Taxus 90, 91, 140
Thuja 89
   T. plicata 87, 131, 153
tiger lily. See *Lilium columbianum*
Tilia cordata Plate 35
toothwort. See *Dentaria laciniata*
tree peony. See *Paeonia suffruticosa*
Trillium 85, 89, 124
   T. chloropetalum 85
   T. grandiflorum 85, 86, 152, 153
   T. ovatum 85
Tsuga 72, 84, 133, 151
   T. canadensis 'Cloud Prince' 186
   T. heterophylla 87, 127, 131, 153
Tulipa 'White Parrot' 170
tulip tree. See *Liriodendron tulipifera*
Vaccinium 105, 107, 108, 120, 152, 154, 157
   V. angustifolium 152, 157
   V. corymbosum 120, 189
   V. macrocarpon 154, 157
   V. macrocarpon 'Hamilton' 105, 110, 157, 186
   V. ovatum 154
   V. oxycoccos 48

   V. parvifolium 152, 157, 158, Plate 41
   V. vitis-idaea 106, 154
   V. vitis-idaea var. *minus* 157
Veronica repens 110
Viburnum 89, 90
   V. acerifolium 152
   V. japonicum 176
   V. lantana 86
   V. opulus 121
vine maple. See *Acer circinatum*
Viola 127
   V. canadensis 85, 153
   V. odorata 123
violet. See *Viola*
Weigela 22
western hemlock. See *Tsuga heterophylla*
western red cedar. See *Thuja plicata*
white heather. See *Cassiope mertensiana*
white oak. See *Quercus alba*
white pine. See *Pinus strobus*
white spruce. See *Picea glauca*
white wake-robin. See *Trillium grandiflorum*
wild bleeding heart. See *Dicentra eximia*
wild columbine. See *Aquilegia canadensis*
wild ginger. See *Asarum canadense, A. caudatum*
winter-blooming bergenia. See *Bergenia crassifolia*
wintergreen. See *Gaultheria procumbens*
Wisteria 191, Plate 51
witch alder. See *Hamamelis virginiana*
witch hazel. See *Hamamelis virginiana*
yellowwood. See *Cladrastis lutea*
yew. See *Taxus*